published 2019.

# CONTRACT LAW

The student's guide to the Law of Contract

# By Vivek Khanna

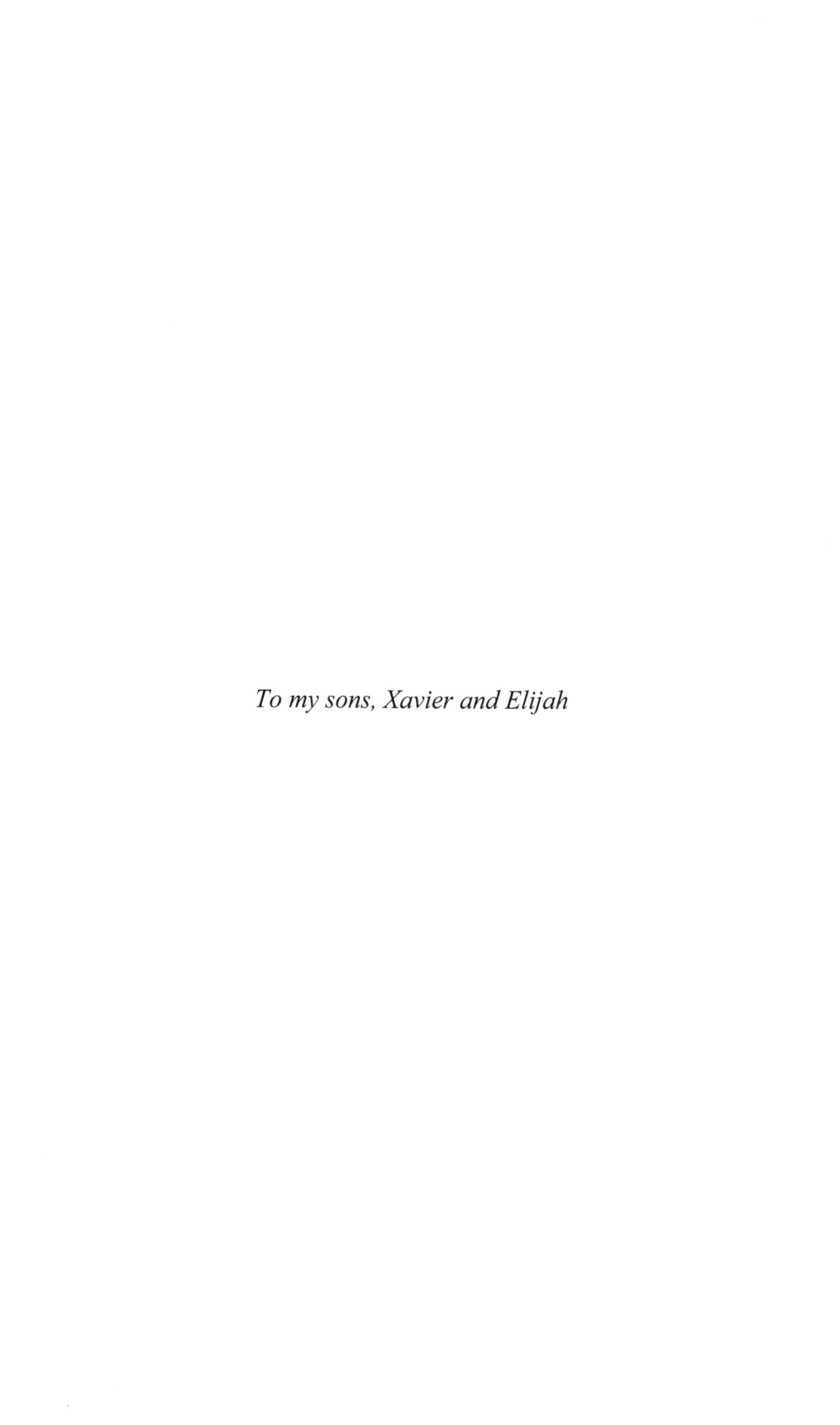

*To my sons, Xavier and Elijah*

# Foreword

Thank you for buying this book. The problem that I encountered when studying law is: knowing everything. There is so much to read and so little time to do it. If you skip some material, or a case you are none the wiser. So throughout my years teaching law I have devised a system and I am going to share this with you.

You may have encountered different methods or formulas to help when advising a client in a mock scenario. One of example is the *IRAC* method or another is *Celo*. These are well documented and you can read about these. I never used them, because I had a method in my head that worked. It was not until I started teaching that I spoke about it. I call my method the "Fact Law Sandwich". Let me explain. If you are asked to advise a party as to their legal rights this is how you present it:

FACTS
GENERAL PRINCIPLE
LAW
APPLY TO FACTS

In **Fact:** simply state what you have been told, this why you can never be accused of not considering the facts. In **General principle:** you simply state what the general rule of the relevant issue is. You express it as if you are speaking to a child who has no knowledge of law. In **Law:** you state "using the authority of.....and you go on to state which statute or case helps prove your point. Lastly in **Apply to Facts**: you apply the reasoning of the case to your factual scenario. Your advice will sound and look structured and professional. The reason it is called the "Fact Law Sandwich", is because the advice contains two outer layers of facts that sandwich the principle and law in the middle.

This book is written to provide the student with a good knowledge of the most important cases on their study. It is written in a way to facilitate the Fact Law Sandwich method. I provide the general principle, the name of the case with full citation, the facts, the

Ratio (the thing the lecturers say you always need to use), and application i.e. how the case should be applied. No other book provides this information at your fingertips. I hope you enjoy using it.

# CONTRACT LAW

## By Vivek Khanna LLB, LLM, MBA Barrister

Question and Answers
- Terms of Contract Essay Question
- Terms of Contract Problem Question

## Chapter 10 - Exemption Clauses
Question and Answers
- Unfair Contract Terms Act 1979 Essay
- Exclusion clause Problem Question

## Chapter 11 – Misrepresentation
Question and Answer
- Misrepresentation Problem Question

## Chapter 12 - Mistake
Question and Answer
- Mistake Problem Question

## Chapter 13 - Frustration

## Chapter 14 - Remedies
Question and Answers
- Remedies Problem Question

# Welcome/Introduction/Overview

This book provides you with basic information as a basis for you to form your own critical opinions on this area of law. Once you have mastered the basics, you will be inspired to question contract principles in your essays and apply them in mock client advisory scenarios. Again, for your convenience, we have provided you with examples of how to answer such questions and how to apply your knowledge as effectively as possible to help you get the best possible marks.

This aid is a fully-fledged source of basic information, which tries to give the student comprehensive understanding for this module. However, it is recommended that you compliment it with the further reading suggestions provided at the end of each topic, as well as read the cases themselves for more in-depth information. This book provides an analysis of the basic principles of modern Contract Law. The following is a summary of the Book content:

- An introduction to the Law of Contract;
- How contracts are formed;
- What goes into a contract: Its content;
- The means of obtaining remedies when there is a breach of contract;

The aim of this Book is to:

- Provide an introduction to anyone studying or interested in studying Law to the key principles and concepts that exist in the Law of Contract.
- To provide a framework to consider Contract Law within the context of examinations.
- Provide a detailed learning resource in order for legal written examination skills to be developed.
- Facilitate the development of written and critical thinking skills.
- Promote the practice of problem solving skills.
- To establish a platform for students to gain a solid understanding of the basic principles and concepts of

Contract Law, this can then be expanded upon through confident independent learning.

Through this Book, students will be able to demonstrate the ability to:

- Demonstrate an awareness of the core principles of Contract Law.
- Critically assess challenging mock factual scenarios and be able to pick out legal issues in the various areas of Contract Law.
- Apply their knowledge when writing a formal assessment.
- Present a reasoned argument and make a judgment on competing viewpoints.
- Make use of technical legalistic vocabulary in the appropriate manner.
- Be responsible for their learning process and work in an adaptable and flexible way.

**Studying Contract Law**

Contract is one of the seven core subjects that the Law Society and the Bar Council deem essential in a qualifying law degree. Therefore, it is vital that a student successfully pass this subject to become a lawyer. Additionally, a knowledge and understanding of contractual principles is needed in order to study other law subjects such as company, employment, international trade, commercial, or even family law. The primary method by which your understanding of the law of contract will develop is by understanding how to solve problem questions. You will also be given essay questions in your examinations. The methods by which these types of question should be approached are somewhat different.

**Tackling Problems and Essay Questions**

There are various ways of approaching problem questions and essay questions. We have provided students with an in-depth analysis with suggested questions and answers at the end of each chapter.

# Chapter 1 - Introduction to Contract law

## The General Ideology

The origins of the principle of a 'contract' can be traced back to the Middle Ages. Much of modern contract law developed in the nineteenth century alongside economics, and played a large part in the Industrial Revolution. Contract Law has an extremely broad application in practice, from consumer transactions in shops and online, to the commercial sale of goods in business and the supply of individual's services and skills. It also includes distribution of goods, franchising products, licensing, intellectual property trade and ownership, finance, security, and even employment, as contracts are essential ingredients in this type of formal relationship. A good understanding of Contract Law is fundamental for all of these many areas of law, because each of them is linked to Contract Law's basic and general principles. This can also be said for many other types of commercial transactions. Many contract disputes are often left to be resolved by law firms, but can also be settled outside of court due to, as you will learn, what the contracts themselves provide in terms of protection.

When reading the easily laid out chapters and sections in this application, you will learn that many modern business transactions are difficult to join with some well-established principles of Contract Law. This is a common thing when you reach the more advanced contract work in practice, where the impetus is mainly directed towards drafting contracts in order to avoid the application of the law. On the other side of the coin, there is equally strong impetus to test and push the boundaries of the existing laws. This is, for the most part, the case in transactions applicable to the Sale of Goods. It is noteworthy to reflect on the words on Professor Mckendrick (2008) here, who has suggested: *"My own view is that we are moving slowly in the direction of a law of contracts [not contract] as the 'general principles' decline in importance."* Despite this, there will always be general principles to guide the courts and upcoming lawyers, such as yourself, when tackling contract disputes.

## Sources of the Law of Contract

As we have established above, Contract Law is a broad subject with many specific applications into different areas of law and aspects of our daily personal and professional lives. We also saw that its origins are in the Middle Ages, with principles largely influenced by judge's decisions in cases at the time. It was, and still is, mainly a common law subject. This means that its rules and principles have been expressed and established by the judiciary when they make judgments in real life cases. The main period of development of the common Law of Contract was in the nineteenth century, which, as a period of considerable commercial and industrial expansion, saw an increasing number of contract disputes brought before the courts.

An overriding principle generally followed by the courts at this time was that of freedom of contract, which states that parties of full capacity (i.e. not children or the mentally infirm) should be free to make whatever agreements they wish so long as they were not for an illegal purpose and subject only to remedies for recognised unfairness, such as misrepresentation or duress. An outcome of the principle of freedom of contract was the principle of sanctity of contract, namely that contracts freely entered into by people with full rational capacity ought to be enforced by the courts.

### The Application of These Principles in Contract Law

The freedom and sanctity of contract principles was expressed by Sir George Jessel in **Printing and Numerical Registering Co v Sampson** (1875):

> *"... if there is one thing more than another that public policy requires, it is that men of full age and competent understanding shall have the utmost liberty in contracting, and that their contracts, when entered into freely and voluntarily, shall be held sacred and shall be enforced by Courts of Justice."*

This expression simply means that any competent and reasonable person has complete choice and mastery over how they enter and conclude their contracts. However, towards the end of the nineteenth century and throughout the twentieth century, there were an increasing number of Acts of Parliament that addressed the principle of freedom of contract. This was because it was increasingly recognised during this period that pure laissez-faire (do it yourself) application of the principle of freedom of contract often led to injustice. As a result of gross inequality of bargaining power between large companies on the one hand, and either consumers or employees on the other, freedom of contract could be abused; for example, in standard form contracts (template agreements) or through the wide use of exemption clauses (a term in a contract that seeks to restrict the rights of the parties to the contract).

**The current position**

A contract is an agreement that is binding and legally enforceable. This kind of agreement is the most frequently used kind of legal dealing and happens in nearly every case where something is sold or purchased, from selling a multi-million pound yacht to buying a lunchtime snack from your local supermarket. Some other examples of contracts include contracts for the sale of goods, sale of land, contracts of employment, contracts of hire, and contracts for the provision of services. Contracts can be made in writing, may be oral (spoken), or may be identified by someone's actions. Most contracts have two parties, but there can be more. However, not every agreement will amount to a contract that can be enforced by law. Some social arrangements between people or contracts that offend public decency (i.e. I will pay you to expose yourself in Lincoln's Inn) and public policy, or those that involve criminal acts, are all examples of contracts that a court would not be willing to consider binding, and are therefore unenforceable.

**Different Ideologies of Contract Law**

With the development of a free market in a globalised world based on the division of work, this capitalistic 21$^{st}$ century society required a flexible legal method of protecting the exchange of goods and services. Many legal practitioners decided to respond to this pressing social need from the beginning of the 20$^{th}$ Century.

They transformed "Contract Law" from the unwieldy and complicated system it was since the sixteenth century into an instrument of virtually unlimited usefulness and applicability. Contract, therefore, became the crucial tool of the modern businessman, allowing him to go about his business in a rational way. Rational behaviour within the setting of modern society is only possible if agreements can be respected. The contract is, however, a tool that everyone can and does use in their everyday lives. For instance, when you buy a mobile phone, you are often receiving it for seemingly nothing on the condition that you pay a specific fee for your chosen telephone service for a certain period of time. In doing this, you are both exercising your own right to freedom of contract, in that you pick which tariff you use, and the sanctity doctrine, in that you expect that service to be maintained for a certain period in exchange for the money you provide the service provider in return.

**The Market Principle**

This principle promotes individualism and is a place for competitive exchange of goods and services. The functions of a contract are to facilitate competition as well as exchange. This ensures bargains must be kept subject to fraud, mistake coercion and so on, because it places emphasis on a duty to honour the agreement and not to behave in a way that will have a negative impact on the other party's interest in the agreement. These include means such as misrepresentation and non-disclosure of information. A contract's security gets recognised in one of the doctrines of law; that is the objective (factual) approach to contract intention. It also accommodates subjective (a subject's personal perspective, rather than that taken from an independent, objective angle) mistakes and third party purchasers. In order to protect an innocent party in the marketplace, Contract Law epitomises that people's expectations measure in damages, as a realistic deterrent for the non-performance of an obligation by any of the contracting parties. The ground rules of contract, therefore, should be clear, with clearly defined penalties. This will, as a result, avoid market inconvenience. This is an underlying principle of Contract Law. It is to comply with creating a level playing field for competition, with no one being placed at a disadvantage at the expense of another taking advantage and benefiting from that profit. English Contract Law holds that it is paramount for a person to be able to achieve his/her goals, but not at the expense of another trying to achieve his/hers.

## The Individualistic Ideology of Contract Law

Judges tend to not intervene with respect to contracts. Any potential party to a contract should enter the market using their own independent reasoning, in order to determine which bargains most potentially benefit them, strike them, and stick to them. The formal names that govern this behaviour are the doctrines of:

1) Freedom of contract
2) Sanctity

This freedom permits parties to freely choose others as consensual contractual partners. They need to be free to formulate and decide upon their own terms, as arguably no single definitive framework can possibly accommodate the unique distinctions of people's characters that form what they want to see in a contract and how they want to benefit from it.

However, the development of many large corporate enterprises in both the public and private sectors has made it impossible for the weaker party to actually exercise freedoms, because of the pressure to forge an agreement with big companies. Therefore, a party could be held to the will of these more economically powerful contracting parties, as opposed to exercising their right to an equal tender on a level playing field. The sanctity of contract is also explicit in that parties should be treated as masters of their own bargains. Those entering into contracts should be able to maintain assurance that the terms of that agreement will be followed without breach, or a way in which the other party can exploit them to gain more than the original terms stated.

## Consumer Welfare Principles

Consumer Welfare principles presuppose that consumer contracts must be regulated closely and commercial contracts, although competitive, must be subjected to far more regulation than market individualism. There are four main principles to consider:

1) **Principle of Constancy:** A person should not encourage another to act in a certain way or form a specific expectation and then act inconsistently with the encouragement.

2) **Proportionality:** Remedies subject to the seriousness of the breach.

3) **Principle of Bad faith:** A party citing a good legal principle in an attempt to exploit another consumer should not be allowed to exercise it. No man should be able to profit from his wrongdoing.

4) **The Principle of Exploitation:** A stronger party should be prohibited from exploiting the apparent weakness of another party's bargaining situation and parties should be taken to have a relationship that will not lead to one exploiting the other.

## The Nature of Agreement: The Objective Approach to Contract

Agreement occurs when one person makes an offer that is accepted by the other person. Provided consideration and intention to create legal relations are also present, there is a contract.

*"A contract is an agreement giving rise to obligations which are enforced or recognised by law. The factor that distinguishes contractual from other legal obligations is that they are based on the agreement of the contracting parties. This proposition remains generally true, even though it is subject to a number of important qualifications."* (Treitel: 13th Revised Edition 2011) Chapter 1 – 1-001.

However, the law applies an objective test rather than a subjective one - if there appears to be an agreement and one person believes there to be one, the other person will not be allowed to say there is not one. There are two exceptions to this. The court will look at the subjective reality, rather than the objective appearance, of agreement if:

1) One party knows that the other party has made a mistake in the terms of agreement - **Hartog v Colin and Shields** [1939] 3 All ER 566

**Hartog v Colin and Shields** [1939] 3 All ER 566
**Facts:** The defendants, Colin and Shields, sold animal hides. Hartog was a furrier (someone who sells fur products). Colin and Shields talked about selling Hartog 30,000 skins taken from Argentinian hares at "10d per skin" (equivalent to £1,250 today). As they were writing up their final offer, Colin and Shields accidentally wrote "30,000 skins at 10d per lb". It was common knowledge in the industry that the skins of hares weigh, on average, 5oz. The final offer amounted to a third of the price originally talked about and verbally agreed to. Hartog attempted to make Shields and Colin honour this offer, which was extremely favourable for him.
**Ratio: The Court held that the claimant must have realised the defendants' mistake. Since this mistake related to a term of the contract, the contract became null and void.**
**Application:** Hartog v Colin and Shields has gradually evolved into a very important precedent (something binding on all courts to apply in practice in future cases). This is especially true in modern society, where much of our shopping is now done on the internet. This is because many online businesses accidentally misprint the prices for their products. A lot of these websites use computer servers to automatically process customer details and payments that they make at the time, thereby creating the contract. All this can happen before the actual company owners find out that there have been misprints on their websites and, as such, the automated systems are selling products far below their actual value. For example, an online computer products retailer such as Amazon™ could advertise a tablet PC, which normally costs £300, for £30 or perhaps even £3. Any company that retails, be it on the high street or online, can evade supplying goods of the misstated lower price if a court is able to find that the would-be purchasers must have known that the advertised price was clearly a mistake and were trying to take advantage of the situation.

2) The second exception is as seen in the cases of **Scriven**

**Bros v Hindley** [1913] 3 KB 564

**Scriven Bros v Hindley** [1913] 3 KB 564
**Facts:** Scriven Bros. lodged a bid at an auction hosted by Hindley and Co., where bales of hemp and tow were offered for auction. Their catalogue made the suggestion that one of the bundles of farm produce contained bales of hemp and tow. In reality, however, the bundle for auction only contained tow.
**Ratio: Lawrence J held that the auctioneer was unable to accept the highest (winning) bid because the bid was placed under misapprehension and mistake.**
**Application:** Two parties cannot create a legal binding contract when the terms of the offer and acceptance do not match.

**General Principle: You cannot escape a contractual agreement by saying you did not intend to form a contract.**

**Storer v Manchester City Council [1974]** UKHL 6
**Facts:** Mr. Storer made an application to purchase the council house he was living in. The Manchester City Council sent him an agreement of sale. The Agreement for Sale had been completed and signed. However, the date on which the tenancy was to end and the beginning of the mortgage repayment period had not been filled. On 20th March, when Mr. Storer signed and returned the agreement, a new political party came into power and the local council's policies changed. They decided to stop selling the properties unless the contracts had already been exchanged. Mr. Storer wanted to get a remedy to enforce what he believed to be an already binding contract. Manchester City Council argued that the clerk did not intend to offer the council house for sale when he sent the agreement of sale.
**Ratio: The court held that agreement of sale was a firm offer which Mr. Storer had accepted. Lord Denning stated, *"In contracts, you do not look into the actual intent of a man's mind. You look at what he said and did."***
**Application:** As Lord Denning says, "A contact exists when there is, to all outward appearances, a contract." Saying you did not intend to create a contract is not a valid defence if all evidence provided demonstrates a willingness to be bound.

## The Nature of Agreement: The Subjective Approach

As we have seen, Courts will set aside what a specific party was thinking at the time (their subjective intentions). Instead, the court places greater emphasis on what a rationally thinking individual would think under the very same conditions and situations. They look at the intentions on a more neutral factual basis (objective intent). Courts do not stray into the zone of what is in a person's mind (such a thing is virtually impossible to prove). Instead, they look at arrangements from the perspective of a reasonable man. The subjective '*meeting of minds*' is not needed for an arrangement or an agreement to become binding at law. The bigger picture is looked at– the whole situation. Courts examine the rationality behind the big picture, and whether or not the parties could be held to have possessed such an intention. If the various stages of this contractual test are not met, then the court will move to assume that the party having their intentions examined did not willingly intend to be bound by a binding legal contract. What we can see is that, in reality, there are somewhat difficult blurred lines crossing over someone's objective and subjective intentions.

**Consider the case of:**

**Leonard v. Pepsi Co. Inc.** 88 F. Supp 2d 1 (S.D.N.Y. 1999)
**Facts:** Pepsi Co. released a commercial advertisement. This televised advert, showed a jet being offered in exchange for seven million of their '*Pepsi points™.*' Mr Leonard gathered the requisite number of points. He then sent a his seven million Pepsi points to stake his claim for the jet, valuing each '*Pepsi Point™*' at $1 each. Pepsi Co. refused to honour Mr Leonard's offer, and he brought action against Pepsi.
**Ratio: The court held that the advertisement on TV was not an offer that Mr. Leonard could accept. The advertisement was a 'sales puff' that was an obviously not meant to be binding.**
**Application:** If the court had fallen on the side of the complainant by looking at his perspective through the subjective approach, it could be remotely (but, ultimately, not convincingly) conceived that Pepsi Co. had given off the impression in their advertising campaign that they were genuinely offering a military fighter jet, which they had in their possession, in exchange for seven million of their '*Pepsi Points ™*'.

## The Elements of a Contract

In order for a contract to come into existence, one of the parties (namely the **offeror**) has to make an **offer that is explicitly clear with certainty at the end** and the other party (the **offeree**) has to respond in providing a statement that is just as clear, and with the certainty that they are willingly accepting the offer.

This can be broken down into three essential elements:

| Agreement | Intention to create legal relations | Consideration |
|---|---|---|
| To include **offer** and **acceptance** | The intention to contract and the necessary **capacity** (capability) | Something being given by each party |

If one of these elements missing = NO contract

## Correct Form of the Contract

It does not usually have to be in **writing**. It can be **oral**, by **inference** or **conduct**, or by a **combination** of these things. Some kinds of contract/agreement must be made and/or evidenced in writing:

1. *Contracts under seal* (also known as 'specialities'): Most formal contracts; all other contracts are called 'simple' contracts, whether in writing or not.

2. *Contracts which must be in writing*: Bills of exchange and promissory notes (The Bills of Exchange Act 1882), hire-purchase agreements (The Consumer Credit Act 1974), the sale of land (The Law of Property (MP) Act 1989).

3. *Contracts which must be evidenced in writing*: Contracts of guarantee (Statute of Frauds 1677).

# Chapter 2 - The Offer

In this section, you will be introduced to the basics of a contract and offers.

One way to describe an offer is that it is a proposal issued by one party towards another party. This proposition is based on terms that are either set in stone and cannot be changed, or ones that are capable of becoming set in stone only when the other party accepts them.

**Opening Negotiations or Statements About Price**

**General Principle: Not everything said in the course of negotiations can amount to a firm offer.**

**Harvey** v **Facey** [1893] AC 552
**Facts:** Harvey (complainant) sent Facey (defendant) a telegram. It said, *"Will you sell us Bumper Hall Pen? Telegraph lowest cash price".* Facey replied that same day, *"Lowest price for Bumper Hall Pen £900."* Harvey responded, *"We agree to buy Bumper Hall Pen for the sum of nine hundred pounds asked by you. Please send us your title deeds in order that we may get early possession."* This was an attempt to try and accept this price.
**Ratio: The Privy Council held that there had been no offer. Facey's statement was one that just concerned the price. As a result, it was something that could not be accepted.**
**Application:** This case distinguished between what an offer is and what an invitation to treat is. The key principle that can be applied from this case was stated by Lord Diplock (then in the Privy Court): *"Intentions that are communicated have to coincide".*

**General Principle: Because merchants have limited supply, the advertisement for their goods is considered an invitation to treat.**

**Grainger v Gough** [1896] AC 325, HL
**Facts:** The Agents were London agents (complainants) for a wine merchant based in France (defendants). They circulated catalogues and took orders, which they then forwarded to the defendants, who

maintained the right to refuse any of them. The case's issue was based on whether or not the defendants were liable to pay tax on legal contracts provided by their agents based in England.

**Ratio: The House of Lords held the advertisement to ultimately be an invitation to treat. As such, it was not an offer. It was just a means of expressing a willingness to listen to offers as the beginning of further negotiations.**

**Application:** Lord Herschell said in this case that it would be incorrect to regard these kinds of advertisements as offers because: *"the merchant might find himself involved in any number of contractual obligations to supply wine of a particular description which he would be quite unable to carry out,"* because the merchant only keeps a finite supply.

**General Principle: An agreement can only exist when a clear offer is made that is then mirrored by a clear statement of acceptance.**

**Gibson v Manchester City Council** [1979] 1WLR 294
**Facts:** This was a case concerning the sale of a council house. Manchester City Council wrote to tenants of some of their council houses. They invited them to apply to purchase their homes. The complainant in this case, Gibson, returned the form that the Council sent out. A price was then agreed between Gibson and the Council. Whilst this was happening, a new political party was elected into power. The new council of Manchester City refused to proceed with the sale of the house to Gibson. **Ratio: The House of Lords held that no legally binding contract existed. Gibson had made an offer that Manchester City Council had still not accepted. Statements in the communications such as *"may be prepared to sell"* and *"please complete the enclosed application form"* all appeared to be elements of an invitation to treat.**

**General Principle: If, during negotiations for a sale, the vendor (person selling) gives a price they will sell at, that statement could be an offer that could then be accepted.**

**Bigg v Boyd Gibbins** [1971] 2 All ER 183
This case concerned the sale of a property. In the course of negotiations, there was a letter from the seller (complainant) that

said, *"...Your offer of £20,000 is a little optimistic. For a quick sale, I would accept £26,000."* The defendant replied, *"I accept your offer."* The last letter that the seller sent stated: *"My wife and I are pleased that you are purchasing the property."*

**Ratio: The court held that there was a contract. An intention to be bound was essential and this was evident by what was said by the complainant in last two letters.**

**Application:** Intention to create legal relations can dictate whether a statement is an offer or an answer to a question.

**Invitation to treat**

**General Principle: Goods displayed on the shelf do not amount to an offer to sell, but are instead an invitation to treat.**

**Pharmaceutical Society of G.B.** v **Boots Cash Chemist** [1953] 1 QB 401

**Facts:** Boots decided to change the layout of their shop from one that used counter services to one that used self-service. A pharmacist was at the tills, but was not at the shelves where the items were. Action was brought against Boots for breaching the legislation, as Section 18 of the Poisons Act 1933 states that is an offense to sell specific items unless the sale took place under the *'supervision of a registered pharmacist'*. The courts needed to decide at which point the offer actually occurred. Was it when the customer took the goods from the shelf and put them in the basket, or was it when the goods were taken to the cash desk?

**Ratio: The Court of Appeal held that a contract came to be when the goods were presented at the till. Displaying the goods on the various shelves in their shops was just an invitation to treat. The sale was in fact legal.**

**Application:** The court also commented on the fact that if taking items from the shelves was indeed an offer, the customer would be held to accept the offer and, as a result, would not have been able to change their mind. Displaying the goods on the various shelves in their shops was just an invitation to treat.

**General Principle: Goods displayed in the a shop window are invitations to treat and not regarded as an offer to sell.**

**Fisher v Bell** [1961] 1 QB 394
**Facts**: Mr. Bell, a shop owner, put a flick pocketknife in the front window of his shop. The Offensive Weapons Act 1959 prohibited the "offer for sale" of these flick knives.
**Ratio: The prosecution against Mr Bell failed. This, the court held, was because putting goods on display in the window of a shop only amounts to an invitation to treat and not an offer.**
**Application:** An offer is made by a customer who wishes to buy the item. The shopkeeper has discretion to accept or reject this offer.

**General Principle: Advertisements in periodicals are typically invitations to treat.**

**Partridge v Crittenden** [1968] 2 All ER 421
**Facts**: The defendant, Crittenden, posted an advertisement in a magazine. It stated that he was willing to sell "Bramblefinch cocks and hens at 25 shillings each". Crittenden was prosecuted under the Protection of Birds Act 1954 for 'offering' wild birds "for sale".
**Ratio: The court held the posted advertisement to be an invitation to treat rather than an offer. It was just an expression of Crittenden's desire to receive offers from potential buyers as the starting point for further negotiation.**
**Application:** Lord Parker CJ stated in this case as obiter: *"I think that when one is dealing with advertisements and circulars, then, unless they come from the manufacturers, there is business sense in* [advertisements] *being construed as invitations to treat and not offers for sale."*

**Bilateral Agreements v Unilateral Offers**

**Bilateral:**

A bilateral contract comes into existence when someone like Adam promises to do something for Josh, if Josh promises to do something for a certain amount of money or something of quantifiable value to Adam in return. Basically, the concept of a promise in exchange for another promise is what will make these kinds of contracts enforceable at law.

**Further Example:** Both parties assume an obligation to each other, e.g. "I will buy your car in return for giving you £500" = "Sold".

**Unilateral Offer:**

Unilateral contracts arise where A promises to do something in return for an ACT to be performed by B. They can be best seen, then, as 'If you do this' types of contract. This is a type of contract where commencing performance is the requisite acceptance

**Example:** I will pay you £10 if you were to take some notes for me at a law lecture I could not attend on a certain day this week.

**Example:** If, during my contract law lecture, I say "I will pay £10,000 to the first student to swim the length of the river Thames by the end of the day," I have just created a unilateral contract that can potentially be accepted by any one of the recipients. If an hour later, a student comes to my office drenched, claiming to have been the first to swim a length of the Thames and claiming the evidence has been put on YouTube, I am bound.

**General Principle: In unilateral contracts, the performance of a requested action amounts acceptance and binds the offeror to give a reward.**

**Carlill v Carbolic Smoke Ball Co.** [1892] 1 QB 256
**Facts:** At the time of an influenza epidemic, the defendants advertised the sale of a device called a 'smoke ball'. They posted the advert in the newspapers, which stated that they would pay £100 to anybody who 'caught influenza, a cold, or any other kind of disease that came from catching a cold' after they used the 'smoke ball' three times a day for fourteen days, in accordance with the instructions they provided with each ball. Carbolic Smoke Ball Company also mentioned in the advertisement that they had put aside £1000 in a bank account to be able to pay such fees. Mrs. Carlill bought a smoke ball and followed all of the instructions, but caught influenza and, as such, went on to claim £100 from the company. The company responded by saying that the advert was

nothing but a 'sales puff,' or a piece of sales talk (e.g. Red Bull gives you wings), and thus there was no offer; furthermore, they argued it would be unreasonable and impossible to contract to the entire world at large.

**Ratio: The Court of Appeal held that the offer was actually a unilateral one; one with the intention to create relations to anyone who met the conditions of the offer to claim £100. The court also rationalised that because it was a unilateral offer, there was no need for communication of acceptance. The court finally addressed the point that an offer to the world at large could be made if it was capable of acceptance, so long as the conditions stated were fulfilled. Mrs. Carlill was, therefore, able to claim £100.**

**Application:** Carbolic Smoke Ball Co. claimed that their advertisement was too vague to be treated as a definite offer. However, if an advertisement is precise and detailed to the point where completing the stated conditions would fulfil a contract, then it is an enforceable unilateral contract and not merely a "sales puff."

**Auctions**

The calling out for bids by an auctioneer amounts to an invitation to treat. Anyone who makes a bid is making offer. The auctioneer has the discretion to accept or reject these offers.

**What the Law Says:** S.57(2) of the **Sale of Goods Act 1979** reinforces the case law rule that a potential buyer makes an offer through bidding, which the auctioneer then accepts at the drop of his hammer. Therefore, anyone looking to buy can withdraw his/her bid right up until the moment that the hammer comes down. Additionally, any item can be withdrawn from sale even after bidding has begun. There are specific rules for auction, however, which mean that the item cannot be sold legally at an auction to anybody other than the person who lodges the highest bid.

**General Principle: If there is an auction without reserve, the auctioneer must sell to the highest bidder.**

**Barry v Davies** (2000) Times 31/8/00, CA

**Facts:** This case concerned an auction of some machines. The auction was advertised as being "without reserve". Two machines, worth £14,000 each, were placed up for auction. Barry bid £200 on each machine. Davies rejected the chance to accept the bid because it was so low. In response, he took the machines down from the auction.

**Ratio: Barry sued. He was awarded £27,600 (The worth of the machines minus the bid). The ruling stood despite an appeal by Davies. Despite the fact that there was no contract between the vendor and the person purchasing the machines, a collateral contract was held to exist between the auctioneer and the highest bidder.**

**Application:** When there is an auction that sells an item or items with 'no reserve price' (that is no minimum fee for a buyer to pay for an offer to be accepted), there is an offer to sell only to the highest bidder. This can only be accepted by the lodging of the highest bid.

**General Principle: Items can be withdrawn before the auction takes place.**

**Harris v Nickerson** (1873) LR 8 QB 286

**Facts:** Nickerson (the defendant) posted a newspaper advert for an auction. The plaintiff took the time to travel, at their expense, to where the auction was being held in order to put in a bid on some office furniture. The listing of the office furniture was unexpectedly withdrawn. The Plaintiff sued for loss of time and expense. The plaintiff argued that the advertisement amounted to a contract between themselves and the defendant.

**Ratio: The court held the advertisement of a sale did not mean that there was a contract to mandate that any specific items, such as the office furniture, would actually be put up for sale.**

**Application:** The important principle that can be applied from this case is that something which advertises that items will be put up for auction does not create nor extend an offer to anybody that the items will really be put up for sale. As a result, the advertiser is actually able to withdraw the items from the auction at any time before the auction is set to begin.

# Tenders

**General Principle: An invitation to tender is usually classed as an invitation to treat.**

**Spencer v Harding** (1870) LR 5 CP 561
**Facts:** Harding (defendant) distributed advertisements that said he was putting some stock up for trade. It also said that he was willing to accept tenders. The defendants decided not to sell the stock to the highest bidder, which was Spencer. Spencer sued, saying that Harding was compelled to accept the highest offer.
**Ratio: The court held that the submission of a tender was an offer, and not acceptance of a contract.**
**Application:** A person has no obligation to accept the highest tender.

**General principle: Referential bidding discouraged by the courts.**

**Harvela Investments Ltd v Royal Trust Co of Canada** [1986] AC 207
**Facts:** Two parties were invited to bid secretly for a block of shares, on the understanding that the shares would be sold to whoever bid highest. Harvela's (complainant) bid $2 175 000, while the other party (Royal Trust of Canada: defendant) bid "$2 100 000, or $10 000 more than any other cash bid, whichever is higher".
**Ratio: The House of Lords said the referential bid was ineffective and that Harvela's cash bid should have been accepted.**
**Application:** If someone who makes a tender says that they will accept the highest offer to buy goods or the lowest for someone to provide certain items, or their services, the tender can be seen as something that is either an offer or an invitation to place offer. Placing a tender that references someone else's' bid will invalidate the tender.

**General Principle: A collateral warranty arises if a bid is properly submitted within time and not considered.**

**Blackpool and Flyde Aeroclub Ltd** v **Blackpool Borough Council** [1990] 1WLR 1195

**Facts:** The Blackpool Aeroclub (claimants) and an additional six potential suitors were invited to submit tenders for the ability to fly leisure flights from Blackpool Airport. The claimant lodged a tender correctly. However, this tender was not considered because there was an admin processing error. The defendant (Blackpool Borough Council) argued that the claimant had simply submitted an offer that had just not been accepted.

**Ratio: The Court of Appeal said there was an implied collateral warranty. Blackpool Council had chosen the parties that they wanted to invite to make tenders. What this implied is that anyone who was invited and who also followed the pre-determined procedure would be allowed to have his tender properly considered.**

**Application:** In Lord Bingham's leading judgement, it was stated that: *"A tendering procedure of this kind is, in many respects, heavily weighted in favour of the person inviting. He can invite tenders from as many or as few parties as he chooses. He need not tell any of them who else, or how many others, he has invited."*

Parties that make invitations to tender are bound to consider a tender that is submitted before a pre-determined deadline.


**Counter-offers**

**General Principle: A counter-offer nullifies the original offer.**

**Hyde** v **Wrench** (1840) 3 Beav 334

**Facts:** Wrench (the defendant) wrote to Hyde (the claimant). Wrench made an offer to sell Hyde his farm for £1000. The claimant responded promptly. He issued an offer for £950. The defendant took time to consider this. He turned down Hyde's offer. Wrench went on to sell the farm to another third party. Hyde tried to accept the first offered price of £1000 whilst bringing action against Wrench for breaching the contract when Wrench sold the farm to the third party.

**Ratio: The Court held that a contract did not exist.**

**Application:** In submitting his own offer, Wrench rejected the offer made by Hyde. The original offer had been completely destroyed and it was not something that was open for Hyde to

accept.
**Request for Information**

**General Principle:** A request for information is not a counter-offer.

**Stevenson Jacques** v **McLean** (1879 – 80) LR 5 QBD 346
**Facts**: The defendant, McLean, sent a telegraph to the complainant, Stevenson. In it he offered to sell 3,800 tons of iron "at 40 shillings a ton…up until Monday". On Monday morning the complainant wired over a telegraph to McLean: *"please wire whether you would accept forty for delivery over two months or if not longest limit you would give"*. McLean did not respond and at 1:34pm the complainant sent another telegram, accepting the original offer. McLean sold the iron off to a third party in that time, later proceeding to advise Stevenson by telegram. Stevenson brought action on the grounds that McLean was in breach of their agreement. His main argument was that the Monday morning telegram amounted to a counter-offer.
**Ratio: The court held Stevenson had not made a counter-offer. Instead, he had just made an inquiry and could not amount to the rejection of the offer.**
**Application:** Is it possible to phrase counteroffers as questions to see if the offeror is willing to accept the new term(s) without nullifying the original offer.

# Chapter 3   Acceptance/Revocation

**General Principle: Silence cannot be used as a means to accept an offer.**

**Felthouse v Bindley** (1863) 142 ER 1037, Exch Ch
**Facts:** Felthouse (the claimant) talked about buying a horse from his nephew. Felthouse wrote to his nephew Bindley stating *"If I hear no more from you, I shall consider the horse to be mine at £30."* The nephew did not reply, no money was paid, and the horse remained in the nephew's custody.
The nephew took action to contact an auctioneer in order to withdraw the horse from an auction. The auctioneer forgot these instructions and the horse was sold to a different person. In order for the uncle to make a claim against the auctioneer, he had to demonstrate that a contract was in place between him and his nephew Bindley.
**Ratio: The Court of Common Pleas held that no contract existed; Felthouse's letter provided an open offer and it had not been accepted.**
**Application:** Silence does not amount to acceptance of an offer.

**The offeror can ask for a specific method of acceptance**

**General Principle: If the offerer requests acceptance through a specific mode, then acceptance can only take place through this mode of communication.**

**Tinn v Hoffman** (1873) 29 LT 271, Exch.Ch.
**Facts:** The claimant wrote to defendant to make an inquiry as to how much it would cost to buy 800 tons of iron. The defendant replied, saying that it would cost £3 per ton and requesting the claimant respond "by return".
**Ratio: The court held that, as the offer was not actually accepted by return of post, no contract existed.**
**Application:** Honeyman J, on the other hand, stated obiter that a telegram, communication verbally or any other kind of communication that was at least as fast as a letter written by return of post would have sufficed. With this in mind, if an offerer asks for acceptance by post and the offeree sends acceptance through

text message, a contract could be held to exist.

**General Principle: The method of acceptance arranged for a tender was not mandatory and if an offeror wants it to be mandatory, this needs to be made explicit.**

**Manchester Diocesan Council v Commercial General Investments** [1969] 3 All ER 1593
**Facts:** The claimants (the Diocesan Council) owned a property that they wanted to sell by tender. The tender form included an additional statement that the tenderer whose application was successful would be notified by letter. It was to be sent through the post to the address that was written in the tender form. The defendant sent in a tender that the council then accepted. In September, they notified the defendant's representative of this acceptance. The secretary of state gave permission for the sale to go ahead in November. During January, the claimant wrote to the defendant in order to provide confirmation of the agreement. The question that arose was when a contract had been formed.
**Ratio: The court held that a contract was formed in September. This is because the way in which acceptance could be carried out, as written in the tender form, was not limited as the only way of doing so. As such, the postal rule (see relevant section) would not apply. However, any other means by which the claimant's acceptance was communicated would be satisfactory.**

**Acceptance can be by conduct**

**General Principle: A contract can be formed in absence of a written agreement if both parties' actions are in accordance with the agreement.**

**Brogden v Metropolitan Railway Co.** (1877) 2 Book Cas 666
**Facts:** For several years, Brogden (complainant) had supplied the railway company (the defendant) with coal in the absence of a written agreement. The parties decided to enter a written contract. A draft contract was prepared and then sent to the complainant. The complainant amended it and marked it as approved before returning it to the railway company. Their agent put the draft in his

desk. Business continued between the complainant and the defendant. The two parties maintained the trade arrangements under this new document until December 1973, at which point Brogden refused to continue to supply coal on that basis. He stated that, since the railway company had never actually made an alternate draft, which they intended to be a counter offer, there could be no legal contract. **Ratio: The House of Lords held a contract did materialise through what the parties' actions that they carried out. The offer was the company ordering coal and the acceptance was Brogden was supplying it.**
**Application:** Actions between the parties can amount to a mutuality of obligations being fulfilled, even in the absence of a written contract.

**The Battle of the Forms**

**General Principle: When accepting a contract, the agreeing party accepts the terms and conditions of the offerer. This is also known as the 'last shot' rule.**

**Butler Machine Tool Co. Ltd v Ex Cell O Corporation ltd** [1979] WLR 401
**Facts:** The sellers responded to the buyers, who were interested in purchasing a machine, by sending them a quote as to how much it would cost to supply it to them. The quote was given on the conditions that the sellers gave. These, it was written, were to be followed above any other terms and conditions that the buyers put in for their order. These clauses contained a price variation clause. The buyers made an order, but letter they sent contained a number of contradictory conditions. In particular, they did not put in a price variation clause. At the bottom of the order was a tear offer confirmation slip that had been put in on the intention of the buyer's terms. The sellers completed this tear off confirmation slip and sent it back. The sellers then asserted that they would now be allowed to make variations to the contract price.
**Ratio: The Court of Appeal rejected this claim. Their reasoning for rejecting the claim was that the sellers had willingly and expressly accepted the buyer's terms on the tear off slip. They had accepted the buyers *"last shot"*. Lord Denning stated: *"In some cases, it is decided by who gets there first. If the offeror intends to sell at a named price on the terms**

*and conditions stated and the buyer orders the goods intending to accept the offer, if the difference is so material that it would affect the price, the buyer ought not to be allowed to take advantage of the difference unless he brings it to the attention of the seller ".*

**Application:** When a party communicates acceptance to an offer, he impliedly accepts the terms and conditions of the offerer.


## The Postal Rule

**General Principle: As soon as acceptance is posted through the mail, a contract is formed. This is known as the 'postal rule'.**

**Adams v Lindsell** (1818) 1 B & Ald 681
**Facts**: Lindsell wrote to Adams, hoping to sell Adams some wool. He requested a reply be sent "in course of post". The letter containing the offer was sent out on the 2$^{nd}$ September. It did not arrive, however, until the 5$^{th}$ of September. On the 5$^{th}$, Adams posted back a letter containing his acceptance. When the letter actually arrived to Lindsell, quite a long period of time had passed. Lindsell had since assumed that the offer had been turned down and he sold the wool to a third party. Adams brought a claim for breach of contract.
**Ratio: The court said Adams was to be awarded damages. The court ruled that Adams accepted when he posted his letter.**
**Application:** Postal rule dictates that a contract takes place as soon as the letter is posted, regardless of whether that letter reaches the offerer in time. The offerer, if he allows acceptance through the post, is held responsible for contracts he may have formed but may not be aware exist.


**General Principle: If acceptance is communicated through a letter that then becomes lost in the post, a contract will still be seen to have formed at the moment it is mailed.**

**Household Fire Insurance v Grant** (1879) 4 ExD 216
**Facts:** Grant took an interest in potentially buying shares in the plaintiff's company. The company was content with the application, and sent Grant a letter in the post stating this, but it got lost in the postal system. The company liquidated soon afterwards.

The liquidator, acting for the company, brought action against Grant in relation to any outstanding balance on the shares. Grant disputed the fact that he had to pay. He said he did not have to because he had not received a reply to his offer to buy the shares.

**Ratio: The court held that a contract came into existence the moment the letter of allotment of shares (the acceptance) was posted.**

**Application:** The "postal rule" still applies if the letter which communicates acceptance is lost in the post. Similarly to Adams v Lindsell, a contract is formed as soon as the letter is mailed, the fate of the letter has no effect on the validity of the contract.

**The Postal Rule and Instantaneous Communication i.e. Email**

The rapid expansion of means of electronic communication has brought up challenging and, as of yet, not fully addressed questions concerning the how the postal rule applies when people communicate using e-mail and any other messaging forum or medium on the whole internet, like Facebook™ and Twitter ™. On one side of the coin, there are those who argue that an e-mail exchange is more or less simultaneous and instantaneous and because of this the postal rule should not apply. What this does not take account of however is that e-mails are occasionally rejected by server service providers such as Google™ or a private server for a company. Even if it does arrive, the recipient of the message might not actually read the message straight away. Many academic commentators have, on that basis, leaned towards the view that e-mail ought to be treated as a kind of mail to which the postal rule should normally apply. This would, of course, be subject to when there is expressly agreed upon exclusion of the rule by the parties' themselves,

It is imperative to remember that the postal rule, should it even be able to be applied, applies to acceptances alone. It does not apply to an offer that has been communicated by post that is being revoked. It is a common misconception that an offer can be revoked by letter at the time it was put into the post box because of the applicability of the postal rule.

As such, the main applicable principle in the postal rule is that acceptance by post comes into effect when it is posted as opposed to when it is delivered.

When an offeror establishes a website that has a reply form included on it, a near instantaneous means of communication is achieved. This is because the offeree can immediately learn as to whether his acceptance has been received or not. There are a lot of theories that advocate that the postal rule should not apply in these situations (and a quite sustainable view that a web page, like a shop window, normally amounts to an invitation to treat as opposed to an offer). However, because the internet facilitates such an expanding means through which people can communicate, there are strong policy reasons that exist to make sure that the rules for accepting offers electronically are consistently the same, regardless of which kind of software is in operation. We have addressed this issue in a full answer in our **Question and Answer Section**.

## Communication of Acceptance

**General Rule: The postal rule cannot be relied on in cases where acceptance mandates actual notification or communication.**

### Holwell Securities v Hughes [1974] 1 WLR 155
**Facts:** Holwell Securities (the claimants) were allowed by the defendant to have an option *"exercisable by notice in writing to* [Hughes, the defendant] *at any time within six months from the date hereof."* On 14th April 1972, Holwell Securities gave notice to Hughes in writing as a means of invoking the option. However, the letter never arrived. The claimants, Holwell Securities, applied for specific performance of the option they agreed with the defendants. They argued that it was complete on 14th April, which is when the letter confirming acceptance was posted.
**Ratio: The courts held that Holwell securities had not legitimately exercised their option. Application:** If acceptance requires actual notice, the notice becomes a term of acceptance. Applying postal rule in these cases results in absurdity as it would violate terms of the offer. As such, postal rule can be set aside.

### When is acceptance communicated?

General Principle: An acceptance via instantaneous communication is not bound by the postal rule; acceptance must be communicated for it to create a binding contract.

**Entores v Miles Far East Company** [1955] 2 QB 327
**Facts**: The claimant was a London based company. They offered to buy, through use of telex, goods from the defendant's agent. The agents were located in Amsterdam. Their offer was accepted by the defendant's agents, again through use of a telex. As there was a dispute between the parties, the location where the contract had been concluded became very important.
**Ratio: The court held that since the acceptance was received in England, when the acceptance was sent via telex and read in England. Lord Denning reasoned that acceptance could not create a binding contract until it notified the offerer.**
**Application:** The onus (responsibility or burden to actually prove something) is on the person accepting to shout back, "I accept your offer" repeatedly until he is heard. Denning utilises many examples to demonstrate this rule. If two men are separated by a river and one attempts to notify the other of his acceptance of an offer (but he is drowned out by the sound of a passing plane), it is his responsibility to voice his acceptance again to create a contract. Because of Entores, no acceptance (outside of the post) can be valid unless it actually notifies the offerer.

**Revocation of offer**

**General Principle: An offer can be withdrawn at any time before it has been accepted. Anything said or done to accept the offer after it has been withdrawn has absolutely no effect whatsoever.**

**Routledge v Grant** (1828) 130 ER 920, Best CJ
Facts: Grant (defendant) made an offer to rent Routledge's (complainant's) building. A definitive answer had to be provided to Routledge within the space of six weeks. After three weeks had passed, Grant retracted his offer. However, just within the six-week period, Routledge decided to accept it. **Ratio: The court held that, in this case, the acceptance had come too late. He**

reasoned that, if one of the parties had six weeks to accept an offer, the other had six weeks to put an end to it. One party cannot be bound without the other.

**Application:** Withdrawal usually needs to be communicated to the offeree. This does not become effective until this kind of communication to withdraw is received. The special rule for postal acceptances (below) is not something that applies to withdrawals.

**General Principle: Revocation of an offer must be communicated and is effective upon its receipt.**

**Byrne & Co v Leon Van Tienhoven & Co** (1880) LR 5 CPD 344

**Facts:** Byrne posted a letter on 1st October, with an offer to sell Van Tienhoven a certain amount of tinplate. Byrne then posted another letter on 8th October intended to be a statement to withdraw the offer. The first letter reached Tienhoven on 11th October and Tienhoven accepted the offer immediately through use of a telegram. They followed this up with a confirmatory letter four days later. The second letter sent by Byrne as a withdrawal arrived on 20th October, by which time the offer had been accepted.

**Ratio: The court ruled that a Bryne's revocation was not valid until it was received by Van Tienhoven, thus a contract had formed when Van Tienhoven telegrammed his acceptance.**

**Application:** These kinds of promises cannot be enforced unless they are supported by some kind of consideration (something of value like money) in return (see relevant section on consideration).

**General Principle: The revocation of an offer does not have to be communicated by one party to another directly; it can be done through a reliable third party.**

**Dickinson v Dodds** (1876) LR 2 Ch D 463

**Facts**: Dodds extended an offer to sell his house to Dickinson. He left the offer open until Friday. On Thursday, Dickinson made a decision to buy the house. He then heard from someone else that Dodds had entered into a contract with a third party for sale. On Friday, Dickinson accepted the offer. He then looked to enforce the agreement.

**Ratio: The Court of Appeal held that the information that was**

provided by a neutral and trustworthy third party about the house being sold was seen to amount to sufficient notice of the withdrawal of the offer for sale. Therefore, his acceptance was not effective.

**Application:** Revocation of an offer does not need to be communicated directly. It is acceptable that the offeror was aware of the revocation of the offer before there was acceptance.

**General Principle: If it can be demonstrated that revocation was sent and could have been reasonably read, then that revocation is valid.**

**Tenax Steamship Co v Owners of the Motor Vessel Brimnes (The Brimnes)** [1975] QB 929

**Facts:** Tenax Steamship hired a ship named The Brimnes, under the condition that the payment be prompt and paid in advance. When the payments arrived late, the owners withdrew their offer as they were entitled to under the agreement. They issued this withdrawal via telex, and no one in the office read the telex although the revocation was sent during business hours. The issue arose as to whether revocation had taken place when the telex arrived with the revocation or when it was picked up and read.

**Ratio: The Court of Appeal held the withdrawal took place when it was received in the charterer's office, not at the point it was read.**

**Application:** If a litigant could prove that his revocation of offer could have been reasonably read, then the offer is officially revoked when it is delivered.

**General Principle: A unilateral offer can be revoked by publishing the revocation in the same method by which the offer was issued. All of the offerees do not need to read the revocation for it to be valid.**

**Shuey v US** (1875) 92 US 73 (persuasive judgement only, not binding)

**Facts:** US authorities placed an advertisement in various newspapers displaying a certain amount of money that would be paid as a reward in exchange for information leading to the arrest of a number of criminals. Later, the President of USA released a

proclamation that cancelled the reward, and once again this was publicized in the newspapers. After this advert had been published, Shuey (who had seen the original advertisement but did not see that the ransom had been revoked) identified one of the wanted men and claimed the reward. **Ratio: The Supreme Court held that, as the offer had been made through a general advert to the world at large, as opposed to him personally, he ought to have realised that it could be withdrawn in the same way.**
**Application:** Where there is an offer that can be accepted through a person's conduct, it is not clear what rules deal with the withdrawal. This is especially so with rewards and "challenges" (i.e I will pay £1000 to the first person here that cycles from London to Liverpool).

**General Principle: When someone has begun to carry out the terms of a unilateral offer and keeps on doing so, the unilateral offer cannot be retracted.**

**Errington v Errington and Woods** [1952] 1 KB 290
**Facts:** Mr Errington purchased a house for both his son and daughter-in-law (Ms. Woods) to live in. He paid £250 in cash and borrowed the remaining £500 from a building society. The house was registered in the name of the father. However, he said that as long as they paid the regular instalments on the mortgage, he would transfer the house to them as soon as it had been repaid. Fifteen years after the father died, his estate brought action to seek possession of the house.
**Ratio: The Court of Appeal held that a unilateral contract existed. Woods and Errington were not obliged to keep paying out money, but if they did so because the father was obliged to transfer the house to them in accordance with his promise, that was acceptable.**
**Application:** Denning LJ said obiter that: "a unilateral contract cannot be revoked once the potential acceptor has started to perform their obligations under the contract arrangements."

**Revocation of a Unilateral Offer**

**General Principle: An offer for a unilateral contract cannot be withdrawn if performance has been started or completed by**

the offeree.

### Daulia v Four Millbank Nominees [1978] 2 All ER 557, CA

**Facts:** Daulia (complainant) wanted to buy a series of different properties from Millbank Nominees (defendant). Inquiries were made and draft contracts were prepared. Millbank agreed that if Daulia co-produced the draft contract and a bankers' draft by a specific time, they would enter into a full contract with her. Daulia obtained the bankers' draft and submitted it to Millbank Nominee's offices before the deadline. However, Millbank ultimately refused to proceed with the deal.

**Ratio: Brightman J rejected Daulia's claim for damages, as the collateral contract did not fall into line with S40 of the Law of Property Act 1925. However, Goff LJ said obiter that** *"while the offeror of a unilateral contract is entitled to require full performance of his condition and short of that is not bound, there must be an implied obligation on his part not to prevent the condition becoming satisfied, and that obligation arises as soon as the offeree starts to perform."*

**Application:** Until the offeree starts to perform, the offeror can revoke the entire offer. However, once the offeree has started to carry out the obligations of the agreement, it becomes too late for the offeror to go back on his offer.

**General Principle: The terms of a contract may allow an offerer to revoke his promise even after it has been partially accepted by performance.**

### Luxor v Cooper [1941] 1 All ER 33, HL

Cooper made an agreement with an estate agent, Luxor, that £10,000 would be paid to them if Luxor was able to find a buyer that would pay £175,000 the land. The agreement between Luxor and Cooper was a standard agreement that could be expected from any seller and estate agent: that Cooper would pay the commission once the house was sold and Cooper would not pay if a buyer was not found. Luxor found a buyer but Cooper actually sold the land (two cinemas) to someone else. Luxor pursued Cooper for the fee stating that they had fulfilled the contract.

**Ratio:** The House of Lords held in favour of Cooper on the grounds that there was no reason to assume a responsibility by not revoking their offer. Lord Wright said obiter: *"it is well recognized that there may be cases where obviously some term must be implied if the intention of the parties is not to be defeated, some term of which it can be predicated that 'it goes without saying'...some term not expressed but necessary to give to the transaction such business efficacy as the parties must have intended."*

**Application:** It is more likely that the courts would agree with an argument for an implied term (see relevant section) if that term were reasonable. They will not imply terms into a contract just because it would be reasonable to do so. This is an important principle to remember when applying it to practical scenarios. A party that has carelessly made a very unfavourable contract will argue that some kind of implied term, which, if it were to exist, would make the contract fair. That, it must be understood, is not a good enough reason to imply a term.

**Lapse of time**

**General Principle:** Offers will expire at the end of the time stated for the lapse (if it's actually said) or after a reasonable time passes.

**Ramsgate Victoria Hotel v Montefiore** (1866) LR 1 Exch 109
**Facts:** In June, the defendant made an offer to buy shares in the plaintiff's company. However, he did not hear back from them. Later, the plaintiffs decided to divide the shares of the company between people who had an interest in it in November, and claimed to accept the defendant's offer. At that point, however, the defendant did not want to through with the deal.
**Ratio: The court said that, although the offer had not been formally withdrawn, it would expire after "a reasonable period of time". Given the ever-changing nature of the subject matter, the time interval had gone beyond what was reasonable.**
**Application:** Ramsgate applies to many cases which deal with lapse of offers. The nature of the goods is critical in applying this case. Stock shares fluctuate in price within seconds, and so it would be incredibly unreasonable to assume that an offer for

shares of a volatile stock would remain valid for days or weeks. If the goods were say furniture, the offer could remain open longer than what would be expected for electronic goods.

## Death of the offeree

**General Principle: Where an offer relies on the continuing existence of the offeror, the offer will terminate when the offeror dies. The offer will be unaffected by the death of the offeror in other cases and can be accepted and will bind the estate.**

**Reynolds** v **Atherton** (1921) 125 LT 690
**Facts:** In 1911, an offer to sell shares was made to "the directors" of a company. In 1919, an attempt was made by the survivors of the directors in 1911, and by the people representing the person who had died.
**Ratio: The supposed acceptance was held to be ineffective. Warrington L.J. said: "The offer having been made to a living person who ceases to be a living person before the offer is accepted, there is no longer an offer at all. The offer is not intended to be made to a dead person or to his executors, and the offer ceases to be an offer capable of acceptance."**
**Application:** If an offeree dies, the offer lapses and living representatives are unable to accept.

## Death of the offeror

**General Principle: If the offeror dies and the offeree does not know about it, acceptance can still occur.**

**Bradbury** v **Morgan** (1862) 1 H & C 249
**Facts:** JM Leigh asked Bradbury to provide credit to his brother. JM Leigh later died, and Bradbury, who did not know of his death, kept giving credit to JM Leigh's brother. The executors of JM Leigh's estate (Morgan) claimed they did not have to pay because these debts were not sustained during JM Leigh's lifetime. They claimed that these contracts were created while JM Leigh had died.
**Ratio: Morgan was held liable for the goods purchased on credit.**

**Application:** A guarantee (i.e being given an overdraft from your bank) is, generally speaking, divisible. The offer is continuous. It is accepted from time to time as the bank makes more loans to its customer. It appears that a guarantee of this kind cannot be established solely by the death of the guarantor. The offer continued to be an active commercial offer and, as such, the guarantee stood.

## Questions and Answers

- Offer and Acceptance problem 1
- Offer and Acceptance Problem 2
- Battle of the forms essay
- Postal rule and instantaneous communication essay

# Offer and Acceptance Problem Question One

On 9th December 2009, Abdul placed a notice on the University noticeboard as follows:

"Second-hand computer. Good condition. Worth £1,000. Selling for £175. Will sell to the first person to notify me by 13ᵗʰ January 2010. Telephone: 020 7320 9876. Email abdul0231@xyz.com Address: 1A, High Street, New Town, London E1."

Samson posted a letter on 8ᵗʰ January 2010, by first class recorded delivery post, agreeing to buy the computer for £175. Owing to the negligence of the Post Office, the letter was delivered to Abdul only on 14ᵗʰ January 2010.

Diana read the notice, telephoned Abdul on 12ᵗʰ January and left a message on his answer-phone, agreeing to buy the computer for £175. She also asked whether she could pay for the computer when she received her student loan money. Abdul listened to this message only on 14ᵗʰ January.

Maggie sent an email on 10ᵗʰ January, agreeing to buy the computer for £175. Abdul read the email on the 12ᵗʰ and sent a reply to Maggie, giving her an appointment to collect the computer on 16ᵗʰ January at 8 pm. Maggie responded by email, saying that she would pay the money when she collects the computer.

On 16ᵗʰ January, a leading computer shop in London decides to do a clearance sale and is selling good, brand new computers at £150 each.

Samson, Diana, and Maggie no longer wish to buy Abdul's computer.

Advise Abdul whether Samson, Diana and Maggie are under a contractual obligation to buy his computer.

# Offer and Acceptance Problem Question One: Answer

## Introduction

This paper is an advice for Abdul, Samson, Diana and Maggie in relation to the recent negotiation in relation to the sale of the computer. First, this paper will advise the parties as to whether a legally enforceable contact has been formed. The paper will do this by advising on the issue of the advertisement, and whether this will be viewed by the courts as a unilateral offer or an invitation to treat. Second, this paper will discuss the issue of Samson's acceptance by post, using the relevant case law. Third, this paper will discuss the issue of whether Diana's message was capable of acceptance. Fourth, this paper will critically discuss whether Maggie's acceptance through email was valid. Lastly, this paper will conclude its findings.

## Unilateral offer or invitation to treat

For a contract to exist one party ("the offeror") needs to make a clear and certain offer and the other party (the offeree) needs to communicate their equally clear and unequivocal acceptance. It is important to establish whether the advertisement placed on the notice board is an invitation to treat or an offer. If it is an offer, it will be capable of being accepted by the parties. However, if it is an invitation to treat, the parties must make the offer to Abdul, who may then choose to accept or reject it.

On 9th December 2009, Abdul, placed a notice on the University notice board as follows: *"Second-hand computer. Good condition. Worth £1,000. Selling for £175. Will sell to the first person to notify me by 13th January 2010. Telephone: 020 7320 9876. Email abdul0231@xyz.com Address: 1A, High Street, New Town, London E1."*

Generally, advertisements are regarded by the courts as statements inviting further negotiations or invitations to treat. An example of this was seen in **Partridge v Crittenden**[1] where a notice reading

'Bramblefinch cocks and hens, 25s each' was placed in the classified advertisement page of a periodical. The Court of Appeal held that newspaper advertisements are ordinarily to be treated as invitations to treat and not offers. The logic of this decision was set out by Lord Parker CJ, who noted the *"business sense in* [advertisements] *being construed as invitations to treat and not as offers"*[2]. Moreover, Lord Parker CJ in agreement cited Lord Herschell in **Grainger & Son v Gough**[3], where he made the point that it would be wrong to regard these types of advertisements as offers because *"the merchant might find himself involved in any number of contractual obligations to supply wine of a particular description which he would be quite unable to carry out,"* because the merchant would have a limited supply.

A possible line of argument that might be raised by the parties is that this advertisement constitutes a unilateral contract. A unilateral offer is where one party makes an offer or proposal, which is open to the world and is capable of acceptance by anyone. The other party 'accepts' the offer by performing the act in accordance with the requirements of the offer. Using **Carlill v Carbolic Smoke Ball Co.**[4], which is the authority on unilateral contracts, it can be argued the advertisement is in very firm terms and because the price and description of the computer are stated, it requires no further negation and is capable of being accepted by performance of payment. The advertisement states Abdul "[w]*ill sell to the first person to notify* [him] *by 13th January 2010"*. This may be interpreted by the court to be a unilateral offer.

However, the opposing argument to this can be drawn from what was argued by Finlay, Q.C., and T. Terrell for the defendant Smoke ball company in **Carlill** that *"the offer, the terms of which are too vague to be treated as a definite offer"*[5]. This argument is on a balance of probabilities likely to prevail because the advertisement is not clear, precise and unequivocal. For example, although the advertisement has a good description of the computer, it lacks information about the way in which acceptance should take

[1] [1968] 1 WLR 1204
[2] Partridge v Critenden [1986] 1 WLR 1204 per Lord Parker para 1209
[3] [1896] AC 325
[4] (1893) 1 QB 256
[5] (1893) 1 QB 256 at p 257

place through performance or the way in which payment should be made, i.e. how is Abdul to be contracted. It is, therefore, merely an invitation to treat and not an offer. This means that the parties must make the offer to Abdul, who can choose to accept or reject it.

Furthermore, Abdul is stipulating when acceptance must take place. This would suggest the offer is only open until *13ᵗʰ January 2010* and will lapse after this time. The leading case on this point is **Ramsgate Victoria Hotel Co. v Montefiore,** in which the courts stated, even an offer that has not been formally withdrawn would expire after "a reasonable time". In this case, the offer was for the sale of shares and the court felt six months was beyond what was reasonable.

**Samson**

Samson has posted a letter on 8ᵗʰ January 2010 by first class recorded delivery post, agreeing to buy the computer for £175. Owing to the negligence of the Post Office, the letter was delivered to Abdul only on 14ᵗʰ January 2010. If the advert is deemed a unilateral offer, then acceptance is normally effectual and the contract binding once acceptance is received by the offeror. However, the courts have introduced the postal rule to overcome the problem of the time a letter spends in the postal system. The problem with the postal system is that it creates a period of uncertainty for the parties, because the offeror is unaware if the offer has been accepted and the offeree is unaware whether the offer has been revoked. The postal rule was laid down in **Adams v Lindsell**. [6] Where post is deemed to be the proper means of communication, the acceptance takes effect from the moment the letter of acceptance is properly posted.

We are not told whether the post was Abdul's preferred method of communication. It would appear the postal rule that applies Samson's acceptance is valid, even though it was only read by Abdul on 14ᵗʰ January 2010. An illustration of this was seen in **Henthorn v Fraser**.[7] Fraser offered, in writing, to sell certain houses to Henthorn, with the offer to remain open for 14 days.

[6] (1818) 1 B & Ald 681
[7] [1892] 2 Ch 27

Henthorn received the offer in person. The next day, at midday, the society posted a letter to Henthorn revoking the offer. At 3:50pm, Henthorn posted a letter to the society accepting the offer. At 5:00pm, Henthorn received the society's revocation. The court in this case held a contract was made at 3:50pm when Henthorn posted his letter of acceptance.

Therefore, applying both cases above, it would appear Samson has benefited under the postal rule and accepted the offer and has a binding contract. However, the lawyers for Abdul may alternatively argue that Samson should not be allowed to benefit under the postal rule and there is no binding agreement, because the advert was at all times an invitation to treat; therefore, his letter will be construed as an offer. The authority for this proposition is **Thornton v Shoe Lane Parking Ltd**[8], which concerned the purchase of a ticket from the machine where he parked his car. In this case, Lord Denning went to great lengths to describe where an offer takes place and where an acceptance takes place.

**Diana**

Diana read the notice, telephoned Abdul on 12th January and left a message on his answer-phone, agreeing to buy the computer for £175, but asked whether she could pay for the computer when she received her student loan money. Abdul listened to this message only on 14th January. Again, if the advertisement is deemed invitation to treat using **Thornton v Shoe Lane Parking Ltd**, Diana's telephone call will be an offer, which Abdul can choose to accept or reject. If the court views this as a unilateral contract, then the offer of £175 could be a binding acceptance.

However, a reason why there is no binding acceptance is because acceptance must communicated. Here, Abdul listened to this message only on 14th January once the offer had expired. The onus is on Diana to communicate acceptance. This principle is found in the case of **Entores v Miles Far East** [9] where Lord Denning said:

> *"Suppose, for instance, that I shout an offer to a man*

---

[8] [1971] 2 QB 163
[9] [1955] 2 Q.B. 327

*across a river or a courtyard but I do not hear his reply because it is drowned by an aircraft flying overhead. There is no contract at that moment. If he wishes to make a contract, he must wait till the aircraft is gone and then shout back his acceptance so that I can hear what he says. Not until I have his answer am I bound."[10]*

Another reason why the courts will not submit to the view that this is a unilateral offer and Diana's message is a valid acceptance is because Diana has varied the contract by asking for late payment. One of the general principles in contract law is that the acceptance must mirror the offer. The "mirror image rule" stipulates that, if Diana wants to accept the offer, she must accept an offer *exactly*, without any modifications; because Diana has changed the offer, this hypothetically becomes a counter-offer that kills the original offer, as seen in the case of **Hyde v. Wrench.**[11] Therefore, we are left in the same position that Diana's message is an offer that Abdul can either accept or reject. Diana may argue that this was only a request for further information as in **Stevenson v McLean**, in which the judge said there was no counter-offer, merely an enquiry that should have been answered. This line of argument is unlikely to succeed, however, because in **Stevenson v McLean**, a variation of delivery was sought. Here, there is late payment that is varying the contract.

**Maggie**

Maggie sent an email on 10th January agreeing to buy the computer for £175. The advertisement is deemed a unilateral offer that will be binding. However, this is unlikely because it may have already have been sold. Thus, Maggie's email will be an offer. Abdul read the email on the 12th with the prescribed period of acceptance **Ramsgate Victoria Hotel Co. v Montefiore** and sent a reply to Maggie giving her an appointment to collect the computer on 16th January at 8 pm. This can be seen as the acceptance of the offer. **Thornton v Shoe Lane Parking Ltd.** Maggie responded by email, saying that she will pay the money when she collects the

---

[10] [1955] 2 Q.B. 327 at 332
[11] (1840) 3 Beav 334

computer, which can be seen as an acknowledgement of the acceptance.

## Conclusion

Abdul has no contract with Samson because he should not be allowed to benefit under the postal rule, and there is no binding agreement because the advert was at all times an invitation to treat. Abdul has no contract with Diana because acceptance must communicated by Diana. Here, Abdul listened to this message only on 14<sup>th</sup> January once the offer had expired. Also, Diana varied the offer and made a counter offer. Abdul has a binding contact with Maggie.

# Offer and Acceptance Problem Question Two

On Monday, Golden Antiques places the following advertisement on their website: 'For sale, three Victorian style beds, gorgeous, £5000 each, cash, will brighten up any bed room!'

David, the manager of White Halls Ltd. Email Golden Antiques, immediately replies: 'White Halls Ltd. Will buy all three beds at £4500 each, please advise if credit facility is available'.

On Tuesday morning, Golden Antiques replies by email to say, 'We are not prepared to sell for less than £5000 each. Credit facility only available if your grantor is acceptable to us. Please confirm by close of business today if interested'.

On Tuesday afternoon, David faxes Golden Antiques to say he is willing to accept their original terms and will buy all three beds at £5000 each. He also faxes a letter he receives from Black Halls Ltd. (the guarantor) which states: 'It is our policy to ensure that our subsidiary, White Halls Ltd., remain solvent at all times". However, the fax was not properly transmitted, as indicated by the status report. David then posts a letter at 5pm accepting Golden Antiques' terms on Tuesday evening, although he knows there is a postal strike that day.

Roger, an accountant, telephones Golden Antiques on Wednesday morning stating that he wants to buy Victorian beds. He persuades the manager of Golden Antiques to sell the beds to him, on the basis that he had prepared the financial accounts for Golden Antiques the year before for half the fee he normally charges. Golden Antiques agrees to sell to Roger, so they send David a fax on Wednesday evening saying that the beds are no longer available for sale.

Golden Antiques receive David's letter at 3.45pm on Thursday. David does not read the fax from Golden Antiques until 4.00pm on Thursday.

Advise the parties as to their legal positions.

# Offer and Acceptance Problem Question Two: Answer

## Introduction

This paper is an advice for Golden Antiques, David, the manager of White Halls Ltd., and Roger, the accountant, ("the parties") in relation to the recent negotiation regarding the sale of three Victorian style beds. This paper will advise the parties as to whether a legally enforceable contact has been formed. The paper will do this by first, advising on the issue of the advertisement, and whether this will be viewed by the courts as a unilateral offer or an invitation to treat. Second, this paper will advise whether a valid offer has been made by Golden Antiques. Third, this paper will critically discuss whether David's acceptance through fax was valid. Fourth, this paper will critically discuss the issue of David's acceptance by post, using the relevant case law. Fifth, this paper will discuss the issue of the sale of the beds to Roger and whether this agreement provided the necessary consideration. Sixth, this paper will discuss whether Golden Antiques revocation took place before David's acceptance. Lastly, this paper will conclude its findings.

### Unilateral offer or invitation to treat

For a contract to exist one party ("the offeror") needs to make a clear and certain offer and the other party (the offeree) needs to communicate their equally clear and unequivocal acceptance. It is important to establish whether the advertisement placed on their website is an invitation to treat or an offer. If it is an offer, it will be capable of being accepted by David. However, if it is an invitation to treat, David must make the offer to Golden Antiques who may then choose to accept or reject it. On Monday, Golden Antiques places the following advertisement on their website *'For sale, three Victorian style beds, gorgeous, £5000 each, cash, will brighten up any bed room!'*.

Generally advertisements are regarded by the courts as statements inviting further negotiations or invitations to treat. An example of this was seen in **Partridge v Crittenden**[12], where a notice reading 'Bramblefinch cocks and hens, 25s each' was placed in the classified advertisement page of a periodical. The Court of Appeal held that newspaper advertisements are ordinarily to be treated as invitations to treat and not offers. The logic of this decision was set out by Lord Parker CJ who noted the *"business sense in* [advertisements] *being construed as invitations to treat and not as offers"*[13]. Moreover, Lord Parker CJ in agreement cited Lord Herschell in **Grainger & Son v Gough**[14], where he made the point that it would be wrong to regard these types of advertisements as offers because *"the merchant might find himself involved in any number of contractual obligations to supply wine of a particular description which he would be quite unable to carry out,"*, because the merchant would have a limited supply. Ewan Mckendrick points out *"this argument is not conclusive because it could be implied that the offer is only capable of acceptance while stocks last"*.[15]

A possible line of argument that might be raised by Golden Antiques is that this advertisement constitutes a unilateral contract.[16] A unilateral offer is where one party makes an offer or proposal that is open to the world and capable of acceptance by anyone. The other party 'accepts' the offer by performing the act in accordance with the requirements of the offer. Using **Carlill v Carbolic Smoke Ball Co.,**[17] which is the authority on unilateral contracts, it can be argued the advertisement is in very firm terms, and because the price and description of the bed is stated, it requires no further negation and is capable of being accepted by performance of payment.[18]

However, the opposing argument to this can be drawn from what was argued by Finlay, Q.C., and T. Terrell for the defendant Smoke ball company in **Carlill** that *"the offer, the terms of which*

---

[12] [1968] 1 WLR 1204
[13] Partridge v Critenden [1986] 1 WLR 1204 per Lord Parker para 1209
[14] [1896] AC 325
[15] Mckendrick E, Contract Law, Palgrove Macmillan Law Masters 7th Ed
[16] G.H. Treitel, The Law of Contract, 11th ed
[17] (1893) 1 QB 256
[18] G.H. Treitel, The Law of Contract, 11th ed

*are too vague to be treated as a definite offer"*[19]. This argument is on a balance of probabilities likely to work because the advertisement is not clear, precise and unequivocal. For example, although the advertisement has a good description of the bed, it lacks information about the way in which acceptance should take place or the way in which payment should be made. It is, therefore, merely an invitation to treat and not an offer. This means that David must make the offer to Golden Antiques who can choose to accept or reject it.

**A valid offer?**

David is the manager of White Halls Ltd. and is acting in his capacity of agent for the White Halls Ltd. He has emailed Golden Antiques saying: *'White Halls Ltd. Will buy all three beds at £4500 each, please advise if credit facility is available'*. It is likely the advertisement is an invitation to treat; therefore, his email will be construed as an offer to Golden Antiques.

Another reason why the courts will not submit to the view that this is a unilateral offer and David's email is a valid acceptance is because David has varied the price of each bed to £4,500. One of the general principles in contract law is that the acceptance must mirror the offer. The "mirror image rule" stipulates that, if David wants to accept Golden Antiques offer, he must accept an offer *exactly*, without any modifications;[20] because David has changed the offer, this hypothetically becomes a counter-offer that kills the original offer, as seen in the case of **Hyde v. Wrench**.[21] Therefore, we are left in the same position that David's email is an offer that Golden Antiques can either accept or reject.

On Tuesday, Golden Antiques replies by email *'We are not prepared to sell for less than £5000 each.* This can be interpreted as a firm refusal by Golden Antiques of the offer presented by David. They have reaffirmed the price of the bed being £5,000. Using the authority of **Hyde v. Wrench** Golden Antiques have made a counter-offer which can now be accepted or rejected by

---

[19] (1893) 1 QB 256 at p 257
[20] Mckendrick E, Contract Law, Palgrove Macmillan Law Masters 7th Ed
[21] (1840) 3 Beav 334

David. Golden Antiques email further reads: *Credit facility only available if your grantor is acceptable to us.'* The statement about the credit facility is quite ambiguous because of the use of the phrase *'if your grantor is acceptable to us'*. Golden Antiques have not specified what the criteria are for the grantor to be acceptable. Lastly, the email reads: *'Please confirm by close of business today if interested'*. Golden Antiques are stipulating by when acceptance must take place. This would suggest the offer is only open for one day and will lapse at close of business. The leading case on this point is **Ramsgate Victoria Hotel Co. v Montefiore**[22], in which the courts said even if an offer has not been formally withdrawn, it would expire after "a reasonable time". In this case, the offer was for the sale of shares and the court felt six months was beyond what was reasonable.

The statement *'please advise if credit facility is available'* will be seen by the courts as a request for further information. Similarly in **Stevenson, Jacques & Co. v McLean**[23], when a customer asked for delivery over two months the courts held the plaintiff had not made a counter-offer but had made a mere enquiry which did not serve to reject the offer. A binding contract had been made when the plaintiffs sent the telegram accepting the offer.

**David's acceptance through fax**

On Tuesday afternoon, David faxes Golden Antiques to say he is willing to accept their original terms and will buy all three beds at £5000 each. David is accepting Golden Antiques offer, but the fax was not properly transmitted, as indicated by the status report. The general principle in contract law is that the acceptance must be communicated to the offeror. This principle is found in the case of **Entores v Miles Far East** [24], where Lord Denning said:

> *"Suppose, for instance, that I shout an offer to a man across a river or a courtyard but I do not hear his reply because it is drowned by an aircraft flying overhead. There is no contract at that moment. If he*

---

[22] (1866) LR 1 Ex 109
[23] (1880) 5 QBD 346
[24] [1955] 2 Q.B. 327

*wishes to make a contract, he must wait till the aircraft is gone and then shout back his acceptance so that I can hear what he says. Not until I have his answer am I bound."*[25]

Furthermore, in **Brinkibon v Stahag Stahl**[26], Lord Wilberforce suggested there was no general rule that could cover all the possible situations in these types of cases. He added each case should be resolved with reference to the intention of the parties, to sound business practice, and, in some cases, to a judgment as to where the risks should lie. The case of Entores suggests that acceptance should take place only upon receipt of the fax. Therefore, the onus is on David to retransmit the fax until he is sure that Golden Antiques have received his acceptance. Failing this, there is no valid or enforceable contract between David and Golden Antiques.

**David's acceptance by post**

David then posts a letter at 5pm accepting Golden Antiques' terms on Tuesday evening; although he knows there is a postal strike that day. Acceptance is normally effectual and the contract binding once acceptance is received by the offeror. However, the courts have introduced the postal rule to overcome the problem of the time a letter spends in the postal system. The reason for this rule is to facilitate business and *"promote certainly within contractual formation at a time when the principle method of communication was slow"*.[27]

The postal rule was laid down in **Adams v Lindsell**. [28] Where post is deemed to be the proper means of communication, the acceptance takes effect from the moment the letter of acceptance is properly posted. We are not told whether the post was Golden Antiques preferred method of communication. But, because David has failed to successfully send the fax, he has opted for the post as a method of acceptance. An illustration of this was seen in

---

[25] [1955] 2 Q.B. 327 at 332
[26] [1982] 1 All ER 293
[27] Capps D, 'You've got Mail' 153 New Law Journal 906
[28] (1818) 1 B & Ald 681

**Henthorn v Fraser**.[29] The court, in this case, held a contract was made at 3:50pm when Henthorn posted his letter of acceptance.

Therefore, applying both cases above, it would appear David has benefited under the postal rule and accepted the offer and has a binding contract. However, the lawyers for Golden Antiques may alternatively argue that David should not be allowed to benefit under the postal rule and there is no binding agreement for two reasons:

First, the offer has lapsed under the **Ramsgate Victoria Hotel Co. v Montefiore**.[30] Golden Antiques stated in their email '*Please confirm by close of business today if interested*'. David had posted the letter at the close of business i.e. 5 o'clock. Thus the acceptance has come a moment too late. Another case which could be used in support of this argument (although this concerns telex and is not directly relevant) is **Tenax Steamship v The Brimnes (The Brimnes)** [31], where Cairns LJ felt that the sender should not rely on the recipients' reading every communication at once, and that, in some circumstances, a notice arriving late in the working day might quite legitimately not be "received" until the following morning.

Second, it could be argued that, because David knows there is a postal strike that day, it would be wrong to allow the postal rule to operate in this way. Lawton LJ in **Holwell Securities v Hughes** [32] seemed to support this proposition, when he said that the rule will not be applied where it would lead to: '*a manifest inconvenience and absurdity.*'[33] However, in the absence of authority on this point, the courts may feel it right to allow the postal rule to apply.

**Sale of the beds to Roger**

Roger, an accountant, telephones Golden Antiques on Wednesday morning stating that he wants to buy Victorian beds. He persuades

---

[29] [1892] 2 Ch 27
[30] (1866) LR 1 Ex 109
[31] [1974] 3 All ER 88
[32] [1974] 1 WLR 155
[33] [1974] 1 WLR 155 at 161

the manager of Golden Antiques to sell the beds to him, on the basis that he had prepared the financial accounts for Golden Antiques the year before for half the fee he normally charges. Golden Antiques agrees to sell to Roger. This is a breach of contract because the contract with David is binding if the postal rule applies.

If Golden Antiques want to change their mind and ultimately sell to David, they are able to do so, because the contract with Rodger may be unenforceable due to lack of consideration. The classic definition of consideration, found in the case of **Currie v Misa**,[34] is that consideration, *'may consist either in some right, interest, profit, or benefit accruing to the one party, or some forbearance, detriment, loss, or responsibility given, suffered, or undertaken by the other'*. This means Roger must provide something in return of the beds, i.e. money. We are told *'the manager of Golden Antiques to sell the beds to him'*. If Roger has paid money, this will be valid consideration.[35] If, however, Roger has not paid any money for the beds and he is relying on the fact he had prepared the financial accounts for Golden Antiques the year before for half the fee he normally charges, this will not be valid consideration for two reasons:

First, consideration must not be past. It is not possible to use consideration as some act that has taken place *prior* to the contract. Consideration must be given *in return* for the beds. This is a matter of fact and it is unlikely that the earlier work done at a discount by Roger will be valid consideration as payment for the beds. The discount was provided probably in order to secure the work rather than as consideration for the future.

The general rule that consideration cannot be past was illustrated in **Eastwood v Kenyon**[36]. In this case, it was held a promise was insufficient where the consideration was wholly past. Moreover, in *Roscorla v Thomas*[37], Roscorla bought Thomas' horse for £30. After the sale, Thomas promised Roscorla that the horse was

---

[34] (1875) LR 10 Ex 153 per Lush J
[35] Chappell v Nestlé [1959] 2 All ER 701
[36] (1840) 11 A & E 438
[37] (1842) 3 QB 234

sound and free from vice. The horse proved to be vicious. The court held there was no consideration to support Thomas' promise and he was not bound. The sale itself could not be valuable consideration, for it was completed prior to the promise being given.

However, in Roger's case, it can be argued that, because this is a transaction of a commercial nature, an implied promise to pay arises. This was acknowledged in the case of **Re Casey's Patents**[38], where the owners of patent rights promised their manager a share in those rights as consideration for his previous services for them. Bowen LJ said,

> *'The fact of a past service raises an implication that at the time it was rendered it was to be paid for, and, if it was a service which was to be paid for, when you get in a subsequent document a promise to pay, that promise may be treated as an admission which evidences or as a positive bargain which fixes the amount of that reasonable remuneration on the faith of which the service was originally rendered.'*

However, the success of this argument swaying the courts is unlikely, because the courts will view this as past consideration.

The second reason this will not be valid consideration is because this is an existing obligation under a contract. The authority for this is **Stilk v Myrick**[39], in which the captain of a ship promised his crew that, if they shared between them the work of two seamen who had deserted, the wages of the deserters would be distributed out between them. The court held that the promise was not binding because the seamen gave no new consideration: they were already contractually bound to do any extra work to complete the voyage.

We have to ask whether Roger has done any more than what he was bound to do under a previous contract with the Golden Antiques. If the answer is no, then there is no consideration. As stated above, it is unlikely that the earlier work done at a discount

---

[38] [1892] 1 Ch 104
[39] (1809) 2 Camp 317

by Roger will be valid consideration as payment for the beds. The discount was provided probably in order to secure the work, rather than consideration for in the future.

**Golden Antiques revocation**

Golden Antiques sent David a fax on Wednesday evening saying that the beds were no longer available for sale. Golden Antiques received David's letter at 3.45pm on Thursday. David did not read the fax from Golden Antiques until 4.00pm on Thursday. The revocation of the offer can only take place if the offer has not been accepted. This will all hinge on whether the courts will apply the postal rule. If the Court applies the postal rule, then acceptance has taken place before revocation and there is a binding contract with David. The authority for this is **Byrne v Van Tienhoven**[40], where an offeror posted a letter on 1 October offering to sell the offeree a quantity of tinplate, then posted another letter on 8 October withdrawing the offer. The first letter reached PP on 11 October and they accepted the offer at once by telegram, following with a confirmatory letter four days later. The second letter purporting to withdraw the offer arrived on 20 October, by which time the offer had been accepted and it was too late for DD to withdraw.

**Conclusion**

First, the advertisement of the beds is not clear, precise and unequivocal and therefore likely to be an invitation to treat. Second, David's email is an offer that Golden Antiques can either accept or reject. Golden Antiques have reaffirmed the price of the bed as £5,000; this is a counter offer. Third, the statement *'please advise if credit facility is available'* will be seen by the courts as a request for further information. David's acceptance by fax is incomplete; he must communicate his acceptance. Fourth, it would appear David has benefited under the postal rule and accepted the offer, and thus has a binding contract. Fifth, if the Court applies the postal rule, then acceptance has taken place before revocation and there is a binding contract with David. If Golden Antiques decides to sell to Roger, this is a breach of contract with David.

---

[40] (1880) LR 5 CPD 344

Lastly, if Golden Antiques want to change their mind and does ultimately sell to David, they can because the contract with Roger may be unenforceable due to lack of consideration.

# Battle of the forms essay

**Question:** Critically appraise whether recent judicial decisions reinforcing a resolute adherence to the rules applied to a battle of the forms scenario actually satisfies the reasonable expectations of businessmen more focused on their commercial transaction than legal doctrine?

**Answer**

There are two components of the essay question which require addressing: (1) what rules are applied to a battle of the forms scenario and whether they have been consistently applied by the courts; and (2) whether or not those rules satisfy the reasonable expectations of businessmen. Naturally, the answer that is to follow will address the above-mentioned matters.

For the sake of convenience and economic efficiency, commercial parties usually enter into agreements between one another via contracts containing standard terms and conditions. The problems begin to surface when both parties have differing terms and conditions and wish to contract on the terms and conditions that protect their interests the most. This gives rise to what has come to be known as the 'battle of the forms' scenario. As was expressed by His Honour Judge Havelock-Allan QC in **Sterling Hydraulics**,[41] the classic example of this type of scenario is in **Butler Machine**.[42]

This was a case where the seller offered to deliver a machine tool on its own terms and conditions, which, amongst others, contained a price variation clause entitling the seller to adjust the price in line with the prices at the date of delivery. The buyer's reply to the offer made the acceptance conditional upon its own terms and conditions. The buyer also included, with the order, a tear-off acknowledgement, which accepted the order on the *"terms and conditions thereon"*. The seller returned the completed and signed acknowledgement form, but with a covering letter stating that

---

[41] *Sterling Hydraulics Limited v Dichtomatik Limited* [2006] EWHC 2004 (QB) *per* Havelock-Allan QC at p. 14, *para.* [21].
[42] *Butler Machine Tool Co. Ltd. v Ex-Cell-O Corporation (England) Ltd* [1979] 1 WLR 401.

delivery was to be *"in accordance with our revised quotation* [as contained in the offer]". A dispute arose between the parties as to whether or not the seller was entitled to the increase in costs of producing the machine. The central issue of the case thus centred on the issue of whose terms and conditions were adopted. If the buyer's terms and conditions were adopted, the seller's demand for an additional fee would be without a valid ground and was thus bound to fail.

Lord Denning MR, having expressed that the rules applied by the courts in battle of the forms cases are out of date, accepted that, in such cases, the approach to be adopted should be the *"traditional analysis of offer, counter-offer, rejection, acceptance"*.[43] This analysis dictates that, where an offer is replied to with any of the terms being modified, that constitutes a counter-offer, since the acceptance must mirror the offer made that must be accepted by the other party to give rise to a valid agreement. According to Lord Denning MR, in such cases, there is a contract as soon as the last of the forms is sent and received without objection being taken to it.[44]

The battle of the forms rules, as established in *Butler Machine*, was recently considered and followed by the Court of Appeal in **Tekdata Interconnections**.[45] Longmore LJ expressed that *"...the traditional offer and acceptance analysis must be adopted unless the documents passing between the parties and their conduct show that their common intention was that some other terms were intended to prevail."*[46] Dyson LJ (as he then was) concurred and ruled that the traditional offer and acceptance analysis is to be applied in battle of the forms cases unless the circumstances of the case leads one to conclude that the parties' intentions were to the contrary.[47]

This is a significant step forward. Although the traditional analysis was applied in both **Butler Machine** and **Tekdata**

---

[43] Butler Machine, *supra* no 2, *per* Lord Denning MR at p. 404(F).
[44] *Ibid*, at p. 404(H).
[45] *Tekdata Interconnections Ltd v Amphenol Ltd* [2009] EWCA Civ 1209; [2009] 2 CLC 866.
[46] *Ibid*, *per* Longmore LJ at p. 870, *para*. [11].
[47] *Ibid*, *per* Dyson LJ (as he then was) at p. 874, *para*. [25].

**Interconnections,** upon a careful examination of both cases, it becomes apparent that the Court of Appeal in **Tekdata Interconnection** did not completely adhere to the traditional analysis, but rather created a system whereby the traditional analysis would be considered as the default rules to be applied to a battle of the forms scenario, unless the common intention of the parties was of such a nature to warrant departure from it. Consequently, if one were to state that the recent judicial decisions reinforce a resolute adherence to the rules applied to a battle of the forms scenario, such an assertion would not accurately portray the current state of the English law as to contract formation. There seems to be a tendency by the courts to *"focus on what the parties must be taken, objectively, to have intended at the time when the contract was made"*.[48]

This, it is submitted, achieves both commercial certainty, which commercial men most desire, and flexibility required to prevent unjust and absurd results. Although **Phillip Morgan** states that the intention required will be difficult to show in a battle of forms case, unless there is a clear course of dealing between the parties and that, consequently, the common intention will be rarely found to exist, he rightfully acknowledges that, if the course of dealing between the parties were permitted to displace the default rule so easily, that would hinder commercial certainty and increase litigation.[49] Upon having read Dyson LJ (as he then was)'s judgment in **Tekdata Interconnections,** one would no doubt become aware of the degree of importance his Lordship attached to the principle of commercial certainty.

Moving on to whether or not the above-mentioned rules satisfy the reasonable expectations of businessmen, one would have to identify what a reasonable businessman should be able to expect when a battle of the forms scenario arises. Richard J. Bragg[50] has accurately identified the considerations that are usually uppermost in a businessman's mind: economic and financial considerations.

---

[48] *Ibid, per* Dyson LJ (as he then was) at p. 876, *para.* [30]. See also, Pill LJ at p. 876, *para.* [34].

[49] Morgan, P., *'Battle of the forms: restating the orthodox'* (2010) Cambridge Law Journal 230 at pp. 231-232.

[50] Bragg, R.J., *'The battle of the forms: another round'* (1986) Company Lawyer 209 at p. 210.

When a businessman enters into a transaction, his ultimate aim is to ensure that it has a profitable return. In the context of the present case, that equates to the avoidance of litigation and, most importantly, the acceptance by the other party of its own terms and conditions. In most cases, if not all, the validity of a disputed clause will determine whether or not a party is obliged to, for instance, make a payment to the other party or be held liable for a loss or damage sustained by the other party. Thus, the terms and conditions that the court holds as adopted and contracted upon will have a crucial effect on the businessman in question.

The most basic expectation of commercial parties would be for the courts to respect the contracts entered into and to refrain from interfering unless strictly necessary. The second, and upon which the first is partly dependent, is for the businessman to be able to ascertain with sufficient clarity the laws and rules that are to be applied when a dispute arises between the parties emanating from the contract. That would not only inform the businessman of the steps that he should take and those he should refrain from taking, but would assist him and his advisors to draft agreements that would reflect the terms upon which he wishes to engage with others.[51] It is without a doubt that those two principles are widely respected and adhered to by the English courts.[52] It is probably the most influential reason why so many agreements are entered into with English law as the applicable law to the contract. Thus, English law on contract formation and the battle of the forms rules in particular, does indeed meet the reasonable expectations of businessmen. It gives them commercial certainty but, at the same time, provides the mechanism necessary for the default rules to be departed from where it is determined from the circumstances of the case that that is what they intended.

---

[51] *See*, Beale, H. Chitty on Contracts, 30th Ed (Sweet & Maxwell: London, 2008), Vol 1, para. 2-037; '*Drafting standard terms and conditions for the supply of services*", Practical Law Company, accessed available at http://uk.practicallaw.com/2-501 7221?q=drafting+standard+terms+and+conditions, accessed on 29 January 2012.

[52] *See*, *Eurico SpA v Philipp Brothers* [1987] 2 Lloyd's Rep. 215 *per* Lord Diplock at p. 218 where his Lordship said: "*A basic principle of the common law of contract ... is that parties to a contract are free to determine for themselves what primary obligations they will accept.*". See also, *Homburg Houtimport B.V. v Agrosin Private Ltd (The Starsin)* [2003] UKHL 12, [2003] 3 WLR 711 *per* Lord Bingham of Cornhill at [57].

# Postal rule and instantaneous communication in a modern age essay

## Introduction

The postal rule can be described as arbitrary, and was created because it was felt, at the time, some rule was essential in the early 19th Century to regulate letter contracting. The principle emerged because the postal service was the only option for distance contracting. Modern technologies and inventions, namely email, makes the postal rule redundant and unfair. This essay explores the advantages, along with the criticisms, of the postal rule and whether it should and can be justified today. The Postal rule is no longer needed, because in the 21st Century, contracts can be concluded in seconds, using both instantaneous and non-instantaneous methods of communication with little or no risk of loss and delay. Therefore, it should be abandoned as an obstacle to fairness in contract law.

### The Postal Rule for Acceptance

The general rule is that, once a letter of acceptance is dispatched in the post, the postal acceptance is already effectual[53]. In other words – as soon as the letter is in the control of the Post Office[54], the contracting parties are legally bound in contract. It was established back in 1818 in **Adam v Lindsell**[55], where it was stated that the rule was essentially a rule of convenience[56]. The postal rule is supported by saying that the offeror takes the risk (i.e. the risk of failing to receive acceptance) by initiating negotiations by post originally[57]. As a result, it does not apply to instantaneous methods of communication (i.e. telephone, telex) on the grounds that all the parties are aware of contract conclusion. Therefore, they are unlikely to face risks such as delays or failure of transmission[58].

---

[53] G.H. Treitel "The Law of Contract, 12th edition (2007), para 2-028
[54] **Brinkinbon Ltd v Stahag und Stahlwarenhandelsgesellschaft mbH** [1983] 2 A.C. 34 at 41
[55] (1818) 1 B & Ald 681
[56] (1999) 1 EBL 5,6 , Issue 5
[57] *Ibid.*
[58] P. Fasciano ''Internet Electronic Mail: A last Bastion for the Mailbox Rule'' (1996 - 1997) 25 Hofstra Law Review 1542

## The Postal Rule for Revocation

However, if it was reasonable to establish a specific postal rule for acceptance, consequently there may be another necessary rule concerning revocations of offers. In the case of communication by post, the general rule is that *"Dispatch of a letter or telegram of acceptance by the offeree terminates the offeror's power of revocation. Loss or delay of the letter of acceptance is immaterial and subsequent death of either party can have no effect on its formation"*[59]. In other words, the letter of revocation is effective only on delivery[60].

## Reasons for the Establishment of the Postal Rule

By and large, the reason for the creation of the postal rule was to raise certainty within contractual formation[61]. Equally, in 1818 the postal service had been comparatively slow; for example, the first train from Liverpool to Manchester had made its first deliveries twenty years afterwards[62]. Therefore, the main predicament at the start of the 19th Century was that the postal service had no substitute method of communication. It was Capps who suggested that, if instantaneous modes of communication were on hand, it is open to question whether an effective-on-dispatch rule would have been required[63].

There is some argument that it is easier to prove posting a letter rather than proving receipt. The reason given is that it is the offeror who chooses to use the post, so they should be at a disadvantage. Although it is true that he can elect to make the offer using telephone, the above-mentioned reason is not very compelling. It

---

[59] (1966) 15 ICLQ 553 at 557
[60] Established by Lindley J in **Byrne & Co v Leon Van Tienhoven** (1880) L.R. 5 (C.P.D.) 344, followed by **Henthorn v Fraser** [1892] 2 Ch. 27 and **Stevenson, Jacques & Co McLean** (1880) L.R. 5 (Q.B.D.) 346; Exceptions are **Hebb's Case** (1867) L.R. 4 Eq. 9 and **Townsend's Case** (1871) L.R. 13 (Eq.) 148 – in both, the letter of revocation was posted, but not delivered before the acceptance took effect. Both regard such withdrawal effective.
[61] D. Capps "You've got mail" (2003) N.L.J 906, See also Adam v Lindsell (1818) 1 B & Ald 681
[62] H. Blake, http://www.telegraph.co.uk/news/uknews/royal-mail/7814591/The-Royal-Mail-a-history-of-the-British-postal-service.html
[63] D. Capps "You've got mail" (2003) N.L.J 906

might have been the offeree who initially started the negotiations by letter[64].

## Was it an arbitrary solution?

In reality, it is to some extent an illogical resolution to the dilemma of which of the participants should bear the risk where they communicate through the post[65]. At the start of the 19th Century, some rule was indispensable. This has led to Evans arguing that the reason for the relevance of the postal rule is *"no more than abdication of responsibility"*[66]. Additionally, it is noteworthy to consider the rule laid down in **Adam v Lindsell**[67] originated at a time when there was no general rule that acceptance needed to be communicated[68]. As a result, Simon Gardner argues that the Adam v Lindsell case provides limited foundation for the original postal acceptance rule[69].

There have always been problems with contract negotiations by post – even at present, letters may either be delayed or lost. Therefore, one of the contracting parties bears a risk by choosing the postal services for a preferred method of communication[70]. Certainly, the offeror is the party who bears that risk, under the effective-on-dispatch postal rule. However, sometimes there will be the case where the offeree starts the negotiations by letter, as mentioned in the previous section. Therefore, the postal rule needs reconsideration, bearing in mind all the technology developments in the 21st Century.

### Justification of the Postal Rule

Thesiger LJ, in Household Fire and Carriage Accident Insurance Co. v Grant[71], argues that it is impossible to produce a rule that

---

[64] L. Koffman (2001) ''The Law of Contract'' 4th edition
[65] *Ibid.*
[66] (1966) 15 ICLQ 553 at 559
[67] (1818) 1 B & Ald 681
[68] L. Koffman (2001) ''The Law of Contract''' , See also A.W.B Simpson (1975), 91 LQR 247
[69] S. Gardner (1992) 12 O.J.L.S. 2, 170-194, p. 171
[70] J. Poole, (2010) ''Contract Law'', p.67
[71] (1878-79) L.R. 4 Ex. D. 216, at 223

would be fair to both of the parties. However, he thinks that it is more convenient for acceptance to be effective on posting, rather than on receipt.

Another reason for justification of the postal rule is that it is logical for the offeror to bear the risk of the distance communications. He is the one who can manipulate the offer and introduce conditions. The offeree is less likely to change the conditions. Even if he does, we know that it will no longer be an acceptance of an offer, but a counter-offer[72].

The offeror can always avoid the postal rule by stipulating actual receipt or a specific way of communication, or even initiating the negotiations by instantaneous method. He can require parties to telegraph instead of using a slower method such as the postal services[73]. The offeror has the choice to set a specific time until which the acceptance should reach him. Consequently, an offer expressed to continue for a fixed time may be legally retracted before the expiration of the time limit unless previously accepted[74].

## Criticism of the Postal Rule

In Household Fire and Carriage Accident Insurance Co v. Grant[75], Thesiger LJ suggested that it is reasonable to treat the post office as the agent of both of the parties[76]. Evans rejected the suggestion on the basis that the post office and telegram company do not fall within the definition of agents,[77] to which acceptance may be communicated. Moreover the, Post Office, as a governmental agency for public services, works under its own regulations. In truth, both the Post Office and telegraph companies are independent contractors for the transmission of messages[78]. Hence, the Post Office is not responsible for the receipt of a letter because

[72] J. Poole (2010) "Contract Law", 57-59
[73] Quenerduaine v Cole (1883), 32 W.R. 185
[74] "Leake's Law of Contracts" (1931) at 24
[75] (1878-79) L.R. 4 Ex. D. 216, at 223
[76] Stocken v Collin (1841) 151 E.R. 870; Dunlop v Higgins (1841) 7 M. & W. 515
[77] Mechem, "Agency" (2nd ed., 1914)
[78] (1966) 15 ICLQ 553 at 559

it is not concerned with possible misdirections[79]. Therefore, the Post Office could never be an agent, but only a carrier between the offer and the acceptance[80].

Evans explains that, under the dispatch rule, if a letter is lost it can be difficult to prove that it was correctly addressed and prepaid[81]. For example, it could be the offeree's fault that the letter did not arrive. Does that mean the offeror is the one who should suffer the consequences? Under the dispatch principle, the postal rule is one-sided and unfair for the offeror. That's why **British and American Telegraph Co v Colson**[82] proposed a compromise rule whereby, "although the letter of acceptance must be received; once received it would be retrospectively effective as from its posting". However, this proposal was rejected[83].

Another common argument for the establishment of the postal rule can be found in the dictum from **Adam v Lindsell**[84]:

> "If the [offerors] were not bound by their offer when accepted by the [offerees] till the answer was received, then the [offerees] ought not to be bound till after they had received the notification that the [offerors] had received their answer and assented to it. And so it might go on ad infinitum".

However, if this reason was acceptable in the 19th Century, it is no longer relevant because of technological development and instantaneous methods of communication. Both of the parties can always check whether the offer or acceptance is successfully delivered by using telex, telephone, etc.

**Postal Rule in the New Era of Technology Development**

Whatever the reasons for the establishment of the postal rule in 1818, currently, the situation is completely different. As time has

---

[79] Ibid.
[80] Ibid.
[81] Ibid.
[82] (1871) LR 6 (Exch) 108
[83] Harris' Case (1871-72) L.R. 7 (Ch. App.) 587
[84] (1818) 1 B & Ald 681 at 683

passed and technology has developed, the speed and range of communication has increased[85]. After the invention of the Press in the 15th Century, the Telegraph System in the 1830s, the Telephone (1876) and Telex System (1930s), the world was ready to face new technologies that would change everything. In current times, the enormous success of Google, Amazon, Facebook, E-bay, Hotmail, and Yahoo illustrates how consumer and businesses alike have embraced internet and electronic commerce in the last decade[86]. Consequently, there are many arguments that the instantaneous methods of communication and internet communications make the postal rule redundant.

## E-mail communications

Unfortunately, there is still ambiguity, uncertainty, and legal arguments about e-mail contracting. The problem derives from the fact that there is no direct authority on the question of whether e-mail communication can be determined as an instantaneous or a non-instantaneous method[87]. The most common argument is that e-mail is not direct between the parties, and messages are broken up into packets that travel around internet networks[88]. Therefore, e-mail is a non-instantaneous method of communication and Murray[89] suggested that "postal rule should apply to e-mail acceptances, because they are neither direct, nor reliable[90] and the acceptor sending his e-mail does not know immediately whether or not the communication was successful"[91]. This is true, but there is a weakness in his judgment, for he has not considered that there is always possibility for the acceptor to check the succession of his e-mail by using telephone. Furthermore, Capps argues that the acceptor has some control over a sent e-mail in that it can often be recalled[92]. Maybe this is why Murray withdraws this interpretation later in his article, in 2005[93].

---

[85] I. Lloyd, D. Mellor(2003) "Telecommunications Law" at p.3;
[86] Edwards, Waelde (2009) "Law and the Internet", at p.89
[87] Ibid., p.105
[88] Ibid, p.105
[89] A.D. Murray (2000) "Entering into Contracts Electronically: The Real W.W.W..", in Edwards and Waelde (eds), "Law and the Internet: A Framework for Electronic Commerce"
[90] Clearly, the delay in e-mail communication will not be as long as the delay using postal services, but uncertainty whether a message has arrived could be just as great.
[91] Edwards, Waelde (2009) Law and the Internet, p.105
[92] D. Capps (2004) I.C.C.L.R. at 209

Edwards and Waelde propose one solution that would be convenient for both of the parties, suggesting that e-mail be deemed to be received when the sender receives the recipient's acknowledgment of the delivery,[94] as in **1996 UNCITRAL Model Law on E-Commerce, Art 14(3).** Under this provision, if a data message has been made conditional on receipt, the data message is treated as though it has never been sent until the acknowledgement is received. This is why the postal rule is not such a burden if manipulated intelligently. In the US, another postal rule regulation can be seen in the **Uniform Computer Information Transactions Act 2000 (UCITA)**, where section **203(4)** states that *"if an offer in an electronic message evokes in electronic message accepting the offer, a contract is formed when an electronic acceptance is received*[95].

A frequently used moral argument for justifying the postal rule is to put the risk of delay on the party choosing the communication method[96]. However, this is no longer convincing because in the 21st Century, companies have a range of communication choices to make a contract. If they would like to protect themselves from the postal rule effect, they could use instantaneous method, which will be more safe and secure. Therefore, if A makes an offer by telephone, and B sends the acceptance by e-mail that never reaches A, then A will not be legally bound and risk is put on B's decision. Another reason why the postal rule is no longer needed is that most e-mail servers have the option to check whether an e-mail has been received and read. If the acceptor receives a failure notification, he can choose to resend it until he is certain about the successful delivery[97]. Therefore, loss and delay are no longer a problem. Even if they occur, they can be traced and corrected.

**Conclusion**

When the postal rule was created, it provided a reasonable answer

---

[93] (2005) L, Edwards (ed), "The New Legal Framework for E-Commerce in Europe"
[94] Edwards, Waelde (2009) "Law and the Internet", p.105
[95] D. Capps "You've got mail" (2003) N.L.J 906
[96] P. Todd, "E-Commerce Law" (2005) para 9.2.1
[97] D. Capps "You've got mail" (2003) N.L.J 906

to a genuine problem, in that the inherent delays in the principle method of communication (Postal services) led to uncertainties in contract formation. Nobody knows for certain what would have been the postal rule if established after the invention of the telegraph, telephone and telex. However, if the same rule were produced in the era of Internet and e-mail communication, it would be absolutely unreasonable. Therefore, the postal rule may have been adequate in the 19th Century. However, at the present time, it is inappropriate because of the technologies in our days, and the postal rule should be abandoned as an obstacle to fairness in contract law.

# Chapter 4    Consideration

## Introduction

A contract that is not established by way of seal (by deed) needs to be backed up with some kind of consideration of value. There are, of course, some exceptions to this main general principle, as you will discover throughout this chapter. Consideration is required in all contracts and is not established by seal, only with its presence will an agreement be deemed legally enforceable.

**General Principle: Consideration is something of value promised by both parties during the formation of a contract.**

**Currie v Misa** (1874-75) L.R. 10 Ex. 153
**Facts:** A company made a sale of four bills of exchange to Mr. Misa, which had been taken out of a foreign bank. Mr. Currie owned this banking franchise and was also Misa's employer. The bills of exchange were sold in February. It was customary for the brokers to be paid on the day after the sale. The foreign bank owned by Mr. Currie had lots of outstanding debts to his bank. Mr. Currie had to cover his debt. He provided his bank with a draft bill for Mr. Misa. This happened on the 14th of February. However, it was actually drafted on 13th February, after which time it was given to the bank. On 14th February, Misa was given a banker's draft. Mr. Currie failed to pay his debts and when Misa learned this, he suspended the cheque from being paid.
**Ratio: Lush J defined the doctrine of consideration as: "some right, interest, profit, or benefit accruing to the one party, or some forbearance, detriment, loss, or responsibility, given, suffered, or undertaken by the other."**
**Application:** Consideration has to be of some kind of value. It is essential to note that the courts have frequently been called upon to look at the adequacy of the doctrine of consideration, but have just as frequently refused to do so. A more concise definition is given by Pollock, which was adopted by the House of Lords in **Dunlop v Selfridge** [1915] AC 847, was namely that, *"an act or forbearance of one party, or the promise thereof, is the price for which the promise of the other is bought, and the promise thus given for value is enforceable."*

## Consideration must be sufficient

**General Principle: Consideration must be present, but need not be adequate. The courts will not measure consideration for adequacy.**

**Thomas v Thomas** [1842] 2 QB 851
**Facts:** Thomas expressed a desire in his will to keep his wife in their home. The executors of Thomas's will entered into an agreement where the wife (the plaintiff) could live in the house and would be charged £1 pound per year as ground rent. Upon the death of one of the co-executors, the defendant refused to uphold the lease, arguing that adequate consideration had not been given.
**Ratio: The courts held that the £1 pound payment was valid consideration.**
**Application:** The courts will not determine whether the consideration is adequate. As long as a detriment of economic value is taken on for someone's benefit, the courts will view this as consideration.

**General Principle: The actual value of the exchanged consideration does not matter; it must only have a value in essence.**

**Chappell and Co v Nestle** [1960] A.C. 87
**Facts:** Nestle offered a record, priced at 1 shilling and 6d, along with three wrappers from their chocolate bars. The copyright for this record belonged to Chappell and Co, and Nestle was paying small percentage of the 1 shilling 6d as royalty. Chappell brought action to prevent Nestle's promotional sales because they were getting a royalty that did not take into account the sale of three chocolate bars.
**Ratio: The Nestle chocolate bar wrappers were deemed by the Court of Appeal to form a part of the consideration. This is despite the fact the wrappers were discarded upon receipt.**
**Application:** Lord Somervell stated that: *"A contracting party can stipulate for what consideration he chooses. A peppercorn does not cease to be good consideration if it is established that the promisee does not like pepper and will throw away the corn."*

**Past Consideration**

**General principle: A promise which is offered after the close of a contract or performance will not be enforced by the courts, as it constitutes 'past consideration'.**

**Roscorla v Thomas** (1842) 3 Q.B. 234
**Facts:** Roscorla decided to buy Thomas' horse. Once the horse had been sold to Roscorla, Thomas assured Roscorla that the horse he had just bought would be "sound and free from any vice". In reality, the horse was ill tempered and prone to violence, making it very difficult to control. Roscola brought action against Thomas for breach of contract.
**Ratio: It was held that Roscorla did not breach any contract. Roscola's sole consideration was the sale price of the horse. Thomas made his assurances on the horse's condition after completion of the contract.**
**Application:** The court cannot force a seller to uphold any reassurances he gives to a buyer, if those promises are made after the close of a contract.

**General Principle: Consideration offered after a voluntary act is performed is 'past consideration' and not considered valid.**

**Re McArdle** [1951] Ch. 669
**Facts:** A daughter in law carried out improvements to a property. After the work was carried out, the remainder of the family agreed that she should be reimbursed the sum of £488. However, the family later refused to pay her.
**Ratio: It was held that the promise to pay was unenforceable as it came after the work was completed.**
**Application:** If someone voluntarily performs an action, or provides consideration without receiving any consideration, he cannot sue for any promises that are made after the work is done.

**Exceptions to the past consideration rule**

**General Principles: If past consideration is offered for an action that was done at requested by the promiser, it can be binding.**

**Lampleigh v Braithwait** (1615) 80 E.R. 255, Common Bench

**Facts:** Braithwait had committed murder, and asked Lampleigh to make endeavours to obtain him a royal pardon to annul his crime. Lampleigh had an audience before the King of England and successfully gained the pardon. Braithwait made a verbal promise to Lampleigh to pay him £100. When Braithwait failed to pay up the £100, Lampleigh brought action against him. His claim was successful.

**Ratio: The overwhelming majority of the judges assembled on the Common Bench held that: "where the promiser makes a request that the other do him some service, and (after the service is performed) promises to pay for it, the promise and the request go together and the contract is binding".**

**Application:** If a person can prove that his action or consideration was done at the request of another, the court can bind the promiser to give the past consideration that was offered.


**General Principle: Past consideration offered in a business context could be enforceable in court.**


**Re Casey's Patents** [1892] 1 Ch. 104

**Facts:** Two people had ownership over a patent for a product. There was also a manager involved, who had assisted in developing the patented product. The two owners of the patented product made a promise to the manager that one third of the shareholding rights would be given to him in exchange for his assistance in developing it. The owners of the patented product argued that their promise regarded services that had already been completed, which was thus past consideration.

**Ratio: The court held that the manager would be able to depend on the agreement.**

**Application:** Despite the fact that the managers consideration was in the past, the consideration had been produced in a business context. This was also done at the owners own wishes and there was mutual understanding between both parties that the manager would get paid and also the further promise that he would be paid a predefined amount.


**General Principle: If past-consideration is offered for an unfulfilled promise, it could be interpreted as consideration for the promise.**

**Pao On v Lau Yiu Long** [1980] AC 614

**Facts:** Pao On (the claimant) made threats that he would not see the primary contract to fruition. This contract concerned share purchases. He said he would not do anything unless some secondary agreements were adhered to, which included both an indemnity and a guarantee. Lau Yiu Long (the defendant) wanted to fulfil the primary contract in haste. This is because the ability to buy shares had been disclosed to the wider world and he did not wish to undermine the company's image in public, nor cause the share prices to drop as a result. Long could have brought an action against Pao for the agreement to be given specific performance. However, this would have caused major disruption and delays to proceedings, not to mention damage to the company's reputation. Long had the benefit of consulting legal representatives before committing to the agreement for indemnity and a guarantee. Pao then tried to invoke his guarantee and Long looked to have the twin agreements struck down because: 1) Pao provided no consideration for these twin agreements, and 2) Long agreed to the agreements while under 'economic duress'.

**Ratio: The Court of Appeal held that the twin agreements should be upheld, and that no economic duress had occurred.**

**Application:** Lord Scarman outlined a number of key factors: "An act done before the giving of a promise to make a payment or to confer some other benefit can sometimes be consideration for the promise."

1) "The act must have been done at the promisors' request..."
2) "The parties must have understood that the act was to be remunerated either by a payment or the conferment of some other benefit...AND"
3) "Payment or the conferment of a benefit must have been legally enforceable had it been promised in advance."

**Contractual duty to a third party**

**General Principle: Despite the fact that performing an existing duty is not valid consideration, performing a duty that is under a contract that a third party is owed can be seen to be valid consideration.**

**Scotson v Pegg** (1861) 6 Hurl. & N. 295

**Facts:** Scotson made a contract to deliver coal to a company (the third party). The company then sold the coal to Pegg (the second contracting party) and asked Scotson to ensure the coal was delivered to Pegg. Pegg made a promise to Scotson that he would be unloading the coal at a set daily rate. Unfortunately Pegg did not carry out his promise to unload the coal. Scotson then tried to sue Pegg for not upholding his promise. Pegg rebutted that the promise could not be legally binding, as Scotson had not given any kind of consideration. He furthered argued that Scotson was obliged to perform his contract with the third party company to actually deliver the coal.

**Ratio: The court ruled that the delivery of the coal was valid consideration because it was a benefit to Pegg and a detriment to Scotson.**

**Application:** If a promisor provides a promise to a third party which he is already contractually bound to, this promise can be used as good consideration for a promise made by the third-party.

**General Principle: Offering a promise to a third party that is already undertaking an action can be valid consideration if the promisee receives a benefit from the promise.**

**New Zealand Shipping v Satterthwaite and Co (The Eurymedon)** [1975] A.C. 154

**Facts:** Satterwaite and Co were a UK based company that made drilling machines. One of their machines had been ordered by New Zealand Shipping. There was a term in the agreement between parties that the liability of the carrier was limited. This applied to anyone who handled the drill whilst it was in transit and assisted in its deployment once it arrived in New Zealand. When the drill was being unloaded in New Zealand, the company who was handling it at the time accidentally dropped the drill, causing damage. The company then looked to be protected by the term in the agreement between Satterthwaite and the shipping company that limited the liability of any other company that handled it.

**Ratio: The Privy Council held that the term protecting third parties that handled the drill was good consideration.**

**Application:** In general, a promisee needs to demonstrate that promise made by a third party benefits him if he would want the promise to be seen as valid consideration. This proposition was illustrated and supported in *Scotson v Pegg* (1861) above which their Lordships consider to be good law.

**Promisee already under a contractual duty**

**General Principle: Performing a contracted duty is not seen as good consideration for a new promise.**

**Stilk v Myrick** (1809) 170 E.R. 1168, KB
**Facts:** Two members of a sailing ship's crew committed mutiny by abandoning the ship they were working on while at sea. The captain was unable to find suitable replacements. In the wake of this problem, the captain made a promise to the remaining crew members to pay them extra wages if they could help get the ship home successfully. When eventually got back to London, the crew members who got the ship back tried to enforce this promise.
**Ratio: The court found that they could not enforce the promise. By staying in their role as crew members, they had done nothing more than their call of duty. They were deemed to have given nothing extra in terms of consideration for the captain's new promise, and were allowed to receive their existing wages only.**
**Application:** The court reasoned that desertions were commonplace problems experienced at sea and because the crew continued to work their contracted roles, they offered no consideration for the captain's promise.

**General Principles: Performing a contracted duty in a capacity beyond normal means, or in potential danger, can be seen as valid consideration for a promise.**

**Hartley v Ponsonby** (1857) 119 E.R. 1471, QB
**Facts:** It also involved sailors mutinying and abandoning ship; however, half the crew abandoned ship on this occasion. Again, the captain of the vessel promised to pay more to the sailors to carry out their existing duty and work harder in the absence of their crew members who had deserted. In this case, half the crew had left and it was quite dangerous to travel with such a small group. The captain refused to pay the additional wages.
**Ratio: The court ruled that the captain had to pay the additional wages he promised. The new hazardous obligations**

on the crew went far beyond their original contracted duties, and so performing the dangerous task of sailing with such a small group was good consideration for the promise of an increase in wages.

**Application:** Once more we can see that where one party to a contract does more than what they were required to do in their original contract, a court can find valid consideration in the form of a new agreement. Additionally, this case has been applied in scenarios that involve third parties.

**General Principle: If one party's contractual obligation confers additional benefit to a party, the fulfilling of the contractual obligation can be good consideration for a binding promise, provided that no economic duress is involved.**

**Williams v Roffey Bros and Nicholls** [1991] 1 Q.B. 1

**Facts:** Roffey Bros were contracted to build a block of flats. In the contract, they put in a clause regarding the action taken if they were not to complete their work on time. This, it was agreed between both parties, would provide incentive to finish the building work on time. Roffey Bros then proceeded to outsource part of the job to Williams for a fee of £20,000. Williams was taking longer than expected to complete the work, their reason being that they were being underpaid for the work they were carrying out. Roffey Bros promised Williams they would pay an extra £10,300 for them to complete their part of the work on the construction site on time. In this agreement, they also settled on other modified working arrangements, such as building the flats one at a time. When Williams completed the work on time, Roffey Bros refused to pay the additional £10,300. They argued that this new agreement with Williams did not apply because there was a deficit of consideration. The reasoning was that Williams was already making good on an existing contractual obligation.

**Ratio: The Court of Appeal held on the facts that Williams had in fact given consideration because they had completed the work on time. As a result, Roffey Bros promise to pay the extra £10,300 was enforceable because Roffey Bros avoided having to pay the penalty for not finishing the work on time.**

**Application:** Glidewell LJ provided the leading analysis on the Stilk v Myrik principle. His aim was to leave the old principle more or less intact, yet elaborate on how it had now expanded. He asserted that Williams had provided valid consideration despite the fact that he was just performing an obligation that already existed. He stated that the concept of promissory estoppel had 'not yet been fully developed'.

**Consideration for the variation of contractual terms**

**General Principle: In general, paying a smaller amount of money will never discharge a larger debt.**

**Penny v Cole** (1602) 5 Co Rep 117a
**Facts:** Pinnel was owed £8 10s by Cole. When Pinnel asked for the money, Cole made a payment of £5 2s 6d a whole month prior to when the bond was due. Cole argued an agreement existed that made sure part payment would count to discharge the whole of the debt.
**Ratio: Pinnel won the case on a technicality. The court said that if it were not for this technicality, they would have ruled in favour of Cole. They acknowledge that Pinnel has received some valued return from Cole (the £5 2s 6d) early, this could be seen to be adequate consideration to ensure that the promise made to wipe the remainder of the debt.**
**Application:** The underpinning principle is that payment of a lesser amount of money might wipe the full debt if and only if some extra form of consideration is provided: *"payment of a lesser sum on the day in satisfaction of a greater sum cannot be any satisfaction for the whole, because it appears to the judges that by no possibility, a lesser sum can be a satisfaction to the claimant for a greater sum...but the gift of a horse, hawk or robe etc. in satisfaction is good...as it is more beneficial to the claimant than the money itself."*

**General Principle: Generally, the party that is in debt is already contractually obliged to repay the larger sum of money and does not provide consideration by agreeing to pay a smaller sum and nothing more.**

**Foakes v Beer** (1884) 9 App Cas 605
**Facts:** Foakes had a debt to pay to Beer. There was an agreement in place between the two parties that Foakes would be able to make payments through monthly instalments. Beer was then

satisfied and agreed that nothing more will be done, if Foakes paid the debt by the date they agreed upon. Sometime after this point, Beer requested that Foakes pay a form of interest in addition to the amount he owed. Foakes did not want to pay it.

**Ratio: Beer was able to claim before the court for Foakes to pay him interest on what he owed. All that was applied was the reasoning from Pinnel's case above.**

**Application:** This cases judgement seems to be, on the surface of things, not fair on Foakes because he had acted in complete reliance and trust on Beer's promise not to do anything else should he pay off the debt he owed. It is all because of Pinnel's cases principle and Foakes v Beer at Common Law that promissory estoppel started to develop through principles of equity.

**General Principle: Paying back a debt in smaller installments, to avoid a company's liquidation and total repayment, does not offer a 'practical benefit' to the borrower.**

Re Selectmove Ltd [1995] 1WLR 474

Facts: Selectmove Ltd had to pay back debts to HMRC (the Inland Revenue). Selectmove's chief executive had a meeting with an Inland Revenue representative. It was agreed that Selectmove would pay taxes in the future as they came in. In regards to the state of arrears the company was in, it was agreed that he pay back at £1000 per month. The Inland Revenue representative said he had to make inquiries within the Inland Revenue and with his superiors to see if this arrangement would be feasible. Selectmove Ltd did not receive any correspondence until a notice was delivered to them by way of post stating that if they did not pay off a now substantially inflated debt, the company would have to go into administration. The chief executive of Selectmove Ltd reacted by claiming that the Inland Revenue had made it clear that he could make a smaller amount of repayments instead of the full amount.

**Ratio: The High Court held that regardless of whether the statement was legitimate or not, the chief executive of Selectmove had not put a binding legal obligation on the Inland Revenue. Additionally, no consideration existed for this arrangement anyway.**

**Application:** The Court of Appeal later made the statement that the doctrine of 'practical benefit' that came out of the case of

Williams v Roffey cannot be applied as another exception to the rule. In Williams v Roffey, it was established, as we have seen, that the doctrine only applies where the original promise was a promise to pay more than the original and not less.

# Question and Answers

- Consideration Essay Question
- Consideration Problem Question

# Consideration Essay Question

## Question

Should the principle in **Williams v Roffey** *be* extended to cover the situation encountered in **re Selectmove Limited**? Give reasons for your answer.

## Answer

### Introduction

This essay will establish the traditional position by looking at case law such as **Stilk v Myrick**; [98]**Hartley v Ponsonby,**[99]**Pinnels case**[100] and **Foakes v Beer.**[101] Second, this paper will examine the decision in **Williams v Roffey Bros** to establish whether the law has departed from the traditional rules of consideration. Third, this paper will examine subsequent case law to see how the courts have applied the principle in **Williams v Roffey Bros.**[102] It will do this by asking the question that should the decision in **Williams v Roffey Bros** be extended to cases concerning part payment. Finally, the essay will conclude its findings.

### The traditional position

In **Stilk v Myrick**, a ships' master promised his crew that the wages of the deserters would be shared out between the crew which remained. The court in these cases held that the promise to pay by the captain was not enforceable on the basis that the crew had provided any consideration. The crew was already under contract to complete the voyage. This can be praised as a good decision because it prevents unscrupulous crew members from blackmailing the ship's master into agreeing to make extra payments. This decision can be interpreted as an early attempt by the courts to protect the ship's master from the possibility of economic duress.

---

[98] (1809) 2 Camp 317
[99] [1857] 26 LJ QB 322
[100]*Pinnel's Case* (1602) 5 Co Rep 117a
[101] (1884) 9 App Cas 605
[102]*Williams v Roffey Bros and Nicholls (Contractors) Limited* [1990] 1 All ER 512

A different approach was taken in **Hartley v Ponsonby** where, where the ships' crew had a large number of desertions. The court held that the crew should be able to recover an extra £40 pay and that this promise to pay had the necessary consideration. The court said the seamen were not obliged to do this under their existing contracts of service and were free to enter into a fresh contract. This recognised exception to **Stilk v Myrick** was approved by the court in **The Atlantic Baron**.[103]

The position in **Stilk v Myrick** seems to have also been applied to cases concerning partial payment in full satisfaction for the debt. In **Pinnel's Case**, the defendant had not provided any consideration for the plaintiffs promise not to sue on partial payment accepted. Sir Edward Coke had stated that:

*"payment of a lesser sum on the day in satisfaction of a greater sum, cannot be any satisfaction for the whole, because it appears to the Judges that by no possibility, a lesser sum can be a satisfaction to the plaintiff for a greater sum."*[104]

This rule was upheld and applied in the case of **Foakes v Beer**, but not without the express doubts of Lord Blackburn, who nevertheless concurred in the judgement in that case, that *"men of business ... do every day recognise and act on the ground that prompt payment of a part of their demand may be more beneficial to them than it would be to insist on their rights."*[105]Therefore, the position according to these old authorities seems to be that any attempt to vary a contract will lack consideration unless what is been received is all together new or different to the original promise.

### The decision in Williams v Roffey

Roffey contracted with Williams to do some carpentry work. The price for the carpentry work was agreed at £20,000. Williams found themselves in severe financial difficulties. Roffey were

---

[103] North Ocean Shipping v Hyundai (The Atlantic Baron) [1979] QB 705
[104]*Pinnel's Case* (1602) 5 Co Rep 117a
[105] [1881–5] All ER Rep 106 at 115

concerned that they would be liable under a penalty clause in the main building contract thus they promised to pay Williams an additional sum for each flat completed on time. Roffey then declined to make any further payments. The plaintiff sued for the additional monies promised. Roffey argued that by completing on time, the Williams had done no more than he was already contractually bound to do. The court held that the promise to pay addition monies was binding. Williams had provided the necessary consideration because Roffey had obtained a 'practical benefit', namely avoiding the penalty and having avoided having to find a new sub-contractor.

Adams and Brownsword argue that the court have taken a 'robust approach' and extended the principle outside of the traditional doctrine of consideration.[106] It can be counter argued that *Roffey* is achieving a major objective. It ensures that a contracting party that makes a promise under no pressure in a commercial context will be bound by this promise, even if there is almost no consideration. The problem that this creates is that it seems to sit uneasily with the traditional common law position of consideration.

There is only one difference (that the court had the ability to deduce) between **Roffey** and **Stilk**: the practical benefit that Roffey gained in that they were prevented from paying under the penalty clause. Glidewell LJ followed **Ward v Byham**[107] where there was consideration because the mother was ordered to do more than what she was supposed to do legally. Williams was only being asked to perform their existing duty. Glidewell LJ avoided referring to **Hartley v Ponsonby** which is distinguishing the same point, that the party brought something totally different to what was in the agreement.

The fundamental issue brought out in this case is not different from the doctrine of estoppel. There are two predictable difficulties. First, estoppel works on the basis that it allows acceptance of part payment of debts to be repaid as consideration for new deals. Second, estoppel works as a protection and not as an

---

[106] Adams and Brownsword 'Contract, consideration and the critical path' (1990) 53 MLR 540
[107] [1956] 1 WLR 496

attack thus it cannot be normally used to find an action. Therefore it can be argued that if the decision in *Roffey* is a good decision, then it should apply to cases concerning part-payment of debts. [108]

**Should we extend the principle in Roffey to part payment cases?**

In **Re Selectmove**, a company owed tax to the Inland Revenue and offered to pay this off in instalments. The tax collector said that he would be in touch with the company if the agreement could not be reached. The IRC ordered to pay all the taxes immediately or they would take immediate actions against the company. The company tried to invoke the principle of **Williams v Roffey** that the promise they made is carrying out an obligation which is existing was supporting the consideration for the deal to pay the debts in parts. The Court of Appeal differentiated **Williams v Roffey** that it contained the precedent of services and goods not debt payments. However, the distinction can be criticised as artificial and it can be suggested that there is no logical reason why the principle should not be extended to apply equally to both types of cases. The precedent that the court followed was **Foakes v Beer** and held that the IRC was not under any agreement binding them to accept part-payments. While the decision in this case shows that it conflicts with the ratio decidendi in **Williams v Roffey**, it could be obvious that the fundamental principle of paying the debts in parts is still unaffected.

It can be argued that extending the principle of **Roffey** to part-payment of debts would have severe consequence for creditors in insolvency. If a business goes into liquidation then the administrator may seek to recover part-payment of debts to discharge the larger debt in full and final settlement. This is damaging to creditors and could as a result have harmful effect on the economy as it shifts the risk of business onto the creditor.

The Court of Appeal could have extended **Roffey** to part-payment of debts in **Selectmove**. However, it must be pointed out that the court's decision not to do so and follow **Foakes v Beer** was

---

[108]See for example the discussion in Trietel, G.H. *Some Landmarks of 20ᵗʰ Century Contract Law*, Oxford University Press, Oxford, 2002, pp38-40,

necessary. The Court of Appeal has no power to overrule **Foakes v Beer** as it was a decision of the House of Lords. More recently in **South Caribbean Trading Ltd ('SCT') v Trafigura Beeher BV** [109]Colman J cast doubt on the decision in **Williams v Roffey Bros**. He noted that the decision was inconsistent with the long-standing rule that consideration must move from the promisee.[110] He further noted that the House of Lords had yet to declare that **Williams v Roffey Bros** was wrongly decided.

## Conclusion

This paper has presented the traditional position as stated in **Stilk v Myrick** and recognised that the principle of **Roffey** seems to be an exception to that. It appears the courts have extended the principle to meet the requirements of justice in **Roffey**. It should not be seen as an overriding principle of law but a rule which courts have decided not to extend in **Re Selectmove**. Further, as this matter seems to also effect the law of insolvency (which is based on who gets paid what on a winding up) the proper body to change the law in this case is Parliament.

---

[109] [2004] EWHC 2676
[110] [2004] EWHC 2676 (paras.106–09 of the judgment)

# Consideration Problem Question

## Question

Debra hired Simon, a builder, to construct a single storey extension on the back of her house. Simon promised to complete the work by 30th December for £10,000. Debra agreed and paid Simon a deposit of £3,000.

Simon commenced the work on time but due to his poor health and a failure to supervise his workers, the job fell significantly behind schedule. Debra, who was hoping to throw a New Year's Eve party in the new extension, was eager to ensure that the work would be completed on time. She promised Simon an extra £2,000 provided that he meets the original 30th December deadline. Simon agreed.

The work was completed on December 29th and Simon sent Debra an invoice for £9,000. Debra told Simon that she was in financial difficulties and could only pay £7,000. Simon needed this money in order to buy materials for his next job and so he felt that he had no alternative but to accept this amount in full and final settlement.

Simon has recently read that Debra has won £1m on the National Lottery.

Advise Simon whether he is entitled to demand the extra £2,000 promised by Debra.

## Answer

### Introduction

This paper advises Simon on his position in relation to his agreement with Debra. The paper examines the difficulties faced by Simon in arguing that he is in fact entitled to the additional £2,000 promised by Debra. In particular, this paper will address the issue of consideration and the possible implications of promissory estoppel and economic duress.

## Consideration for the variation

It is first necessary to address whether the variation of the terms in this case is a binding variation of the contract. This variation will only be enforceable where it satisfies the formal requirements governing the formation of contract, and therefore consideration must be present. In the case of **Currie v Misa**, Lush J referred to consideration as *'[...] some right, interest, profit or benefit accruing to one party, or some forbearance, detriment, loss or responsibility, given, suffered or undertaken by the other'*.

On the facts of this case, it does not appear that there has been any further consideration to support the variation of the agreement. Whilst it is clear that Simon will receive the further benefit of the additional £2,000, it is more difficult to establish the benefit received by Debra. This suggests that the variation is not mutually beneficial and therefore not enforceable. It may however be possible to argue that Debra will gain the benefit of having the new extension built in time for her New Year's Eve party which may be a practical benefit.

It is important to consider the case law in this area in determining whether Simon can argue that Debra received a practical benefit, which amounted to consideration. In **Stilk v Myrick**, after failing to find replacements, the captain promised his crew that the wages of the deserters would be shared out between them if they fulfilled the duties of the missing crewmen as well as their own. The court held that the promise was not binding, as the crew had not given consideration in respect of the promise. Applying this to the facts of our case, it seems unlikely that Simon would recover the additional £2,000. Debra could argue that Simon merely discharged their pre-existing duty, and therefore no additional benefit was conferred on them. As a result, Debra may argue consideration was not present and the variation was therefore not binding on them.

The exception to this principle was established in **Hartley v Ponsonby** where a ship's crew had been seriously depleted by a number of desertions. The captain promised the remaining crew members £40 extra pay if they would complete the voyage. It was held by the court that this promise was binding. The crew had provided valid consideration because it was dangerous to sail so undermanned. The seamen were not obliged to do this under their contracts of service and were; therefore, free to enter into a fresh contract, which would include the extra remuneration, for the remaining part of the voyage.

This exception was developed even further in **Williams v Roffey Bros. & Nicholls (Contractors) Ltd**. Here a building contractor was refurbishing a block of twenty-seven flats. The building contractor subcontracted with the plaintiff, who undertook to provide certain carpentry work for the price of £20,000. The plaintiff later found himself in severe financial difficulties despite having received £16,200. The building contractor promised to pay the plaintiff an additional sum for each flat completed on time, as they were concerned that they would be liable under a penalty clause and realized that the contract was under-priced. The plaintiff completed eight further flats and the building contractor paid a further £1,500, but would not pay any additional monies. In a similar way to **Stilk v Myrick**, the building contractors argued that the plaintiff had merely done what he was already bound to do. Unlike **Stilk v Myrick** however, the court held that the building contractor received certain practical benefits including not losing out on money under the penalty clause and the cost and inconvenience of finding an alternative contractor.

On the basis of this decision, it may therefore be a valid argument that the benefit received by Debra in having the extension built before the 30th December deadline was a practical benefit. However, it is not clear that the principles in **Williams v Roffey** would extend this far. Whilst it is not addressed in the facts of our case, it may be that Debra wants no sign of building work if she is having guest over, which would not be there if the extension is built. This would certainly be a situation covered by the concept of practical benefit, although more details would be required to determine whether such practical benefits did arise.

**Economic duress**

If consideration can be established, the second issue to consider is economic duress. In particular, it is necessary to determine whether Simon's behaviour could be characterized as either illegitimate commercial pressure, which would render the contract voidable, or merely 'the rough and tumble of normal commercial bargaining', which would potentially allow Simon to recover the £2,000. This appears to be relevant as Debra states that she reluctantly agreed to the additional monies, as it needed to have the extension built before the 30th December deadline. The most recent definition of economic duress can be found in **DSND Subsea Ltd v Petroleum Geo-Services ASA**, in which Dyson J stated that:

> *'[...] there must be pressure, (a) whose practical effect is that there is compulsion on, or lack of practical choice for, the victim, (b) which is illegitimate, and (c) which is a significant case inducing the claimant to enter into the contract.'*

It may be arguable that the compulsion or lack of practical choice for the victim was not illegitimate, but was instead the exertion of pressure to be expected in a normal commercial environment. It is necessary to gain further information to determine whether this is a possible argument. Dyson J set out a number of principles to determine whether the pressure was illegitimate. In particular, it would be important for Simon to demonstrate that they were acting in good faith, that Debra had a realistic alternative but to submit to the pressure and that Debra did not protest to the variation. Whilst the threatened breach of the contract by Simon would suggest illegitimate compulsion, evidence of the other factors discussed could still lead to a finding in favour of Simon.

**Promissory estoppel**

The next issue to be examined is the application of promissory estoppel. The doctrine of promissory estoppel applies where *"a promise was made which was intended to create legal relations and which, to the knowledge of the person making the promise, was going to be acted on by the person to whom it was made and which was in fact so acted on"*. It is clear in this definition that the doctrine of promissory estoppel may therefore apply in our case. It can be argued that Debra made an unequivocal promise, which was intended to affect the legal relationship between the parties. It is also arguable that Debra knew that the promise was going to be acted on, as Simon made it clear he would finish before the 30th December deadline on the basis of Debra' promise. Finally, Simon then relied upon this promise.

There are two limitations to the doctrine of promissory estoppel however. First, it must inequitable for the promisor to go back on the promise (**D & C Builders v Rees**). It is arguable that it is unfair for Debra to go back on their agreement to pay the additional £2,000 to Simon. However, because she has won the lottery it would seem to be inequitable for her to go back on her word considering she is no longer in financial trouble.

Second, and more problematic, is that promissory estoppel cannot be used as a separate cause of action. This may provide difficulties for Simon, as they will want to make a claim to recover the £2,000. There may be two ways in which this problem can be addressed. First, Simon could make a claim based on Debra' promise and then only rely on promissory estoppel as a defence to Debra's argument that the terms of the original contract were still binding. Second, Simon could argue that, in not relying on promissory estoppel, they provided good consideration for the promise to pay the extra £2,000. However, promissory estoppel is merely suspensory and therefore it is possible that Debra could bring the promissory estoppel to an end by giving reasonable notice. It is not clear what reasonable notice would be, although the short length of the contract may mean that little notice would be required.

**Conclusion**

In conclusion, it is possible that Simon will be able to recover the £2,000 on the basis that consideration was present. Whilst this argument appears weak, Simon may be able to rely upon **Williams v Roffey** in establishing consideration, which appears to be their strongest argument. The next issue to overcome is economic duress. It seems arguable that economic duress was not present in our case, although further information is necessary to determine the strength of this argument. The doctrine of promissory estoppel may also be useful in establishing Simon's claim for the additional monies, although again limitations do exist. Whilst it is possible that Simon could therefore recover the monies on the basis of these arguments, it is by no means certain and further information is necessary before it is possible to determine the likelihood of recovery.

# Chapter 5   Duress and Economic Duress

## Introduction

One of the defining mechanisms in the Law of Contract is that parties can only establish contracts of their own free will and enter into them of their own free will. As a result, any party that has been influenced or forced into entering an agreement could evade the obligations of that contract by using the principle of duress. This largely rests, however, on the kinds of influences and pressures that the affected party is subjected to.

## Duress to the person

**General Principle: When a contract is established by undue pressure, it can be cancelled out altogether.**

**Williams v Bayley** [1866] LR 1 HL 200
**Facts:** Bayley's son made a forgery of his father's signature on some bank cheques and then gave them to Mr. Williams. Mr. Williams threatened Mr. Bayley, claiming he would bring criminal prosecution against his son unless he allowed an equitable mortgage to get the notes back.
**Ratio: The House of Lords held that the cancelling of this contract was acceptable on the grounds that there had been undue influence in the returning of the notes.**
**Application:** An agreement will be set aside when it can be shown that a person was unable to make a decision of their own free will.

**General Principle: Pressure has to be proven by the party that claims to be put under duress, but it does not need to be the only reason.**

**Barton v Armstrong** [1976] A.C. 104
**Facts:** The former chairperson of a company, Armstrong, made a threat towards Barton. He threatened to kill him if he did not agree to buy all of his shares. Barton quickly made the agreement. Later, evidence arose that Barton's purchase of the shares was also potentially motivated by his belief that it was a good business

decision.

**Ratio: The court held that "if Mr. Armstrong's threats were a reason for Barton buying the shares...he is entitled to seek remedy". Armstrong had to prove his threats were not what made Barton buy out all the shares, and duress did not have to be the only reason for Barton's purchase.**

**Application:** The burden of proof lies with the person accused of duress to prove that he was not putting the other party under duress.

### Economic Duress

**General principle: The central idea of duress is that someone does something 'or else' something bad will happen to them, but you must remember that it does not have to come as a direct threat to them. As long as a party can prove their free will was twisted, then duress can stand as a defence to enforcing a contract.**

**Pao On v Lau Yiu Long** [1979] 3 All ER 65

**Facts:** Pao On (the claimant) made threats that he would not see the primary contract to fruition. This contract concerned share purchases. He said he would not do anything unless some secondary agreements were adhered to, which included both an indemnity and a guarantee. Lau Yiu Long (the defendant) wanted to fulfil the primary contract in haste. This is because the ability to buy shares had been disclosed to the wider world and he did not wish to undermine the company's image in public, nor cause the share prices to drop as a result. Long could have brought an action against Pao for the agreement to be given specific performance. However, this would have caused major disruption and delay to proceedings, not to mention would have damaged the company's reputation. Long had the benefit of consulting legal representatives before committing to the agreement for indemnity and a guarantee. **Pao On** then tried to invoke his guarantee and Long looked to have the twin agreements struck down because he believed they would cause economic duress.

**Ratio: The Court of Appeal held that no economic duress had occurred.**

**Application:** Lord Scarman outlined a number of key factors as guidelines for whether economic duress existed:

"An act done before the giving of a promise to make a payment or to confer some other benefit can sometimes be consideration for the promise."

1) "The act must have been done at the promisors' request..."

2) "The parties must have understood that the act was to be remunerated either by a payment or the conferment of some other benefit...AND"

3) "Payment or the conferment of a benefit must have been legally enforceable had it been promised in advance."

**General principle: The central idea of duress is that someone does something 'or else' something bad will happen to them, but you must remember that it does not have to come as a direct threat to them. As long as a party can prove their free will was twisted, then duress can stand as a defence to enforcing a contract.**

**DSND Subsea Ltd v Petroleum Services ASA** [2000] BLR 530

**Facts:** DSND were hired by Petroleum Geo-Services (PGS) to work under the sea as part of developing oil rig sites and drilling platforms in the North Sea. The original subcontract had been amended by subsequent agreements. These had changed the terms of payment for important aspects of the work. Having made these agreements, PGS wanted to have them struck down in court. One of the reasons they brought up was that the agreements had been made while PGS was under economic duress.

**Ratio: The court held that PGS could have pursued alternative kinds of action that would have clearly allowed for them to avoid this situation, therefore they could not claim for duress.**

**Application:** In this important case, Dyson J formulated a list of the general principles that applied when trying to show that there has been economic duress in a commercial setting. These are:

(i)     "Economic pressure can amount to duress, provided it may be characterised as illegitimate and has constituted a 'but for' cause inducing the claimant to enter into the relevant contract or to make a payment."

(ii)    "A threat to break a contract will generally be regarded as illegitimate, particularly where the defendant must know that it would be in breach of contract if the threat were implemented".

(iii) "It is relevant to consider whether the claimant had a 'real choice' or 'realistic alternative' and could, if they had wished, equally well have resisted the pressure and, for example, pursued practical and effective legal redress. If there was no reasonable alternative, that may be very strong evidence in support of a conclusion that the victim of the duress was in fact influenced by the threat."

(iv) "The presence, or absence, of protest, may be of some relevance when considering whether the threat had coercive effect. But, even the total absence of protest does not mean that the payment was voluntary."

**General Principle: Economic Duress exists when there is compulsion of the will to the point where the party under duress is without any practical alternative, outside of complying with the threat.**

**Universe Tankships Inc. v International Transport Workers' Federation (The Universe Sentinel)** [1983] 1 AC 366
**Facts:** International Transport Workers' Federation, a trade union, had called a strike action amongst its members. This significantly disrupted the construction work that was happening on the Sentinel, a ship that transported cargo containers across the sea. The ship was being built for the claimants, Universe Tankships Inc. The union decided to end the strike but said that they would only do so if the tanker company made payments into its welfare fund, which they used to purchase materials, amongst other things. The tanker company put a payment through to those working on the construction of the ship, but at the same time, tried to recover the payment on the grounds that they had to pay under duress.
**Ratio: The Court determined that the payments were made under duress. Furthermore, the Court of Appeal held that it was not applicable to discuss the principle of duress in this context of involuntary agreements. This is because the victimised party always maintains a choice, even if this left them with undesirable outcomes from not doing what the other said. Lord Diplock asserted that it was far more fitting to**

"formulate a test in terms of whether the innocent party was given any practical alternative other than to comply with the other party's demands."
Application: This decision was reached on the rationale that the victimised party always maintains a choice, even if this leaves them with undesirable outcomes from not doing what the other said.

General Principle: Economic duress amounts to the kind of pressure being put on a contracting party. In these situations, these are acts designed by the other party to damage their financial situation as opposed to their physical well-being.

North Ocean Shipping Co. Ltd v Hyundai Construction Co. Ltd [1979] QB 705(The Atlantic Baron)
Facts: There was a contract that governed the building of a ship called 'The Atlantic Baron'. The party building the ship, Hyundai, wanted to make an increase to the overall price of the ship just after they started working on it. This decision came as a result of unpredictable changes in the stock market and exchange rates. North Ocean Shipping Co. Ltd refused to be bound by this proposed amendment to the original terms of the contract. However, they were worried that in doing so, the ship's construction would be delayed and they, as a result, would suffer potential loss of a multimillion-pound charter deal with another company. As a result, they paid Hyundai the extra amount that they wanted. A number of months after they did this, however, the company brought action against Hyundai on the basis that they had been forced to pay through duress.
Ratio: The court held that the kind of pressure Hyundai put the North Ocean Shipping Co under could actually amount to duress, but it could not be applied in this case due to the fact the shipping company had put off bringing action for too long afterwards.
Application: The court added that: *"the essence of duress...[is that]...there needs to have been some compulsion of the will...which could arise from just as much from economic pressure as it would from threats of violence."*

**General principle: The threat of withdrawing a line of credit doesn't amount to illegitimate pressure.**

**CTN Cash & Carry Ltd v Gallaher** [1994] 4 All ER 714
**Facts:** The claimants, CTN Cash and Carry, were in dispute with Gallaher Ltd, the defendants, in regard to whether CTN ought to make a payment for a batch of cigarettes that were delivered to the wrong warehouse. Additionally, the cigarettes had been stolen from the warehouse before Gallaher could retrieve them. Gallaher continued to request payment for the stolen cigarettes, in addition to the new shipment. CTN was unwilling to pay for the second shipment, but Gallaher threatened to withdraw CTN's credit for any dealings they might have with them in future. CTN paid for the misplaced stolen cigarettes.
**Ratio: The court held that withdrawing credit did not amount to duress, and dismissed CTN's claim.**
**Application:** Steyn LJ said that *"extending the law of Duress to cover lawful act duress" would be going too far...and there were policy reasons for not doing so".* So normal pressures in the course of business would be acceptable and would not amount to Duress. It would have to be something more extreme.

**General Principle: Economic duress can come about when parties enter into a contract and then one party decides to take advantage of the other's bad situation and then force the terms of the contract to be renegotiated to be more favourable to himself.**

**D & C Builders v Rees** [1966] 2 Q.B. 617
**Facts:** D and C Builders were an independent building contractors company. Rees, a client of theirs, owed the company £500 as payment for work they had carried out for him. After a lengthy wait, Rees' wife made an offer to pay £300 as the final amount to settle the contract. She attached a statement saying that, if her offer was not accepted, the building company would not be paid. D and C Builders agreed, but in extreme reluctance. After receiving the £300, they returned and brought action to claim the remaining £200.
**Ratio: The Court of Appeal approved the claim that was made by D and C Builders. In their judgement, they distinguished between Sibree v Tripp and this case. They also expressed**

their disapproval of some later cases, crucially stating that "a cheque was no different from cash."

**Application:** Lord Denning said: "When there is a genuine agreement in place between someone receiving credit and those giving it out and it is expressly stated that the party giving credit would accept a smaller amount of money than originally given to pay off a debt…equity might then intervene to prevent his insisting on his full legal rights if it would be unjust and unreasonable for him to do so, but this was not such a case".

**General Principle: There is a 'dividing line' between economic duress and so called 'hard and fair bargaining'. The line will always be difficult to draw; because of this, it is a question of fact whether a party has been forced into unduly accepting unfavourable terms or just entering as a result of normal contractual negotiations.**

**Atlas Express Ltd v Kafco (Importers and Distributors) Ltd** [1989] Q.B. 833; [1989] 3 W.L.R. 389

**Facts:** Kafco Ltd was party to a contract with the now former high-street retail chain 'Woolworths'. The contract involved the delivery of baskets to 'Woolworths'. The contract's duration was set to last for a minimum of six months. During the course of this contract, Atlas Ltd came to realise that it had miscalculated the size of the baskets and, as such, were losing money by having to pay extra fees to ensure they were delivered to 'Woolworths'. Kafco did not want to change the pricing agreement. Atlas sent one of their drivers in an empty lorry to Kafco's head office, where he delivered a letter stating that, if the company did not agree to pay a higher charge on deliveries, the driver would refuse to accept the cargo and leave. Kafco were not in a financial position to take risks with their main supplier, nor were they able to find a replacement supplier, so they reluctantly agreed. Kafco then refused to make any payments and brought forward a claim for economic duress. They also argued that no new consideration existed.

**Ratio: Tucker J held that economic duress was present in this particular case; therefore, Kafco was allowed to avoid their contractual duty. When Kafco agreed they did so, according to Tucker J, "unwillingly and under compulsion…there was no bargaining power at all".**

**Application:** Economic duress can, in the words of Tucker J, "vitiate" a new agreement made with a party being subjected to duress.

**R v Attorney General** [2003] E.M.L.R. 24
**Facts:** This case concerned a solider that fought in the SAS for the UK military. He was told by his superior officers that he had to sign a confidentiality agreement or go down a rank through demotion. He signed the non-disclosure agreement. He then went back to New Zealand. While he was there, he decided to write and then publish his memoirs. The Court of Appeal in New Zealand did not disallow the memoirs of the soldier from being published. What they did instead was apportion a set amount of the profits from the book as a means of compensation for the breach of contract. The soldier then appealed to the UK Privy Council. He contested that the contract only came about because he was put under duress when he signed it. Also, the soldier said that army had a lot of control over his actions and authority, which is why there was undue influence when he signed the agreement.
**Ratio: The Privy Council held that duress could not apply to avoiding the contract. Lord Hoffmann said there "was no illegitimate pressure, therefore no duress could exist".**
**Application:** The main element for duress, according to Lord Hoffman, is: "pressure amounting to compulsion of the will of the victim and the second was the illegitimacy of the pressure".

# Question and Answers

- **Duress Essay Question**

## Question

"The doctrine of duress is without rational foundation and unjustifiably violates the basic principle of freedom of contract." Critically discuss.

## Answer

### Introduction

This paper will discuss the proposition that the doctrine of duress and its justification. It will examine the doctrine and critically discuss if it violates and sit uncomfortably with the principle of freedom of contact. In order to do this, the paper will discuss the basic principle of freedom of contract. Second it will discuss what duress is? Third it will discuss the tests of economic duress laid down by Dyson J in **DSND** and the application of the test in *Carillion*. Fourth this paper will examine the jurisprudence of economic duress. Fifth this paper will argue restitution is a better remedy than duress. Last this paper will conclude.

### The principle of freedom of contract

In the nineteenth century the common Law of Contract saw a huge growth where due to significant commercial and industrial development, witnessed numerous contract disputes being brought to the courts. A superseding rule of freedom of contract followed which outlined that parties who were of full capacity should have full freedom to make any terms as long as they were legal. The result of this resulted in the rule of freedom of contract was the rule of sanctity of contract, where contracts that were willingly entered into by individuals that were of rational capacity should be enforced by the courts. In **Printing and Numerical Registering Co v Sampson,**[111] Sir George Jessel stated:

---

[111] (1875) 19 Eq 462

*"...men of full age and competent understanding shall have the utmost liberty in contracting, and that their contracts, when entered into freely and voluntarily, shall be held sacred and shall be enforced by Courts of Justice."*

This statement indicates that where a person is reasonable and capable then they have a choice over how they both start and complete their contracts. Nevertheless, towards the latter of the nineteenth and during the twentieth century, there was a rise in numbers of Acts of Parliament that focused on the rule of freedom of contract. This was due to it becoming more frequently recognised that the do it yourself application in regards to the rule of freedom of contract on more occasions resulted in injustice. Freedom of Contract therefore could be abused as a result of gross inequality of bargaining power between both large companies and consumers or employees; an example of this is ecominic duress or template agreements.

Potential parties to contracts should enter the market using their own thinking to ensure that they decide which bargains will work in their favour and stick to them. This freedom authorises parties to openly choose others as consensual contractual partners. Parties need to be free to express and choose their own individual terms due to each contract needing to be unique, based on the differences of people characters and what they want to expect to see from their contracts and how it can benefit them. Nevertheless the growth of both private and public sector large corporate enterprises made it almost impossible for the fragile party to exercise freedom, this is due to the pressure on for forming agreements with larger companies. Hence a party could be apprehended to the will of these more economically powerful contracting parties rather than practising their rights to an equal tender.

**What is duress?**

Judges have a tendency not into get involved with contracts.[112] On the other hand parties that are entering contracts need to be able to

---

[112] Atiyah " Economic Duress and the ' Overborne Will" ' (1982) 98 L.Q.R. 197

preserve assurance in terms that the contract will be adhered to which will ensure that no other party will be exploited.[113] An example of where intervention by the court is seen in duress.[114] Economic duress was known under the common law in 1976 as an acceptable ground to avoid an agreement. The first case where the doctrine arose was **Occidental Worldwide Investment Corp v Skibs**.[115] In this case it was insisted by charters of two ships that the cost to rent a ship must be reduced due to the fall in market rates by intimidating the owners about their assets and stated that unless costs were to be reduced then they would go into bankruptcy. The charterers were aware that if the ships were returned then given the slump they would face monetary difficulty and therefore would be unable to find substitute charterers. The result of this was that the threats that were made were false and deceitful meaning that owners were able to escape the renegotiated terms. Nevertheless Kerr J. acknowledged that in principle economic duress can be used to void the agreement.

In **North Ocean Shipping Ltd v Hyundai Corporation Co**, shipbuilders without any legal explanation threatened to dismiss the contract unless an increase of 10 per cent was settled by the plaintiff. The ship owners agreed to additional payment due to dreading a loss in the charter if the ship was not supplied on time. Mocatta J detailed: *"compulsion may take the form of 'economic duress' if necessary facts are proved. A threat to break a contract may amount to such 'economic duress".* Similarly, Lord Scarman in **Pao On v Lau Yiu Long**[116] concluded: *"there is nothing contrary to principle to recognising economic duress as a factor which may render a contract voidable".[117]*

**The tests of economic duress**

In a number of small cases Economic duress has been applied.[118] Two cases important cases are **DSND Subsea v. Petroleum Geo-Services**[119] and *Carillion Construction Ltd v Felix (UK) Ltd.[120]*

---

[113] Chitty on Contracts (29th ed., Sweet & Maxwell, London, 2004)
[114] *Barton v Armstrong* [1976] AC 104
[115] [1976] 1 Lloyd's Rep. 293
[116] [1980] A.C. 614
[117] [1980] A.C. 614 at 636
[118] *Atlas Express Ltd v Kafco Ltd* [1989] Q.B. 333

Dyson J was the judge who decided both of these cases. Ecominic duress was discovered in the latter case but was not in *DSND*. According to Dyson J in the *DSND*:

*"The ingredients of actionable duress are that there must be pressure, (a) whose practical effect is that there is compulsion on, or a lack of practical choice, for the victim, (b) which is illegitimate, and (c) which is a significant cause inducing the claimant to enter into the contract ... In determining whether there has been illegitimate pressure, the court takes into account a range of factors. These include whether there has been an actual or threatened breach of contract; whether the person allegedly exerting the pressure has acted in good or bad faith; whether the victim protested at the time; and whether he affirmed and sought to rely on the contract. These are all relevant factors".*

Dyson J ended this test by placing a proviso, which has famously made economic duress very hard to argue:

*"Illegitimate pressure must be distinguished from the rough and tumble of the pressures of normal commercial bargaining."*

**DSND**

DSND were hired by Petroleum Geo-Services (PGS) to work under the sea as part of developing oil rig sites and drilling platforms in the North Sea. The original contract had been altered by succeeding agreements. These had changed the payment terms for aspects of the work. Having made these agreements, PGS wanted to have them struck down in court because of economic duress. The court held that PGS could have pursued alternative kinds of action that would have clearly allowed for them to avoid this situation, therefore they could not claim for duress. Dyson J relating the test to the evidence, said:

*" [a] suspension of the work on the RTIAS pending resolution of the insurance/indemnity question, even if it was a breach of*

[119] [2000] BLR 531
[120] [2001] B.L.R. 1

*contract, and even if it amounted to pressure, did not amount to*
*illegitimate pressure. It was reasonable behaviour by a contractor*
*acting bona fide in a very difficult situation".*[121]

## Carillion

In **Carillion**, the test for economic duress was awarded. Carillion
was the core contractor asked to build an office building. Carillion
delegated the supply, manufacture and design of the cladding to
Felix. If the office was to be completed late then a charge of
£75,000 per week would have to be made by Carillion to the
developer for liquidated ascertained damages. Knowing Felix had
fallen behind with completion, it asserted that Carillion sign the
contract in relation to the monetary account which at the time was
being disputed, prior to Felix completing the delivery of the
cladding. Dyson J referred to his test for economic duress laid
down in *DSND* and applied it to the facts of **Carillion.** Unless an
agreement was made Felix threatened not to complete any more
deliveries, which would result in a breach of contract.

Carillion needed to complete the job and were unable to do so
without the cladding from Felix. The cladding was an important
part of the task and Carillion were frantic for the cladding to be
completed. Unless the cladding was to be completed the other
trades would be unable to begin their tasks and would result in the
whole project being delayed. Felix provided bespoke cladding and
there were no other options for Carillion. There was no
opportunity for settlement as it would have still taken a further six
weeks to gain a decision and there were major complications in
gaining a mandatory injunction. Felix had no power when asking
for their final account to be paid before the completion of work nor
did Felix have the right to stop deliveries until payment was made
as this was not stated in the contract. In addition to this, Felix was
claiming in excess of what they were contractually entitled to were
mindful that Carillion had no other substitute and therefore would
have no other option but to concede to their demands for the sum.
Based on the facts Carillion would have never entered the
commercial settlement agreement if Felix had threatened not to
deliver the cladding. Additionally, Carillion indicated in their

---

[121] [2000] B.L.R. 530 at 546

correspondence at the *"extreme displeasure at being required to enter into such an agreement"*.

**The jurisprudence of economic duress**

Due to the broad nature of Dyson J's test judges are now not willing to break the parties' bargain. The main ideology operating in this area seemed to be market individualism.[122] This involved two principles one being the market philosophy and the other individualistic philosophy. Market philosophy views the operation of the law of contract as the result of competitive exchange. Individualism is about *"freedom of contract"* and *"sanctity of contract"*. It is fundamental to ensure that individuals have full licence in making the terms of their agreements, but also to ensure that parties are held to their contracts. Indications of this can be seen in *Pao On*, where Lord Scarman stated:

> *"Where businessmen are negotiating at arm's length it is unnecessary for the achievement of justice, and unhelpful in the development of the law to invoke such a rule of public policy. It would also create unacceptable anomaly. It is unnecessary because justice requires that men, who have negotiated at arm's length, be held to their bargains, unless it can be shown that their consent was vitiated by fraud, mistake or duress".[123]*

In addition, in **CTN Cash and Carry v Gallagher Ltd**,[124] Steyn L.J. was extremely cautious when arguing out the significance of commercial certainty:

"[allowing lawful act duress] *would introduce a substantial and undesirable element of uncertainty in the commercial bargaining process. Moreover it will often enable bona fide settled accounts to be reopened when parties to commercial dealings fall out".*

Steyn L.J. was unhappy about the courts delving to see if the contracts where socially or morally unacceptable. Part of market individualism contains reducing or completely eradicating any

---

[122] J. N. Adams and R. Brownsword, *Understanding Contract Law* (4th ed., Sweet & Maxwell, London, 2004)
[123] [1980] A.C. 614 at 634
[124] [1994] 4 All E.R. 714 at 719

moral or legal factors that as a result could lead to uncertainty. Freedom of contract theory can explain the decisions in *Atlas Express Ltd v Kafco* and *North Ocean Shipping*. It is argued whilst the difference between economic duress and legitimate commercial pressure may in some ways be unclear; the courts will usually find economic duress where the facts are captivating.[125] An example of this would be in *Atlas*, where the plaintiff carriers under-priced a contract where they were to transport basket-ware to numerous retail outlets which commanded that costs should be modified upwards. The plaintiffs further developed a new agreement and gave drivers strict directions stating that unless the defendants signed the agreement they were to drive away with the defendant's goods. The defendants had no other choice but to sign this agreement as it was so close to Christmas and as a result they could not make any further substitute provisions nor could they let down retail outlets.

It is argued duress is fact specific. If facts do not appear captivating then as a result may not fall within the test for economic duress. It is said that decisions of the court based upon market-individualism show us the test of economic duress is hard to satisfy for those involved in the rough and tumble of commercial business, but who have in turn been unfairly exploited. It is advised that's victims should look elsewhere for remedy. The remedy of restitution is not dependent on making contracts void and so the *"freedom of contract"* theory should not present a hurdle.

**Restitution to the rescue**

The law of restitution dictates that a claimant is able to recover a benefit rather than receive compensation for breach of contract. Lord Wright stated in 1943 that:

> *"It is clear that any civilised system of law is bound to provide remedies for cases of what has been called unjust enrichment or unjust benefit, that is, to prevent a man from retaining the money of, or some benefit derived from, another which it is against conscience that he should keep".[126]*

---

[125] D. Tan, " Constructing a Doctrine of Economic Duress" (2002) 18 Const. L.J. 87

Restitutionary remedies are widely different from remedies in the law of both contract and tort and have been recognised under English law by the House of Lords.[127] It is said in the present situation that victims should, rather than seeking a rescission should seek restitution.[128] In the present case, *"unjust enrichment"* is the main theory based for restitution required by the victim. Unfair restitutionary remedies are only accessible where the defendant has been unfairly enriched at the cost of the victim.[129] This is the presumption upon which the victim is looking for redress because the obstacle of avoiding the contract is impossible to overcome or deal with successfully.[130] Lord Hoffmann said that the ingredients of restitution are:

*"First, whether the defendant would be enriched at the plaintiff's expense; secondly, whether such enrichment would be unjust; and thirdly, whether there are nevertheless reasons of policy for denying a remedy".*[131]

## Conclusion

In conclusion, it is shown that the test for economic duress is broad ranging. The idea of Freedom of Contract puts courts under pressure therefore leaving them unwilling to get involved with commercial contracts. Only when accurate circumstances are presented then there is a possibility that they may thrive to avoid the contract, although affirmation still remains. It may be more useful for victims to instead depend on restitution. There are categories of unfair enrichment that may be held open. It may be easier to bring an action in unjust enrichment than it is to satisfy the requirements of duress. The reason behind this is that the court is happy to set aside market-individualism theory in protecting unjust enrichment. The court justifies this because it is not voiding a contract rather neutralising opportunistic commercial behaviour. Restitution seems to be the way to go.

---

[126] *Fibrosa Spolka Akcyjna v Fairbairn Lawson Combe Barbour* [1943] A.C. 32 at 61
[127] *Lipkin Gorman Ltd v Karpnale Ltd* [1991] 2 A.C. 548
[128] *B&S Contracts v Victor Green Publications* [1984] I.C.R. 419
[129] R. Halson, " Opportunism, Economic Duress and Contractual Modifications" (1991) 107 L.Q.R. 649-678
[130] G. Virgo, The Principles of the Law of Restitution (Clarendon Press, Oxford, 1999).
[131] *Banque Financière de la Cité v Parc (Battersea) Ltd* [1999] 1 A.C. 221 at 234 per Lord Hoffmann

# Chapter 6   Promissory Estoppel and Waivers

## Waivers

**General Principle: Waivers allow parties to agree to not enforce their rights that are included in a contract.**

**Hickman v Haynes** (1874-75) L.R. 10 C.P. 598
**Facts:** Hickman asked Haynes to make a delivery of some goods significantly later than they agreed to do. When Haynes finally made the delivery, Hickman refused to accept the goods shipment. Hickman brought action against Haynes for breach of contract and Haynes argued that Hickman had in fact breached the contract because he had delivered the goods later than they had agreed in the contract.
**Ratio: The court rejected the claim. Hickman had openly requested Haynes deliver the goods later.**
**Application:** Waivers can allow for promises to be binding, even in the absence of consideration.

**General Principle:  Terms of a contract, even very critical or important ones, can be amended by waiver.**

**Charles Rickards Ltd v Oppenheim** [1950] 1 K.B. 616; [1950] 1 All E.R. 420
Facts: Oppenheim (defendants) requested that Charles Rickards Ltd (plaintiffs) to make some repairs and modifications to his Royals Royce. He asked that the plaintiff finish the job within a period of 6 or seven months. The work was not completed on time and Oppenhiem allowed an additional three months for the work to be completed. It work was not completed after this period and Oppenhiem demanded that the work was finished in one month or he would cancel the order. The work wasn't finished for an additional two months after this demand and Oppenhiem refused to accept the car.
**Ratio: The Court of Appeals held that not finishing the work in time was a breach of contract.**
**Application:** What this means is that if the Royals Royce had had its work completed on time for that extended deadline, the defendants would then have had to accept it, regardless of the

original completion date. Once Oppenheim provided Charles Rickards Ltd with notice that the completion time had been extended yet again, Charles Rickards Ltd fiasco of completing the work within that time meant that they were in breach of contract.

## Promissory Estoppel

Promissory Estoppel can be seen as a development of the waiver doctrine, because both operate in equity. It can make a promise binding even if consideration has not been provided. Hughes and Metropolitan Railway Co (1887) was the basis for the doctrine.

**General Principle: If you promise a person something, and that person relies on said promise, then you cannot operate on previous agreements modified or postponed by that promise.**

**Hughes v Metropolitan Railway Co** (1887) 2 App. Cas. 439
**Facts:** Metropolitan Railway Co. had leased property from Hughes. The lease between the two stipulated that the tenants had to keep the property in a good state of repair. In October 1874, the landlord gave a notice period of six months to the tenants to complete some repairs and said that, if the repairs were not completed, the lease would be forfeited. Come November, both parties started discussing the potential of the tenants buying the lease out and taking possession of the property. The landlord indicated that he would not enforce the notice during the course of negotiations, so the tenants did not make the repairs. In December, the parties fell out and negotiations stalled. At the end of the six months, Hughes said that the lease was null and void due to the fact that no repairs had been made by the tenants to the property.
**Ratio: The House of Lords held that there was an implied promise in the landlord's behaviour that the voiding of the lease would not happen at the end of the six month notice period. Metropolitan Railway Co. had been relying on the landlord's promise. The six month period was seen by the court to have restarted right after the point where they disagreed and negotiations for the tenants to buy out the lease had come to a halt. The promise was held to be a good and binding one.**
**Application:** The equitable principle of promissory estoppel provides a limited exception to the rule that requires consideration

to be given. This happens by way of exchange for an undertaking not to enforce a debt. There also has to be a pre-existing legal relationship for the doctrine of promissory estoppel to apply.

**General Principle: Promissory estoppel can operate as an equitable exception to the general rule that part payment of a debt without fresh consideration does not discharge the debt obligation.**

**Central London Property v High Trees House** [1947] KB 130
**Facts:** In 1937, the landlords of a block of flats entered into a lease with the defendants at an annual rent of £2,500. Due to the outbreak of war, the tenant was unable to sub-let the property and in 1940, the contract was varied to a reduced rent of £1,250. Nothing was expressed as to how long this arrangement was to last. In 1945, the war ended and the tenant was able to sublet the property fully. The landlords wrote to the tenant and asked for the full rent and £8,000 worth of arrears. However, the landlords chose only to sue for the rent due from May 1945 onwards.
**Ratio: Denning J decided that the 1940 agreement was only intended to be temporary because of the war and that the agreement had now come to an end. The landlords could sue for the rent from May 1945 onwards, because the financial pressures caused by the war no longer existed.**
**Application:** In obiter, Denning J claimed that the plaintiffs were not eligible to claim the rent from the years during the war, despite there being no consideration for their rent reduction. He argued that the promise was expected to be binding and was relied upon by the tenants. He maintained that there was a general equitable principle, stating: *'A promise intended to be binding, intended to be acted on and in fact acted on, is binding so far as its terms properly apply.'*

**When does promissory estoppel exist?**
Promissory estoppel is only possible under limited circumstances. These steps include the following:

1. Promissory estoppel can only arise in cases where a contractual or legal relationship exists.

2. In order for promissory estoppel to exist, a person must

promise that he or she will not enforce his or her legal rights.

3. Promissory estoppel appears when the promisee relies on the promise.

4. Promissory estoppel necessitates that it be inequitable for the promisor to go back on his or her promise and revert to his or her legal rights.

5. Promissory estoppel can only be used as a defence; it cannot be used as the basis of a case, but "as a shield, not a sword."

6. Promissory estoppel can only suspend contractual rights – it cannot remove them.

**General Principle: In order for promissory estoppel to exist, a person must promise that he or she will not enforce his or her legal rights.**

**Woodhouse A.C. Israel Cocoa Ltd. S.A. and Another v Nigerian Produce Marketing Co. Ltd.** [1972] A.C. 741; [1972] 2 W.L.R. 1090
**Facts:** In Lagos, a provision was made for payment in Nigerian pounds (£N), but the buyers inquired whether the sellers would accept pounds sterling. The sellers agreed that 'payment [could] be made in Sterling and in Lagos.' However, the pound sterling was later devalued to fifteen percent less than the Nigerian pound. The buyers tried to keep the sellers from going back on their agreement to accept both currencies after the decrease in value.
**Ratio: The House of Lords determined that, in order to claim promissory estoppel, there must be a clear and precise promise or representation made; in this circumstance, such a representation had not been made.**
**Application:** Lord Hailsham, L.C., commented: "Counsel for the appellants was asked whether he knew of any case in which an ambiguous statement had ever formed the basis of promissory estoppel, as contended for here, as distinct from estoppel of a more familiar type based on factual misrepresentation… it would really

be an astonishing thing if, in the case of a genuine misunderstanding as to the meaning of an offer, the offeree could obtain by means of the doctrine of promissory estoppel something that he must fail to obtain under the conventional law of contract." Here, the need for a precise, unequivocal promise is made clear; claims of promissory estoppel cannot rely on unclear promises.

**General Principle: Promissory estoppel appears when the promisee relies on the promise.**

**Emmanuel Ayodeji Ajayi v R.T. Briscoe (Nigeria) Ltd.** [1964] 1 W.L.R. 1326
The plaintiff loaned several Lorries to the defendant, and agreed to 'withhold instalments due [on the lorries] as long as they are withdrawn from active service' after learning of the defendant's difficulty in putting the Lorries to use. After the plaintiff sued, the defendant claimed that promissory estoppel should prevent the plaintiff from recovering the instalments.
**Ratio: The Privy Council determined that claims of promissory estoppel would not undermine the plaintiff's claim, maintaining that the defendant did not prove that the Lorries were actually not used, despite their claims.**
**Application:** Lord Hodson further explained promissory estoppel as 'when one party to a contract in the absence of fresh consideration agrees not to enforce his rights, an equity will be raised in favour of the other party. This equity is, however, subject to the qualification a) that the other party has altered his position.'
In determining whether the promisee has relied on the promise, one should consider whether the promise influenced the conduct of the promisee.

**How can Promissory Estoppel be used?**

**General Principle: The doctrine of promissory estoppel only ever suspends contractual rights – it does not diminish them altogether. Remember, because the doctrine is one that exists in equity, it is only something that can be used at the court's discretion when a judge examines the facts of a case.**

**Tool Metal Manufacturing Co. v Tungsten Electric Ltd (No.2)**
[1955] 1 WLR 761
**Facts:** Tool Metal owned a patent which they allowed Tungsten Electric to use on payment of a royalty. Payments were suspended during the war pending the making of a new agreement, which was not made. After the war, Tool Metal struggled to get Tungsten Electric to make a new agreement, and tried to claim the compensation expected for the time following the war, arguing that the previous litigation was sufficient notice.
**Ratio: The House of Lords held that notice had been given and that Tool Metal could claim their money from 1947.**
**Application:** A person can promise to suspend their legal rights and thus be stopped from going against their promise, but they are able to return to their legal entitlement, upon reasonable notice.

**General Principle: You can only use estoppel as a defence, not as something that can be construed as a detriment to the other party – as "a shield, not a sword"**

**Combe v Combe** [1951] 2 KB 215
**Facts:** During divorce proceedings, a husband promised to give his wife £100 per week in maintenance. The wife did not provide any consideration for this promise. The wife did not claim any maintenance in her petition. No payment was made, so she sued.
**Ratio: The judge initially stated that the wife should succeed in relying on the High Trees principle; however, in the Court of Appeal, Lord Denning overruled this and set out the principle that promissory estoppel could only be used as a defence.**
**Application:** Estoppel can be used, in Lord Denning's words, as a *"shield, not a sword."*

**General Principle: Estoppel can only be used if it is not inequitable for the promisor to go back on their promise.**

**D&C Builders v Rees** [1966] 2 Q.B. 617
**Facts:** D and C Builders were an independent building contractors company. Rees, a client of theirs, owed the company £500 as payment for work they had carried out for him. After a lengthy wait, Rees' wife made an offer to pay £300 as the final amount to settle the contract. She attached a statement saying that, if her offer was not accepted, the building company would not be paid. D and

C Builders agreed but in extreme reluctance. After receiving the £300, they returned and brought action to claim the remaining £200.

**Ratio: While the court maintained that this case fell under Pinnel's Case, Lord Denning also addressed promissory estoppel, claiming that Mrs. Rees could not claim estoppel because they had enacted it in a malicious manner, intending to take advantage of D and C Builders. The variation was not binding, so the builders could sue. Promissory estoppel could only be used if it would be inequitable for a creditor to enforce their legal rights.**

**Application:** A part payment can be accepted as full payment in situation where economic duress occurs.

# Question and Answer

1. Promissory Estoppel Essay

**Question**

"A promise to accept a smaller sum [in satisfaction of a greater debt], if acted upon, is binding notwithstanding the absence of consideration" Per Denning J in *Central London Property Trust Ltd v High Trees House Ltd* [1947] KB 130.

Explain the statement with reference to consideration and the doctrine of promissory estoppel. To what extent does this statement represent an accurate view of the law?

**Answer**

**Introduction**

This paper will discuss that promise to accept smaller amount of money in satisfaction of a greater debt is not enforceable and the concept of promissory estoppel will be discussed.

**Promise to accept smaller amount of money**

In **Pinnel's Case** the defendant had not provided any consideration for the plaintiff's promise not to sue on partial payment accepted. Sir Edward Coke had stated that:

> *"payment of a lesser sum on the day in satisfaction of a greater, cannot be any satisfaction for the whole, because it appears to the Judges that by no possibility, a lesser sum can be a satisfaction to the plaintiff for a greater sum."*[132]

This rule was upheld and applied in the case of *Foakes v Beer*, but not without the express doubts of Lord Blackburn, who nevertheless concurred in the judgement in that case, that *"men of business ... do every day recognise and act on the ground that*

---

132 *Pinnel's Case* (1602) 5 Co Rep 117a

*prompt payment of a part of their demand may be more beneficial to them than it would be to insist on their rights.* "[133] Therefore, the position according to these old authorities seems to be that any attempt to vary a contract (and promise to accept a smaller sum [in satisfaction of a greater debt]), will lack consideration unless what is been received is all together new or different to the original promise.

## Where payment of a lesser sum discharges an obligation to pay a greater sum

The rule as stated above is only applicable if the promise of the creditor to accept a lesser sum is unsupported by fresh consideration from the promisee. However, if, at the creditor's request, some new element is introduced, such as payment at a different place, or at a different time, compliance with this request will amount to consideration for the waiver. This concept was acknowledged in **Pinnel's Case** itself.

**Pinnel's Case** (1602): here Pinnel sued Cole in debt for £8 10s due on a bond on 11 November 1600. Cole's defence was that, at Pinnel's request, he had paid him £5 2s 6d on 1 October and that Pinnel had accepted this payment in full satisfaction of the original debt. Judgment was given for the plaintiff on a point of pleading but the court made it clear that, had it not been for a technical flaw, they would have found for the defendant on the ground that the part payment had been made on an earlier date than that stipulated in the bond. Early payment was a 'new element' which clearly would benefit the creditor and would therefore amount to consideration for the promise to accept a lesser sum.

It is also clear from the case itself that the tender of a different chattel at the request of the creditor could amount to fresh consideration. The chattel may totally replace the money owed or may be tendered along with a partial payment. Consistent with the law as already stated, the court will not enquire as to whether the chattel is of an equivalent monetary value to the debt as if there is sufficient consideration it matters not whether it is adequate. It is stated in the case that 'a hawk, a horse, or a robe may clear the

---

133 [1881–5] All ER Rep 106 at 115

debt but an offer of 19s 6d in the £1 on the due date at the appointed place will not suffice'.

This view was affirmed in **Sibree v Tripp** (1846) 15 M & W 23, where Baron Alderson said: *'It is undoubtedly true that payment of a portion of a liquidated demand, in the same manner as the whole liquidated demand ought to be paid, is payment only in part; because it is not one bargain, but two; namely payment of part and an agreement, without consideration, to give up the residue . . . But if you substitute a piece of paper or a stick of sealing wax, it is different, and the bargain may be carried out in its full integrity. A man may give, in satisfaction of a debt of £100, a horse of the value of £5, but not £5. Again, if the time or place of payment be different, the one sum may be in satisfaction of the other.'*

In the case itself it was argued that the tender of a promissory note was a sufficient novelty to constitute consideration for the creditor's promise to accept a lesser sum. This was based on the argument that, by accepting the peculiar obligation inherent in a negotiable security, the debtor would be doing something which he was not already bound to do. Baron Alderson said, *'if for money you give a negotiable security, you pay it in a different way. The security may be worth more or less; it is of uncertain value. That is a case falling within the rule of law as enunciated.'*

An attempt to draw on this decision was made in **D & C Builders v Rees** [1966] 2 QB 617 where it was suggested that part payment by cheque (a negotiable instrument) was a sufficiently new element to exonerate the partly paid debt. The plaintiffs here had done some building work for the defendants and payment of £482 was still outstanding 6 months after payment had first been demanded. The defendant's wife (acting on his behalf) offered the plaintiffs £300 in full and final settlement. The plaintiff's reluctantly accepted the cheque marked, 'in completion of account' because they were in severe financial difficulties; a fact known to the defendant's wife. The plaintiffs then brought the action to recover the balance. Lord Selbourne distinguished the **Sibtree** case. He said that in no way in 1965 could it be better to have a cheque for a lesser amount than to have the whole amount in cash. The court also took into account the element of economic duress here and said that the defendants have used their knowledge of the plaintiffs' financial difficulties in order to intimidate them. There was some suggestion at the time that this decision heralded the death knell for the rule in *Pinnel* and that a watchful eye on economic duress would negate the need for such a rule. To date, this has not proved to be the case: **Re Selectmove** (1995). Part payment of a debt at a different place can amount to valuable consideration but only if the payment at the different place confers a benefit on the creditor.

**Promissory Estoppel**

Promissory estoppel can operate as an equitable exception to the general rule that part payment of a debt without fresh consideration does not discharge the debt obligation. **Central London Property Trust Ltd. v High Trees House Ltd**: in September 1939 the plaintiffs leased a block of flats to the defendants, who planned to lease out the individual flats. When the Second World War broke out the defendants had difficulty in leasing all of the flats and so the landlord agreed in 1940 to accept just half of the ground rent stipulated in the lease. This arrangement continued until 1945 by which time all the flats were fully let and the plaintiffs sought to return to the terms of the original agreement. The plaintiff brought an action against the defendant claiming the full original rent both for the future and the last two quarters of 1945. Denning J held that the action should succeed. The parties intended the reduction of the rent to be a temporary measure while the flats could not be fully let. The flats were fully let early in 1945 and therefore Denning held that the plaintiffs should be able to recover the full rent from the last two quarters of 1945 onwards. Denning J expressed the view, *obiter*, that the plaintiffs would not have been able to recover the rent for the 1940 – 1945 period even though there was no consideration for the promise to accept reduced rent. The reason for this was that he thought that there was a general equitable principle whereby:

*'A promise intended to be binding, intended to be acted on and in fact acted on, is binding so far as its terms properly apply.'*

The decision is controversial since it appears to conflict with **Foakes v Beer** (1884) 9 App Cas 605. The case of **Foakes v Beer** established that part payment of a debt could never be good consideration for satisfaction of the whole of the debt. However, despite the adoption of the doctrine by the courts, there has been acute judicial keenness to constrain it within very strict parameters, and these will now be considered. One of the ways the courts have tried to get around this problem is by adding the requirement that it must be Inequitable for the promisor to go back on his promise for the promise to raise promissory estoppel.

The use of promissory estoppel, as an equitable doctrine, and is at the discretion of the courts. Even if all the other elements of the doctrine are made out, it may still not be applied because it would be inequitable in the circumstances to do so. This point is well illustrated by **D & C Builders v Rees** [1965] 3 All ER 837 where the builders agreed to accept a cheque for the sum of £300 in full and final settlement of a debt of £482. Lord Denning said that because this promise had been extracted from the plaintiff creditors by intimidation on the part of the debtor, the debtor could not rely on the doctrine of promissory estoppel, since *he who seeks equity must do equity*. Thus although in **D & C,** A acted upon a promise to accept a smaller sum and **Rees** the courts prevented them from availing from the argument of promissory estoppel, as an equitable doctrine on the basis they had acted in a unequitable way.

# Chapter 7   Intention to Create Legal Relations

## Introduction

A legally binding contract can only exist when the contracting parties intend to form a legal relationship. Depending upon the relationship, one may assume that the parties either intended or did not intend to create legal relations. However, the intention to create legal relations can exist or not exist in a variety of circumstances; persons with a social or domestic relationship may indeed intend to create legal relations, while persons outside of these relationships may not. Contracts may fall into the category of domestic and social agreements, which are most likely to be considered without intention to create legal relations, or commercial agreements, which will typically possess intention to create legal relations.

### Social and Domestic Agreements

**General Principle: Unless indicated, it is assumed that a married couple that makes an agreement does not intend to create legal relations.**

**Balfour v Balfour** [1919] 2 KB 571
**Facts:** A husband promised to pay his sickly wife £30/month, upon returning to Sri Lanka while she recovered in England. However, the couple later separated, and the husband ceased his monthly payments.
**Ratio: The Court of Appeal determined that there was no intention to create legal relations between the married couple at the time of the agreement; as such, the husband was not obligated to continue paying the monthly allowance.**
**Application:** Despite the fact that courts are still largely hesitant to honour agreements made while couples are still married, there have been recent cases where couples in the process of separating were seen as possessing the intention to create legal relations.

**General Principle: A married couple in the process of separating or divorcing can be considered to possess the intention to create legal relations.**

**Merritt v Merritt** [1969] 119 NLJ 484
**Facts:** After abandoning his wife to live with his mistress, Mr. Merritt agreed to pay his wife £40/month to cover the mortgage for their home. He also agreed to give her complete ownership of the house after the mortgage was paid. Mr. Merritt signed a document agreeing to these terms; however, he refused to give his wife ownership of the home after she had paid the remaining mortgage fees. Ratio: The Court of Appeal maintained that the parties had intended to create legal relations, and supported the plaintiff's claim.

**General Principle: Unless indicated, it is assumed that domestic agreements between parents and children do not possess intention to create legal relations.**

**Jones v Padavatton** [1969] 2 All ER 616
**Facts:** A child and her mother agreed that, if the daughter quit her job in the United States and moved to England to become a barrister, the mother would pay her a monthly allowance to support her studies. Later, after the daughter had moved to England and began her studies, the mother purchased a house for the daughter to live in and rent out, so long as the daughter continued her studies. However, after the daughter repeatedly failed her Bar Examinations, the mother tried to reclaim the house.
**Ratio: The Court of Appeal determined that both agreements were not legally enforceable; as such, the mother was entitled to reclaim the house.**

**General Principle: While the courts can determine that a social agreement does not possess intention to create legal relations, even if it is between non-familial parties, this concept can be refuted depending on the context of the agreement.**

**Simpkins v Pays** [1955] 3 All ER 10
**Facts:** The claimant was sharing a residence with the defendant, where they jointly entered weekly competitions in a newspaper. They shared the entry cost and the defendant promised to give the claimant an equal share of any possible winnings. When one of the entries resulted in a £750 prize, the defendant refused to give the claimant his portion of the winnings. She argued that their

agreement was contractually invalid, as she had no intention to create legal relations.

**Ratio: The court determined that their agreement was legally binding; as such, the claimant was entitled to his share of the winnings.**

**Application:** The context by which intention to create legal relations exists is often determined by each case's unique factual circumstances. Debates over the intention to create legal relations in non-familial relationships often arise in agreements over shared winnings, as seen in this case. For example, **Peck v Lateu** [1973] involved a similar situation, where two people had made an agreement to share any winnings from their bingo games; here, the courts found a similar intention to create legal relations. However, the latter case of **Wilson v Burnett** [2007] illustrated a lack of intention to create legal relations when the parties claimed to have had an oral agreement to share winnings. The situations, on the face of it, appear nearly identical; in each case, the courts will have to evaluate the circumstances before deciding whether intention does, indeed, exist.

**Commercial Agreements**

**General Principle: It is largely assumed that, in commercial agreements, the parties possess intention to create legal relations. It is unlikely that the courts will consider this differently without strong evidence otherwise.**

**Esso Petroleum Co Ltd v Customs and Excise** [1976] 1 All ER 117, HL

Facts: Esso Petroleum promised to provide one collectable coin with every four gallons of petrol purchased from their stations. An investigation into the existence of a contract of sale led the court to determine whether there was, indeed, intention to create legal relations in this circumstance.

**Ratio: The House of Lords maintained that, as these promises were made in a commercial/business setting, there was intention to create legal relations.**

**Application:** This case originally arose as a question of whether the collectable coins were liable for taxation, and the House of Lords determined that the coins did not qualify as taxable goods.

**General Principle: If two parties are in the process of conducting business with each other, the courts are almost certainly going to consider an agreement as possessing the intention to create legal relations.**

**J Evans & Son** (Portsmouth) **Ltd v Andrea Merzario Ltd** [1976] 2 All ER 930, CA

Facts: The claimants had contracted with the defendants to manage the transport of their machinery, with the specification that all machinery had to be transported below deck to avoid damage. Later, the defendants gave the claimants a 'courtesy call,' where they proposed shipping the goods on a container ship. The caller assured the claimants that, despite the fact that most vessels transport cargo above deck, the machinery would be stored below deck. The claimants agreed to have the machinery transported via container ship; however, one of their shipments was later damaged after it was transported above deck. The defendants asserted that their promise was only made during the course of an unspecific 'courtesy call,' and did not possess any intention to create legal relations.

**Ratio: The Court of Appeal determined that, given the commercial history between the defendant and the claimant, there was an intention to create legal relations. The owners of the machinery would not have agreed to transport it on a container ship if the defendants had not promised it would be handled properly.**

Commercial Agreements: Exceptions

**While the courts are very likely to find intention to create legal relations in agreements conducted within a commercial relationship, several exceptions do exist.**

1. 'Mere Puffs'

**General Principle: The courts will not recognise intention to create legal relationships in a situation where an offer is obviously not serious or is exceptionally ambiguous or vague.**

**Weeks v Tybald** [1604] Noy 11

Facts: In this case, the defendant offered £100 to any man who would marry his daughter, so long as he deemed him acceptable. **Ratio: The courts determined that his offer was clearly not meant to be taken seriously, and that there was no intention to create legal relations.** Application: This case is reminiscent of Carlill v Carbolic Smoke Ball Co, while Carbolic's attempts to categorise their offer as a 'mere puff' were unsuccessful, this case illustrates a clear example of the level of vagueness required for the courts to accept an offer as not serious or intentional.

## 2. Honour Clauses

**General Principle: Even in business transactions, the inclusion of an 'honourable pledge clause' can render an agreement legally unenforceable, as both parties have agreed to consider the document informal and not legally binding.**

**Rose and Frank Co v JR Crompton & Bros Ltd** [1923] 2 KB 261 CA
Facts: The two parties had been engaged in a commercial relationship, and signed an agreement extending the relationship to a future point in time, at a fixed price. The agreement contained an 'honourable pledge clause,' which claimed the agreement was informal and could not be enforced in court; rather, the agreement simply documented the objectives of the parties and was not meant to be used as a binding agreement. Later, the claimants sued for breach of this agreement, as well as for the non-delivery of items requested before the defendants terminated the agreement.
**Ratio: The court rejected the claimant's first claim, stating that the agreement was not legally binding, as the clause made clear the informal nature of the document. However, they did uphold the claim for non-delivery of goods, maintaining that the acceptance of the order created a new, legally binding contract.**
Application: Scrutton LJ illustrated the relevance of an 'honourable pledge clause' in his statement: 'I can see no reason why, even in business matters, the parties should not intend to rely on each other's good faith and humour, and to exclude all idea of settling disputes by an outside intervention…'

**General Principle: If an agreement specifies that it is 'binding**

in honour only,' then it is not legally enforceable because there is no demonstrated intention to create legal relations.

**Jones v Vernon's Pools** [1938] 2 All ER 626
**Facts:** The claimant argued that he was entitled to money won during a football pool. However, the terms on the pool's coupon made clear that it was 'binding in contract only'. The defendants argued that the agreement was never intended to be legally binding.
**Ratio: The courts rejected the claimant's argument, stating that the coupon's specification as 'binding in contract only' demonstrated a lack of intention to create legal relations. As such, the claimant could not raise a legal complaint against the defendants for failing to pay him the money.**
**Application:** In this case, Atkinson J stated, *"the defendants wish it to be made quite clear that ... they intend to say by these conditions: Everybody who comes into these pools must understand that there are no legal obligations either way in connection with these pools".*

## 3. 'Subject to Contract'

**General Principle: If an agreement incorporates the phrase 'subject to contract,' it may indicate that there is no intention to create legal relations; however, this may differ if the parties choose to act upon the agreement as a contract.**

**Confetti Records v Warner Music UK Ltd** [2003] EWHC 1274
**Facts:** The defendants wanted to use a music track, the copyright of which was held by the claimants. The defendants issued a document with terms 'subject to contract,' which the claimants signed and returned. Later, the claimants provided a copy of the music track accompanied by an invoice specifying the license period.
**Ratio: The courts stated that the first document was not a valid contract, as its terms were 'subject to contract'; however, they also maintained that the later invoice qualified as an offer, which the defendant accepted by including the music track in their album.**
**Application:** It is worth noting that, if the parties act upon the agreement as if it were a binding contract, the courts may construe

this as an intention to create a contract.

## Commercial Agreements: Ambiguous Phrasing

**General Principle: The courts are likely to find intention to create legal relations in circumstances where the phrasing in a commercial agreement seems vague or ambiguous.**

**Edwards v Skyways Ltd** [1964] 1 WLR 349
**Facts:** Skyways Ltd promised their employee an ex gratia payment if their employee agreed not to claim his entitlement to his entire pension as part of his redundancy agreement. However, Skyways later refused to make the payment, arguing that their inclusion of the phrase 'ex gratia' indicated a lack of intention to create legal relations.
**Ratio: The Court of Appeal held that the agreement did possess intention to create legal relations, as it was a commercial agreement and the term 'ex gratia' did not prevent the defendants from being bound by their agreement.**
**Application:** The term 'ex gratia,' in Latin, means 'by favour.' In this case, the court interpreted it as removing any possible pre-existing liability on the defendant's behalf; however, it did not entitle them to refuse payment to their former employee.

## Commercial Agreements: Collective Bargaining

**General Principle: Collective bargaining agreements, where terms of employment are discussed with all employees instead of a single individual, are not meant to be legally binding unless explicitly stated.**

**Ford Motor Co Ltd v Amalgamated Union of Engineering and Foundry Workers** [1969] 2 QB 303
**Facts:** Ford had reached an agreement with several unions that forbade the unions from striking without first adhering to certain protocols. Ford later sought to keep the unions from striking, after they ignored this part of the agreement.
**Ratio: The courts stated that the unions were not obligated to follow the terms of the agreement, as it was known in the industry that collective bargaining agreements were not legally binding.**

**Application:** This case, if considered today, would be further supported by the Trade Union and Labour Relations (Consolidation) Act 1992. This act underscores the principle explained in this section, and is frequently relied upon by modern judiciaries.

# Question and Answers

- Problem Question Intention to Create Legal Relations

**Question**

Michael has made the following promises:

a. He promises to sell his 3 year old BMW car to Chithra for £100.00 as he has recently won a new expensive car in a competition
b. On returning from holiday he promises Rachel, his daughter, £50.00 as she had cleaned his house for him whilst he was away

c. He has engaged Daniel to build a conservatory, at an agreed price of £15,500, the work to be completed in 6 months, in time for his wife's birthday party. After 3 months, it became apparent to Daniel that he would not be able to complete the job for the agreed price. He tells Michael that he needs another £2000, otherwise he will quit. Mindful of not wanting to upset the birthday plans, Michael promises to pay the extra £2000. Michael has now changed his mind about the extra payment.

You are required to advise Michael:

The rules relating to the requirement of consideration and intention to create legal relations in the law of contract and If he can be required by the law of contract to fulfil these promises.

**Answer**

**Introduction**

This paper will be advising Michael on whether he has intended to create legal obligations through promises he has made, and whether he is required to fulfil these promises under the requirement of consideration, also considering his intentions to be legally bound. This paper will cover the issues determining whether Michael; promising to sell his three-year old BMW to Chithra for £100.00, promising his daughter Rachel £50.00 as she had cleaned his house for him while he was away. Finally this advice will discuss whether Michael is legally obligated to pay Daniel an extra £2000 for building his conservatory. The advice will specifically examine consideration, economic duress and promissory estoppel. Lastly this advice will conclude its findings.

**Relevance of consideration**

In all of the different scenarios, the persons will have enforceable contracts, only if they can show consideration was provided by them for the promises made. It is first necessary to address the fact that consideration must be present within an agreement to make it a legally enforceable contract. In the case of **Currie v Misa**[134], Lush J referred to consideration as *"some right, interest, profit or benefit accruing to one party, or some forbearance, detriment, loss or responsibility, given, suffered or undertaken by the other"*.[135]

**Michael's promise to sell the BMW**

Michael promised to sell his 3 year old BMW car to Chithra for £100.00 as he won a new expensive car. The question is: was there sufficient consideration and can Chithra bring an action against Michael for this promise? Consideration must be sufficient. It can range from some form of payment to other interests of value under the law. Consideration must also be 'adequate', in terms of a bargain being made, although it is not imperative. Sufficiency remains of prime importance when forming a contract. A case authority establishing this principle is **Thomas v Thomas**,[136] where the court held that as long as there is valid consideration under the authority of **Currie v Misa**[137] then the agreement has some benefit or detriment to the parties. Furthermore in **Chappel v Nestle**,[138] the courts stated the chocolate wrappers purported consideration. It was held that the offer Nestle made for the exchange of chocolate wrappers provided that they were of some

---

[134] [1875] LR 10 Ex 153, 162
[135] Currie v Misa [1875] LR 10 Ex 153, 162
[136] (1842) 2 Q.B. 851
[137] ibid
[138] [1960] A.C. 87

value. In advice to Michael, if Michael promised to sell his 3 year old BMW to Chithra for £100, this may not be the market value of the car. However, the £100 will still be deemed to be of some value, hence valid consideration, making the promise to sell the car enforceable by Chithra.

### Relevance of Intention to create legal obligations

A vital component in the formation of contract is the intention to create legal relations. If there is no clear intention to be legally bound by the parties then no contract has been formed. The courts pursue the expressed or assumed, objective intentions, of both persons in the contract. In **Rose and Frank Co. v Crompton Bros.**[139]Atkin LJ said, in the Court of Appeal, that: *"To create a contract there must be a common intention of the parties to enter into legal obligations, mutually communicated expressly or impliedly."* Moreover in the same case, Scrutton LJ said:

> *"Now it is quite possible for parties to come to an agreement by accepting a proposal with the result that the agreement does not give rise to legal relations. The reason for this is that the parties do not intend that their agreement shall give rise to legal relations. This intention may be implied from the subject matter of the agreement, but it may also be expressed by the parties. In social and family relations such an intention is readily implied, while in business matters, the opposite result would ordinarily follow".*

### Intention to create legal obligations

Michael promised to sell his 3 year old BMW car to Chithra for £100.00 as he won a new expensive car in a competition. Did Michael intend to be legally bound by this promise to sell Chithra his BMW? Or was this simply a social agreement to a friend? Intention to be legally bound generally differs depending on what kinds of agreements are being made. It is essential in forming a binding contract. Commercial agreements are decided upon a

---

[139](1925) AC 445

strong probability that the agreement was to be legally enforceable. In a social and domestic context there is a presumption that it is not intended to be legally binding. Therefore evidence to rebut the presumption should be provided. In **Lens v Devonshire Club**[140] where the winner of a golf competition held by a golf club could not file a claim for his prize in court due to the fact that, in the competition no one ever insinuated that there were legal implications. In advice to Michael, promising to sell his 3 year old BMW car to Chithra for £100.00, in the courts will not create an impulsion to be legally bound because it is a social agreement. *'to offer a friend a meal is not to invite litigation'*[141].Therefore Michael's agreement may not be binding and he does not have to sell the BMW.

**Enforceability of the promise to Rachel**

On returning from his holiday, Michael promises Rachel, his daughter, £50.00 as she had cleaned his house for him whilst he was away. Can Rachel legally enforce this promise or has consideration past? If a person freely carries out an action of their own accord, after the other party makes a promise, then consideration is in the past. Therefore it is not valid. In the case of **Roscorla v Thomas**,[142]Roscorla brought a horse from Thomas'. After buying the horse it was promised that the horse was *"sound and free from vice"*. It materialised that the horse was vicious and the buyer sued. The court held that because the promise was made after the sale consideration was past and could not be enforced. Likewise, in **Re McArdle**[143] a daughter in law carried out improvements to a property. On completion the family agreed that she should be reimbursed the sum of £488, but the money was not paid. It was held that the promise to pay was unenforceable as it came after the work was completed. Past consideration is generally seen to be something that purports invalid consideration. Using the above two authorities we can advise Michael that, the promise to pay constitutes past consideration. Therefore since the promise to pay Rachel has come after his return and after she has cleaned the

---

[140]Unreported. See The Times Newspaper, December 4, 1914.
[141]G.C Cheshire, C.H. Fifoot and M.P.Furmston, Law of Contract, (15thEdn, OUP, 2007), 148.
[142](1842) 3 QB 234
[143] [1951] Ch 669

house, then this establishes past consideration and he does not have to pay her.

**The exception to this rule**

There are certain exceptions to the past consideration rule. In **Lampleigh v Braithwait**[144], the overwhelming majority of the judges assembled on the Common Bench held that *"where the promisor makes a request that the other do him some service, and (after the service is performed) promises to pay for it, the promise and the request go together and the contract is binding"*.[145] **Re Casey's Patents**[146] in a commercial context judgement held was despite the fact that the manager's consideration was past; the consideration had been produced in a business setting. This was also done at the owners own wishes and there was mutual understanding between both parties that the manager would get paid and also the further promise that he would be paid a predefined amount. In advice to Michael if Rachel has understood that she was to be paid for cleaning the house, she falls into the exception that consideration was past. It will largely depend on the judgement laid down by Lord Scarman above. Therefore Michael does not have to pay Rachel as Rachel's services has constituted past consideration.

**Intention to create legal obligations**

Another argument that Michael can raise in his defence is that there was never an intention to create legal obligations, because this is a social/domestic agreement in which a payment between a father and daughter should not be enforceable. In **Balfour v Balfour**[147] this was an agreement between a husband and wife, who promised to pay £30 per month to his separated wife. It was held the wife could not recover the money because it was a domestic agreement and not legally binding. Furthermore in **Jones v Padavatton**[148] A mother offered her daughter an allowance if the daughter gave up her job in the US and studied for the Bar in

---

[144](1615) Hob 105
[145]Lampleigh v Braithwait(1615) Hob 105
[146] [1892] 1 Ch. 104
[147][1919] 2 KB 571
[148][1969] 1 W.L.R. 328

London. The court held the agreement was vague and uncertain and therefore was a social arrangement. Using the above authorities it is likely on a balance of probabilities that the court will express this to be no more than a social agreement. Hence this agreement between Michael and Rachel is not enforceable.

**Pay Daniel the addition £2000**

Daniel is asking for more money for a job he is already contractually obliged to perform. Can he ask for the additional £2000 and is this an acceptable variation? Performing an action that is already required under a contract will not amount to valid consideration. The leading case on this issue is **Stilk v Myrick.**[149]I n this case the court held that the crew had not provided consideration for additional payment of the deserted seamen's salary. The seamen were still under an obligation to carry out their pre-existing duties. In application to the facts of Michael's case it seems unlikely that Daniel would recover the additional £2,000. Michael could argue that Daniel merely discharged their pre-existing duty, and therefore no additional benefit was conferred on them. As a result, Michael may argue consideration was not present and the variation was therefore not binding.

Exceptions to the traditional consideration principle can be found in **Hartley v Ponsonby.**[150]A ship's crew was seriously unmanned and the captain promised the remaining crew members additional pay. The crew provided substantial consideration as it was dangerous to sail so understaffed and this was not within their contracts. It is unlikely that Daniel will be able to avail from this argument because the work has not been rendered completely different or extra and it cannot be said that a fresh contract has arisen in the circumstances.

In **Williams v Roffey Bros. & Nicholls (Contractors) Ltd**[151]the exception progressed further. A building contractor subcontracted with the claimant to carry out some carpentry work on a block of 27 flats being refurbished. For the carpentry work, Mr Williams

---

[149]70 E.R. 1168;(1809)2 Camp 317
[150](1857) 7 El &Bl 572
[151] [1990] 1 QB 1

was to be paid £20,000. Mr Williams ended up in financial difficulties even though he had already received £16,200. The building contractor pledged to pay Mr Williams extra for every flat he completes on time. This is because the company was worried they would be liable under a penalty clause for late completion and that the contract was priced too low. Mr Williams finished 8 flats, but had only received an additional £1,500 alone. The building contractors replaced Mr Williams with new carpenters and Mr Williams filed a claim. This is similarly related to **Stilk v Myrick**,[152]w here again building contractors disputed that the claimant carried out tasks previously set out, that he was legally obliged to perform. On the other hand in **Williams v Roffey Bros.**[153]the courts adjudicated that the building contractor obtained practical benefits, not losing money under the penalty clause and avoided the disrupt effects of extra fees and the nuisance of finding a different contractor.[154]In **Williams v Roffey Bros**[155] Glidewell LJ delivered the primary evaluation on the theory established in **Stilk v Myrik**[156]M r Williams had stipulated binding consideration even though he was performing a currently existing duty. Glidewell LJ developed on how the old principle had expanded, but his goal was not to change the old principle. He expressed that promissory estoppel had 'not yet been fully developed'. In addition he made the following points on existing law;

1)    "If A enters into a contract with B to do work for, or to supply goods of services to B in return for payment by B and

2)    At some point before A has finished performing his obligations that have been made out under the contract B has reason to doubt whether A will, or will be able to, complete his side of the bargain AND"

3)    B then makes a promise to A to provide additional payment in return for A's promise to perform his contractual obligations on time AND"

---

[152]70 E.R. 1168;(1809)2 Camp 317
[153][1990] 1 QB 1
[154] Stone, Williams v Roffey: the death of Stilk v Myrick?, S.L. Rev. 1991, 2(Spr), 17-18
[155][1990] 1 QB 1
[156]70 E.R. 1168;(1809)2 Camp 317

*4)	As a result of giving his promise, B gets a benefit in practice, or obviates a disbenefit and*

*5)	B's promise is not given as a result of economic duress of fraud on the part of A, THEN*

*6)	The benefit to B is capable of being consideration for B's promise, so that the promise will be legally binding".157*

Therefore in relevance to this present case, it could be argued that Michael has received a practical benefit as the conservatory was built before his wife's birthday party. Nonetheless it is not clear that the principles in **Williams v Roffey**158 would extend this far.159 Whilst it is not addressed in the facts of our case, it may be that Michael wants no sign of building work if she is having guests over, which would not be there if the conservatory is built. This would certainly be a situation covered by the concept of practical benefit, although more details would be required to determine whether such practical benefits did arise.

**Economic duress**

For **Williams** to apply there must be an absence of economic duress. If's Daniel's behaviour can be categorised as illegitimate commercial pressure this would either render the contract void or simply be *'the rough and tumble of normal commercial bargaining'*160. Absence of economic duress would allow Daniel to recover the £2000. Michael reluctantly agreed to pay the additional money not wanting to upset the birthday plans. In **DSND Subsea Ltd v Petroleum Geo-Services ASA**161 in which Dyson J stated that;

> *"[...] there must be pressure,*
> *(a) whose practical effect is that there is compulsion on, or lack of practical choice for, the victim,*

---

157[1990] 1 QB 1, pp. 15-16

158 [1990] 1 QB 1

159South Caribbean Trading Ltd v TrafiguraBeheer [2004] EWHC 2676 (paras.106–09 of the judgment) in the Privy Council Colman J cast doubt on the decision in Williams v Roffey Bros.

160DSND Subsea Ltd v Petroleum Geo-Services ASA [2000] All ER (D) 1101

161[2000] All ER (D) 1101

*(b) which is illegitimate, and*
*(c) which is a significant cause inducing the claimant to*
*enter into the contract. "*[162]

It is therefore debatable whether the lack of practical choice or compulsion was illegitimate, it would be inaccurate to determine whether the application of pressure is to be expected in this kind of environment. In reference to this case, Daniel must prove that Michael has a realistic alternative but chose to appease the pressure he was involved in. Daniel must show he was acting in good faith and Michael did not protest the variation. Otherwise this would lead to breach of contract by Daniel.

### Promissory estoppel

The doctrine of promissory estoppel applies where; *"a promise was made which was intended to create legal relations and which, to the knowledge of the person making the promise, was going to be acted on by the person to whom it was made and which was in fact so acted on".*[163] The dispute is that Michael can be seen to have made an unequivocal promise, which was intended to legally affect both parties. Daniel stated that he would finish before Michael's wife's birthday party for the extra £2000. In Michael's acceptance Daniel would have relied on this promise. Initial requirements are that it should be inequitable for the promisor to invalidate the promise **D & C Builders v Rees**[164]. It is arguable that it is unfair for Michael to go back on their agreement to pay the additional £2,000 to Daniel. However, promissory estoppel cannot be used as a separate cause of action[165]. This would prove challenging for Daniel to recover the £2000. First Daniel could claim relying on Michael's promise and use estoppel as a defence that he was still bound to the terms of the initial agreement. Second is that Daniel can prove he supplied valid consideration for the promise to pay the additional £2,000 by using **Wiliams**.

### Conclusion

---

[162] ibid.
[163] Central London Property Trust v High Trees House Ltd [1947] KB 130.
[164] [1966] 2 QB 617.
[165] Combe v Combe [1951] 2 KB 215.

Overall this advice for Michael consists of the following. Consideration must be sufficient and of some benefit or detriment to each party[166]. Michael has given sufficient consideration and would be legally enforced to sell his 3 year old BMW to Chithra as it has been established that it is worth £100 which is of some value. In social and domestic agreements the courts assumption is that they are not intended to be legally binding. This means that in concern of the same issue through the principle of intention to create legal obligations. Michael does not have to sell his 3 year old BMW to Chithra for £100 because this was a social agreement which the courts would assume neither Michael nor Chithra intended it to be legally enforceable. The promise for Rachel cleaning his house for £50.00 is enforceable relies on the principle of whether Rachel's act can be determined as past consideration. In this instance because Rachel's act was done on return of her father this constitutes past consideration.[167]Moreover, the court will express this as a social agreement hence not enforceable. In respect of Daniel, he may be able to recover the £2,000 from Michael on the basis that fresh consideration was present. Whilst being weak this argument is a question of fact. Daniel may choose to rely on the case of **Williams v Roffey** in establishing that Michael received a practical benefit from the conservatory being finished in time for his wife's birthday. In order for Daniel to rely on the practice benefit doctrine he will have to show the absence of economic duress. It seems clear that economic duress was not present. The doctrine of promissory estoppel will not be of any use to Daniel because it can only be used as a shield and not a sword. This advice has given a firm conclusion in respect of each point on the information we have before us.

---

[166]Currie v Misa[1875] LR 10 Ex 153, 162.
[167]Roscorla v Thomas(1842) 3 QB 234.

# Chapter 8   Privity of Contract

## Introduction

It is a fundamental principle of English law that no one can derive rights or obligations from a contract to which he has given no consideration and is hence not a party. This doctrine, known as privity of contract, is still substantially valid but has been modified in various ways. In a number of situations, some parties are third parties to contracts. Nevertheless, they can still gain rights and certain liabilities as more distant parties and, in some cases, even if they are not party to the original contract at all.

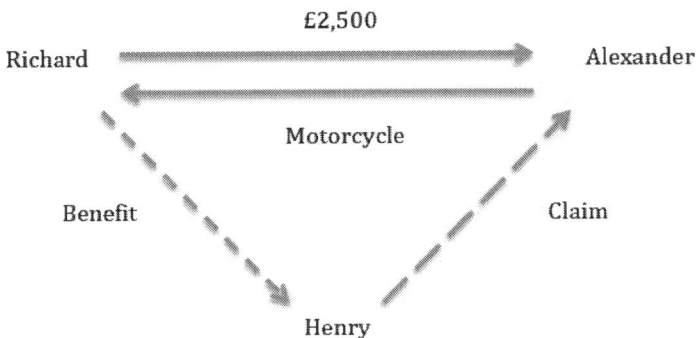

There have been multiple criticisms of the doctrine of privity and its associated common law exceptions. Some argue the privity rule enables parties to circumvent contractual obligations intended to benefit an outside party, while disregarding the decisions of the original parties. It can also prevent the victimised party from suing the party who is truly responsible, which can create multiple lawsuits focused on settling one issue. Additionally, the sheer number of exceptions to the doctrine of privity has been condemned as overly complex and contradictory; however, the Rights of Third Parties Act 1999 succeeded in clarifying the rights of a third party in a contract.

**Definition**

General Principle: Only parties that are associated with a contract are able to gain rights and liabilities under that particular contract. Thus, if someone is not a party to a contract, they cannot bring action with it. Conversely, it follows that if someone cannot bring action with the contract, they cannot be sued by one of the parties to the contract either.

**Dunlop Pneumatic Tyre Co Ltd v Selfridge & Co Ltd** [1915] AC 847
**Facts**: Dunlop entered into an agreement with Dew and Co. It was established that any wholesale contract that was agreed with retailers should include a price maintenance clause. Additionally, any retailer who breached this clause would have to pay £5 per breach to Dunlop. Dew and Co sold tyres to Selfridge, who retailed them at a discount. Dunlop did not receive any payment and sued Selfridge.
**Ratio: Dunlop's claim failed. Despite the fact that there was a contract between Dunlop and Dew and Co., Selfridge were not a party associated with that contract. As such, they could invoke any of the terms on either party.**
**Application:** Only a person who is a party to a contract can sue on it. Dunlop was not party to the contract between Dew and Co and Selfridge, so their action failed.

**General Principle: Generally, if you are not party to a contract between other parties, you cannot bring a claim.**

**Tweddle v Atkinson** (1861) 1 B & S 393
**Facts:** Tweddle's father and father in law entered a contract in order to pay Tweddle a sum of money. However, the money was not paid and Tweddle later sued.
**Ratio: The court held that Tweddle was not a party to the contract, so his attempts to sue were unsuccessful.**
**Application:** The application of the principle of privity and third parties' abilities to claim are largely limited. However, following Tweddle's case and Dunlop v Selfridge, a number of exceptions to the rule have been developed. In the case of Darlington Borough Council v Wiltshier Northern Limited (1995) 1 WLR 68, Lord Steyn was critical of the doctrine of privity of contract. He said:

"there is…no doctrinal, logical or policy reason why the law should deny effectiveness to a contract for the benefit of a third party where that is the expressed intention of the parties."

### Rights of Third Parties Act 1999

There are a number of exceptions to the doctrine of privity of contract, which stemmed from the court's dissatisfaction with the way the doctrine was being used in practice. The amount of common law rules that were developing was becoming increasingly complex; as such, Parliament drafted and passed the **Contracts (Rights of Third Parties) Act 1999**. This Act imposed limits on the doctrine of privity.

There are two circumstances under which the Act enables contractual provisions to be enforced by a non-contracting party:

- The contract contains an express provision allowing the third party to sue
- The contract intends to provide a benefit to the third party. However, this is not applicable if the parties entering the contract did not intend this benefit to be enforceable.

The Act is vast and contains many different provisions; however, the key changes that aimed to clarify the common law rules can be found in sections 1 (1) to (3):

1(1) *Subject to the provisions of this Act, a person who is not a party to a contract (a third party) may in his own right enforce a term of the contract if:*
 *(a) The contract expressly provides that he may, or*
 *(b) Subject to subsection (2) the term purports to confer a benefit on him*
*(2) Subsection (1) (b) does not apply if on a proper construction of the contract it appears that the parties did not intend the term to be enforceable by the third party.*
*(3) The third party must be expressly identified in the contract by name, as a member of a class or as answering a particular description but need not be in existence when the contract is entered into.*

**Note:** The Rights of Third Parties Act 1999 does **not** apply to exchange bills, cheques, employment contracts, or transportation of goods by sea.

**General Principle: As maintained in the Rights of Third Parties Act 1999, a third party can enforce a term of a contract if the contract intended to provide an enforceable benefit to the third party.**

**Nisshin Shipping Co Ltd v Cleaves and Co** [2003] EWHC 2602 (Comm)

**Facts:** Cleaves and Co were a broker's firm. They negotiated charter agreements between the shipping company Nisshin Shipping Co Limited and other shipping companies. Although Cleaves was not a party to any of the agreements, Nisshin expressly agreed in each contract to pay Cleaves a commission fee. Under each contract, there was also a term that allowed for arbitration to occur to settle disputes. Nisshin went on to decline to pay the commission fee to Cleaves. Cleaves commenced arbitration against Nisshin in an attempt to recover the commission. They argued that, under S.8 of the Rights of Third Parties Act, Cleaves maintained a right to enforce the commission term through arbitration using the clause in the Nisshin's contracts with all of their other shipping company associates.

**Ratio: The court decided that it had jurisdiction to settle the dispute because, under S.1 of the Contracts (Rights of Third Parties) Act 1999, Cleaves had a right to enforce the provisions under the contracts where Nisshin had agreed to pay Cleaves commission.**

**Application:** This case made an interpretation of the Rights of Third Parties Act 1999. The common law principles that emerged in this test case were: (1)If the contract is neutral on the question of whether the term was intended to be enforceable by the third party, then section 1 (2) does not negate section 1 (1) (b).

**Remedies for Third Parties**

Section 1(5) of the Act provides that the third party has any kind of remedy that would have been available to them for breach of contract. Essentially, the third party will be on an even footing with a direct party to the main contract. However, both the third party and the direct party cannot receive equal recovery from the promisor. To do so would create double liability; as such, any award given to the third party will reduce the award available to the promisee.

**The Exceptions:**

There are other common law exceptions that existed before the introduction of Contracts (Rights of Third Parties) Act 1999.

**1. Tort**

**General Principle: A third party may also be able to pursue a concurrent action in tort.**
**Donoghue v Stevenson** [1932] AC 562, HL
**Facts:** A woman went to a café with a friend, who bought her a bottle of ginger beer. After drinking most of it, the woman found a decomposed snail in the bottle and became ill. The woman had no contract with the café (the contract was between her friend, who purchased the bottle from the cafe), so she sued the manufacturers in delict (the Scottish equivalent of tort).
**Ratio: The House of Lords said the manufacturers had a duty of care to the consumer of their product.**
**Application:** Even if a third party does not have a claim under the doctrine of privity, they still may have a claim through another form of action, such as tort liability.

**2. Collateral Contracts**

This is one of the examples of an area that exists as an exception to the traditional rules of privity of contract.
**General Principle: A collateral contract can be utilised to avoid the traditional rule of privity.**
**Shanklin Pier v Detel Products Ltd** [1951] 2 KB 854
**Facts:** The plaintiff (Shanklin) had to repaint their pier, and contacted Detel to ask about the quality of their paint. Detel claimed their paint would last for 7-10 years, so Shanklin hired painters to refurbish the pier with paint produced by Detel. However, the paint only lasted for roughly 4 months. The painters

could not be liable, as they had never promised the paint would last for 10 years. Shanklin had also never contracted with Detel, having instructed the painters to use Detel paint. Shanklin Pier decided to sue Detel for breach of contract.

**Ratio: As well as the contract between Shanklin and the painters, there was a collateral contract between the plaintiff and Detel. The defendants had promised that the paint would last 7 – 10 years and, in return, the plaintiffs had instructed the painters to buy the paint.**

**Application:** Collateral contracts can be viewed as a means of identifying a contract between the party that makes the promise and another party. This is because the promise has induced the other party to enter into a completely different contract with a third party. As such, the party that makes the promise gets some kind of benefit by being able to sell their goods with reliance on the original contract between the first two parties.

**General Principle: If a participant enters a contract with the organisers of an event, they can also enter into a collateral contract with all of the participants of that event.**

**Clarke v Dunraven** [1897] AC 59
**Facts:** A yacht club advertised a regatta. Both Clarke (the appellant) and Dunraven (the respondents) entered their yachts into the race. They were required to send a letter to the secretary of the club agreeing that, if they damaged another yacht during the race, full damages would be payable by the owner of the yacht who had caused the collision. The appellant's yacht collided with the respondents and it sank.

**Ratio: The House of Lords held that a separate contract had been created between the individual yacht owners.**

**Application:** A contract between two parties can be coupled with a collateral contract between either one of those parties and a third party whose business relates to the same subject matter.

**General Principle: A third party subcontractor may benefit from a limited liability clause, provided they satisfy the necessary conditions.**

**Scruttons v Midland Silicones** [1962] AC 446

**Facts:** A clause in a contract regarding the shipment of a drum of chemicals provided a limited liability of $500 to the carriers. Scruttons were contracted by the carriers and tasked with unloading the chemicals. Unfortunately, Scruttons damaged the drum, and tried to utilise the limited liability outlined in the contract between the carriers and the owners of the shipment.

**Ratio: Lord Reid said that there might be a contract between owner and subcontractor, making this limitation effective, if four conditions were satisfied. In this case, the four conditions were not satisfied, and the liability clause did not apply to the third party.**

**Application:** Lord Reid defined four conditions that must be satisfied for a third party to have an exemption clause when they are not an original party in the contract. He stated:

*"(first) the bill of lading makes it clear that the stevedore is intended to be protected by the provisions in it which limit liability, (secondly) the bill of lading makes it clear that the carrier, in addition for contracting for these provisions on his own behalf, should apply to the stevedore, (thirdly) the carrier has authority from the stevedore to do that, or perhaps later ratification by the stevedore would suffice, and (fourthly) that any difficulties about consideration moving from the stevedore were overcome.."* These conditions are often defined as the 'Lord Reid Test.'

**General Principle: A collateral contract can provide the benefit of an exemption clause to a third party who was not originally a party in the contract.**

**New Zealand Shipping Co Ltd v Satterthwaite & Co Ltd (*The Eurymedon*)** [1975] AC 154

**Facts:** The facts were similar to those in Scruttons; however, in this case, the limited liability clause extended to all parties contracted by the original parties to the contract.

**Ratio: The Privy Council determined a collateral contract existed between the owner of the damaged items and the contracted party who unloaded the items. As such, the third party was protected by the exclusion clause.**

**Application:** This case illustrates the benefit of a Himalaya Clause, which have often been utilised in shipping contracts after

Scruttons v Midland Silicones. A Himalaya Clause allows third parties to benefit from a contract, and are frequently included in contracts relating to maritime endeavours.

## 3. Contracts over Land

The doctrine of privity is not applicable in contracts over land, when dealing with restrictive covenants. Covenants over land may operate in favour of (or against) future owners of the land involved, and s.56 of the Law of Property Act 1925 provides that a person *"may take an ... interest in land or other property ... although he may not be named as a party to the conveyance or other instrument."* This consolidates some of the earlier common law rules relating to real property, which clearly saw certain rights and obligations as belonging to the land rather than to any individual.

**General Principle: A covenant in land can pass to successors in title and be enforceable because, (although there is no privity of contract as between original covenantee and coventor) there is privity of estate.**

**Smith & Snipes Hall v River Douglas Catchment Board** [1949] 2 All ER 179, CA
**Facts:** Ellen Smith held land adjacent to a riverbank and entered into a covenant with the River Douglas Catchment Board. The River Douglas Catchment Board agreed to maintain the quality of the riverbanks. Ellen Smith later sold the land to John Smith. After John purchased the land, the riverbanks flooded and the property was damaged.
**Ratio:** The Court of Appeal allowed the new owner to enforce the previous agreement that River Douglas Catchment Board maintain the land, since it was clearly intended to attach to the land rather than to the individual who originally made it.

**General Principle: Restrictive covenants in land cases can be applicable to future owners; in this case, the covenant applies to the land – not the owner.**

**Tulk v Moxhay** (1848) 2 Ph 774

**Facts:** Mr. Tulk sold a plot of land in Leicester Square to another person, under the condition that the central square not be built upon. The defendant received the property after it had been sold several times. He argued that the restrictive covenant did not apply to him, as he was not a party in the original contract.

**Ratio: Lord Cottenham maintained that a purchaser of land could be bound by a restrictive covenant to which he was not an original party. The new owner of the land was restricted from building upon the central square.**

**Application:** This case established certain requirements, in order for a restrictive covenant to remain applicable to future owners. The restrictive covenant must relate to the land itself, and the original parties are required to have intended for the covenant to extend to future owners. Additionally, the future owner must have knowledge of the covenant, and must hold interest in the property equal to the original promissor.

## 4. Right to Claim Damages

Apart from the exceptions to the doctrine of privity, a third party has no way of enforcing a contract. One of the main parties to the original contract would have to bring action against another first. On the other hand, if the contract gives a third party some kind of benefit, it is unlikely that the party who issues a claim for damages will have suffered loss themselves. As such, if a court awards damages, this can compensate the party who issues the claim. If they have suffered little or no loss, then they would only be allowed a small amount of money in damages.

**General Principle: If a contracting party purchases something on behalf of others, they may also be compensated for their loss, in addition to their own.**

**Jackson v Horizon Holidays Ltd** [1975] 1 WLR 1468

**Facts**: Jackson had booked a family holiday through Horizon Holidays Ltd. Horizons brochure described the hotel to be one of the highest standards; however, for many reasons, the holiday was ruined. The accommodation was poor and all of the services the brochure had flaunted to be present were either discontinued or not as advertised. Jackson brought action against Horizon Holidays on behalf of his family, but Horizon argued that it should not pay damages to the family, as it was not a party to the contract.

**Ratio: The Court of Appeal awarded Jackson damages, both for his own distress, as well as the additional distress caused by the disappointment of his wife and children.**

**Application:** This case has been criticised for being too wide and conflicting with the doctrine of privity. Lord Denning attempted to clarify this distinction by explaining that the wife and children were not being compensated; rather, Mr. Jackson was being compensated for their disappointment, after purchasing the vacation for their benefit. However, this case would have been decided under the Contracts (Rights of Third Parties) Act 1999, illustrating the value of this Act when evaluating the doctrine of privity.

**General Principle: In cases of repudiatory breach (a severe case of breach) the rules of Privity could be ignored.**

**Woodar Investment Development Ltd v Wimpey Construction (UK) Ltd** [1980] 1 WLR 277

**Facts:** The party that was purchasing, Wimpey Construction, entered into a contract to buy some land from Woodar for £850,000. It was agreed that £150,000 had to be paid to a third party company called Transworld Trade upon completion. Wimpey Construction later terminated the contract, and Woodar sued them for both the £850,000 amount as well as the £150,000 promised to Transworld.

**Ratio: The House of Lords held, by a majority, that no repudiatory breach existed under the circumstances of this case. Lord Salmon and Lord Russell both dissented. In Obiter, they agreed that Woodar would have been able to claim damages for Transworld Trade Ltd, if they did indeed have a claim for repudiatory breach.**

**Application:** The House of Lords had admitted that no general principle existed to support a party to bring action against another on behalf of a third party who had suffered a loss for breach of the original contract. The use of the doctrine, it appears, has been restricted by the House of Lords to holiday contracts only, or other contracts involving special circumstances such as ordering meals for others, etc.

**General Principle: A third party may circumvent the doctrine of privity and sue for their own benefit, provided they are the executor of the original party's estate.**

**Beswick v Beswick** [1968] AC 58
**Facts:** Peter Beswick transferred his business to his nephew, provided the nephew pay him annually and, after his death, pay his widow an annuity of £5 per week. After Peter Beswick's death, his nephew failed to pay the annuity to the widow. She sued, both in her personal capacity as a beneficiary under the contract and in her capacity as executor of her husband's estate.
**Ratio: The widow failed in her personal capacity, as she was a stranger to the contract, but succeeded as the executor of her late husband's estate.**
**Application:** Lord Denning stated: *"Where a contract is made for the benefit of a third person who has a legitimate interest to enforce it, it can be enforced by the third person in the name of the contracting party or jointly with him or, if he refuses to join, by adding him as a defendant. In that sense and it is a very real sense, the third person has a right arising by way of contract."*

# Question and Answer

- Privity of Contract Problem question

## Question

Jo books a holiday to Italy for her and her family through a tour operator based in the UK. She specifies that the accommodation must provide facilities for young children. When Jo and her family arrive they are told that their specified accommodation is no longer available. The tour company offer Jo alternative accommodation located in the city centre. Due to its location the alternative accommodation does not provide any facilities for children; in fact, guests must be at least 18 years old in order to stay at this alternative accommodation.

Jo brings an action for breach of contract against the tour company claiming damages for the ruined holiday for herself and on behalf of her family.

Discuss the legal issues.

## Answer

## Introduction

This is an advice that discusses the legal issues in relation to Jo who books a holiday to Italy for her and her family through a tour operator based in the UK. This paper will highlight and critically discuss all the legal issue that arise. It will start by discussing the liability of the tour operator, for the additional cost of accommodation incurred by Jo. It will then look at liability of the tour operator for disappointment or 'mental distress' or loss of amenity caused by the ruined holiday. It will examine the case of **Jarvis v Swans Tours Ltd**[168], which is a similar fact authority. It will then examine the issue of privity of contract and how this stops Jo from bringing an action on behalf of her family. It will then discuss the case of **Jackson v Horizon Holidays Ltd**[169], to show

---

[168] [1972] EWCA Civ 8, first instance
[169] [1975] 1 WLR 1468

how the rule of privity was circumvented. This paper will then examine the Contract (Rights of Third Parties) Act 1999, to see how Jo can rely on this to claim damages for her family. Lastly this paper will conclude its findings.

### Liability of the tour operator

Ultimately Jo is unhappy with what she has received under the contract for her holiday. The legal issue is whether she can claim damages for her loss. She cannot repudiate the contact for the holiday because she has received some of the benefit.[170] She booked a family holiday. The hotel she booked was no longer available. It can be argued this is a breach of warranty.[171] A breach of warranty entitles the innocent part to damages.[172] The tour company makes an attempt to remedy the situation by offering an alternative hotel. The hotel however, did not offer facilities for children. Moreover, the hotel did not accept guests under the age of 18. This is a breach of contract. The breach fundamentally alters the nature of the contract. This means Jo has to find alternative accommodation. Jo can sue the tour operator for i) cost of hotel; ii) any additional expense; and iii) loss of enjoyment or distress. She will have to satisfy the principles of remoteness, causation and mitigation.

### (i)    Recovering the cost of alternative accommodation

The purpose of contractual damages is to put the party back in the position had the breach of contract not occurred. Jo can recover the cost of finding new accommodation. Hotel can be quite expensive at short notice. If this cost of Jo's hotel outweighs the cost of the initial holiday, the court may award here a difference in value between the performance received and that promised in the contract (diminution in value), i.e. a difference in value between what way paid for the holiday and what it was worth. In **Jarvis v Swans Tours Ltd**[173] the judge in the court of first instance believed Mr. Jarvis had got half of what he paid for. So the judge gave him half

---

[170] This is known as a quantum meruit. See **Sumpter v. Hedges** (1898) 1 QB 673
[171] Section 62 of the Sale of Goods Act 1979 states a warranty is 'collateral to the main purpose of the contract'.
[172] **Bettini v Gye** (1876) 1 QBD 183
[173] [1972] EWCA Civ 8

the amount which he had paid.

Another example is the case of *Ruxley Electronics and Construction Ltd v Forsyth*.[174] The court decided in Ruxley that it would be unreasonable to claim the cost of cure as the relation between the work fulfilled and the benefit obtained would be unfair to the defendant and therefore a difference in value should be awarded. [175] In that sense Jo is likely to be awarded the difference in value in what her holiday was worth and what she received.

**(ii)    Additional expense**

Moreover, if Jo has incurred additional expenses, i.e. taxi fares to and from the new hotel which are also recoverable.

**(iii)    Damages for disappointment or 'mental distress' or loss of amenity**

The question arises if Jo can claim for mental distress, anguish or annoyance caused by breach of contract? The authority of **Addis v Gramophone Co Ltd**[176] says that usually for mental distress, anguish or annoyance caused by breach of contract damages are not awarded. The House of Lords has refused to award damages in Addis v Gramophone Co Ltd that has been created as to the 'harsh and humiliating' way the defendant has released the Addis from his job in breach of contract. The House of Lords again confirmed their decision in **Johnson v Unisys Ltd**[177] by stating that "damages for distress and injury to feelings resulting from the manner of dismissal are unavailable in the law of contract"[178].

Nevertheless, as to most rules, there are also exceptions to this rule. In a small number of cases, which have had the main purpose of relaxation, pleasure and peace of mind mental distress may be compensated,[179] as stated also confirmed more recently in **Farley v Skinner**[180]. The House of Lords in **Farley** stated damaged could be

[174] [1996] A.C. 344
[175] McMeel, Gerard, Common sense on cost of cure, L.M.C.L.Q. 1995, 4(Nov), 456-461
176 [1909] AC 488
177 [2001] UKLH 13
178 Lord Hoffmann in Johnson v Unisys Limited [2001] UKHL 13
179 Jarvis v Swan Tours [1973] 1 All ER 71

recovered where a major object (though not the whole purpose) of the contract was to provide pleasure, relaxation and peace of mind".[181]

This can also be seen from the authority of **Jarvis v Swans Tours Ltd**[182] in which a brochure has promised a holiday with an enjoyable time but in fact it fell short of the promise. Jarvis has then sued for his disappointment and the Court of Appeal decided that damages for Jarvis' disappointment and distress can be awarded in circumstances like this. Lord Denning MR remarked that the decision in Addis that under the above stated circumstances damages may not be awarded is out of date. Furthermore he said that in terms of holiday contracts or other contracts which promise enjoyment and entertainment exceptions should be made.

Another authority which can be brought into relation with Jo's case is **Jackson v Horizon Holidays Ltd**[183]. Mr Jackson has purchased a holiday from Horizon Holidays Ltd which has promised in their brochure the accommodation to have excellent facilities, but when Jackson has arrived with his family the hotel's facilities were substandard. Lord Denning MR stated in his judgement: *"they were greatly disappointed. Their room had not got a connecting door with the room for the children at all. The room for the children was mildewed - black with mildew, at the bottom. There was fungus growing on the walls. The toilet was stained. The shower was dirty. There was no bath. They could not let the children sleep in it...They were so uncomfortable at Brown's Hotel, that after a fortnight they moved to the Pegasus Reef Hotel."[184]* The judge had followed the authority of **Jarvis v Swans Tours Ltd** and the judge awarded just a little bit less than the initial cost of the holiday as damages in distress. In Jarvis Lord Denning MR held that Mr Jarvis could recover damages for the cost of his holiday, but also damages for "disappointment, the distress, the upset and frustration caused by the breach

In light of the authorities Jo will be able be able to recover damages

---

[180] [2001] UKHL 49
[181] Pearce, David, Farley v Skinner: right or wrong?, C.L.J. 2002, 61(1), 24-27
[182] [1972] EWCA Civ 8
[183] [1975] 1 WLR
[184] [1975] 1 WLR

for mental distress, anguish or annoyance caused by breach of contract, because the whole purpose of the contract was to provide pleasure and relaxation in the form of a holiday for Jo and her children. The fact that when Jo and her family arrive at the hotel they are told that their specified accommodation is no longer available appears to be a breach of warranty that can be remedied if alternative accommodation is provided.

**Privity of contract**

One problem Jo faces is claiming damages on behalf of her family. It can be argued that the family was not in contract with the tour operator and thus cannot enforce the contract against them. The doctrine of privity of contract, a fundamental principle in common law, says though, that a rights and obligations created by contracts are only applicable to the parties of the contract.[185] This means that it does not confer enforceable rights or impose any obligations on a person who is not a party to the contract.[186] How then can Jo's family bring an action? One possibility is Jo can bring it on their behalf as in the case of **Jackson v Horizon Holidays Ltd**.[187]

**Circumventing Privity: Jackson v Horizon Holidays Ltd**

As already addressed above, the authority of Jackson is highly relevant to Jo's case. The Jackson case is representing the difficulties with the general principle of privity in a family context. The court's decision in Jackson was that when the buyer of a holiday contracts for the benefit of himself and his family, then the buyer may be able to sue for his family. Jo, can according to the authority of Jackson, sue for damages suffered by her family as well as for herself. This exception to the principle of privity is therefore applicable in the sense that the family was not a party to the contract and not able to sue for damages by themselves for want of not being one of the contracting parties. [188]

---

[185] Flannigan, Robert (October 1987). "Privity - the end of an era (error)". Law Quarterly Review p.103
[186] Dean, Meryll (2000) Removing a blot on the landscape - the reform of the doctrine of privity. Journal of Business Law, March. pp. 143-152
[187] [1975] 1 WLR
[188] Jacobs, Edward (1986). "Judicial reform of privity and consideration". Journal of Business Law (6):

## The Contract (Rights of Third Parties) Act 1999

The Jackson case has been decided 1975, which has been before the implementation of the Rights of Third Parties Act in 1999. If it would have been decided after 1999, it would now be partly resolved by the Act's section 1(1) (b). The Act permits Jo's family to sue for the damages by themselves. This is an enormous change to the rule of privity which has been undertaken as to the concerns of the judiciary and the Law Commission to review the rule of privity.[189] Though the Act only allows special circumstances, a third party to enforce terms of contracts to which they are not a party.[190] In that sense, Jo's family may now after the implementation of the Act enforces a term of the contract to which only Jo is a contracting party but the contract cannot be enforced against Jo's family. In s.1 of the Act, a two-limbed test is used in order to find out whether the third party can sue for a contract or not.[191]

Jo's family may enforce the term if: i) The contract expressly says that they may (section 1(1)(a)); or ii) it purports to confer a benefit upon them (section 1(1)(b)) unless, if on a proper construction of the contract (s1(2)) it is clear that the parties, Jo and the tour operator, did not intend the term to be enforceable by the third party, meaning the family. For section 1(1)(b) to apply, it must be established that the agreement indeed 'intended to confer a benefit' on Jo's family.[192] Furthermore, it can be found in section 1(3) that Jo's family would have to be expressly identified. This would have to be done either by description, by being a member of a class or simply by name. This was applied in the authority of **Avraamides and another v Colwill and Another**.[193] There has been a transfer agreement and Lord Justice Waller held that it did not confer a

---

[189] Bridge, Michael (2001). "Privity of contract; Third parties", Edinburgh Law Review 5 (1): 85–102
[190] Flannigan, Robert (October 1987). "Privity – the end of an era (error)". Law Quarterly Review 103 (4): 564–593
[191] MacMillan, Catharine (2000). "A Birthday Present for Lord Denning: The Contracts (Rights of Third Parties) Act 1999". Modern Law Review 63 (5): 721–738
[192] Dolphin & Maritime & Aviation Services Ltd v Sveriges Angfartygs Assurans Forening, The
Swedish Club [2009] EWHC 716 (Comm) summarised in Poole's Textbook
on Contract Law (Chapter 11)
[193] [2006] EWCA civ 1533

benefit to the Avraamides as they have not been expressly identified in accordance with section 1(3).[194]

## Conclusion

Moreover, the question arises if Jo could recover the full expenses. According to the authority of **Ruxley** she would not be obliged to the full price of the booked holiday paid and the full price of the alternative accommodation and the extra expenses but she may be able to recover the difference between the original price paid and the final expenses, in that sense the difference in value. She will also be able to recover the additional expenses and damages for mental distress, anguish or annoyance as the purpose of the contract was to provide pleasure and relaxation. Additionally it is essential to identify her family relevant third parties and whether they should be given enforceable rights in order to draw the right conclusions with the use of the Act. Moreover, it should be questioned whether, when third parties receive enforceable rights, there ability on enforcing these rights should be restricted.

---

[194] Furmston, Michael (2007). Law of Contract (15th ed.), Oxford University Press

# Chapter 9 Terms of Contract

The duties and obligations of each party to the contract are laid out in the terms of a contract. These terms of contract can be **express terms** laid down by the parties themselves, or **implied terms** which are inferred from the intention of the parties and facts of the agreement.

### Express terms of the contract

**General Principle: Statements made during the course of negotiations are either representations or terms.**

**J.Evans & Son (Portsmouth) Ltd v Andrea Merzario** [1976] 1WLR 1078
**Facts:** The plaintiffs contracted with the defendants for carriage of machines to England by sea. The defendant gave an oral assurance that the containers would be shipped below the deck. The plaintiffs therefore agreed to the transport as their machines were liable to rust if carried on deck. During the course of the voyage, a container shipped on deck and fell overboard. The plaintiffs claimed damages from the defendants citing a breach of contract.
**Ratio: It was held that since 'the oral assurance was an express term of the contract, and as the contract was partly oral and partly written, evidence of the oral term was admissible'. As a result, the defendants were held liable for breach of this oral promise.**
**Application:** when a contract is partly oral and partly in writing then the court will consider all the evidence from the beginning in order to see what bargain was struck between the parties.

### Importance of statement

**General Principle: a statement is considered important if the aggrieved party has made it clear to the other party that had it not been for the statement, the party would have never entered into the contract in the first place.**

**Bannerman v White** (1861) 10 CB NS 844
**Facts:** White was considering buying hops from Bannerman, and

he enquired whether Sulphur had been used on them, he added that if they had been there was no point in even continuing the discussion. Bannerman said that the hops were not treated with Sulphur (believing this to be true) and consequently a contract of sale was made. It was later discovered that some of the hops were treated with sulphur, when Bannerman sued for the price, White claimed that the contract had been breached and he was justified in his refusal to pay.

**Ratio: this statement was a term of the contract and the buyer was entitled to terminate in case of breach.**

**Application:** The importance of the statement is a determining factor in deciding if a representation remains so or becomes a term.

## Timing of statement

**General Principle: the more time that elapses between the statement being made and the contract being concluded, the less likely is that the court will consider it as the term of the contract.**

### Routledge v McKay [1954] 1 WLR 615

**Facts:** In a private sale of a motor bike, since the defendant had no specialist knowledge of motorcycles he relied on the registration book which listed 1942 as the manufacturing date of the bike. A written contract was drawn up a week later which didn't mention the age of the bike. It was discovered that the bike was a `1930' model and worth much less than what had been paid for it. The buyer claimed that the date of manufacture was a term of the contract.

**Ratio: The Court held that the interval between the making of the statement and the writing of the contract meant that the statement as to the age of the bike was not a term.**

**Application:** The timing of the statement is a determining factor in deciding if a representation remains so or becomes a term.

### Schawel v Reade [1913] 2 IR 81

**Facts**: The plaintiff wanted to buy a stud and went to the defendant's stables where he started examining the horses. The defendant claimed, "You need not look anything; the horse is perfectly sound. If there was anything wrong with the horse I would tell you". The plaintiff stopped the examination. Three weeks later a contract of sale was concluded between the two parties, it was found that the horse was totally unfit for stud purposes. The question that arose before the Court was whether the defendant's statement amounted to a term or representation.

**Ratio: The House of Lords held that the importance of the seller's statement which the buyer completely relied on makes it a contractual term even though some time had lapsed between making the statement and the conclusion of the contract.**

**Application:** If the buyer has relied on the express warranty of the vendor, then it becomes a term of the contract even though some time would have passed between making of the statement and conclusion of the contract.

**Reduced term into writing**

**General Principle: where the parties put their contract in writing, any statement that appears in the written contract will be regarded as a term.**

**Duffy v Newcastle United Football Ltd** (2000) All ER (D) 892
**Facts:** The club offered its season ticket holders to buy a 'bond' for £500. The bondholder was to be given a 'designated seat' for ten years. The bond had a condition that the designated seat could be taken away at the discretion of the club. The club tried to change the seats of a few bondholders to make way to increase the capacity of the football stadium.

**Ratio: The Court held that since there was nothing in the Club's literature which amounted to a binding representation that the claimants would have an absolute right to use of their seats for the lifetime of the bond. On the facts, the stadium development was a good and sufficient reason and the action failed.**

**Application:** the written terms and conditions of the bond were considered as a part of the contract.

**Special knowledge and skill**

**General Principle: If a statement is made by a person with special skill or knowledge it is more likely to be considered as a term by the Court as opposed to a statement being made by an**

amateur with no special knowledge.

**Oscar Chess v Williams** [1957] 1 WLR 370
**Facts**: The defendant sold his car to the plaintiffs who were motor dealers, for £290. The registration book listed the car to be a 1948 model and the defendant honestly believed it to be so. Later, it was discovered that the car was a 1939 model and therefore sued for the price difference.
**Ratio: The Court held that it was an innocent misrepresentation which meant that it was non-fraudulent (damages were only available if the misrepresentation was fraudulent). The Court of Appeal stated that the private individual did not have any special skill or knowledge to rely on and moreover the buyers were experienced car dealers who would have been more likely to spot the car's real age. Therefore, the defendant's statement was not considered as a term.**

**Dick Bentley Productions v Harold Smith (Motors)** [1965] 1 WLR 623
**Facts**: The plaintiff was looking for a 'well vetted' Bentley car. The defendants were dealers who claimed to have found such a car and that this car had been fitted with a replacement engine and gearbox and had travelled only 20,000 miles since then. Bentley purchased the car but found that it had done closer to 100,000 miles and was unreliable. The plaintiffs sued claiming damages for the breach of contract.
**Ratio: The court held that the dealers were experts and thus their statements became part of the contract. This statement amounted to a warranty, and hence the plaintiff was awarded damages.**
**Application:** The importance given to a statement depends on who makes it, if it is made by a person with special skill or knowledge about the subject matter then it becomes a term and if it is made by a person who has no claim to special knowledge it might not always become a term of the contract.

**Parol Evidence Rule**

**General Principle: where there is a written contract, extrinsic (parol) evidence cannot change the express terms of the**

contract.

## Henderson v Arthur (1907)

**Facts:** Both were partiers to a lease, which contained a covenant for payment of rent quarterly in advance, although before the lease was drawn up the parties had agreed that the rent could in fact be paid in arrears. On being sued, the tenant pointed out this agreement.

**Ratio: The Court held that the terms of a prior oral agreement are superseded by a written contract; it effectively destroyed the previous oral agreement about rent.**

There are a few exceptions to the rule: rectification, partially written agreements, implied terms, evidence about the parties and following a custom.

## Implied Terms of Contract

### Implied by Custom

**General Principle: terms can be implied into a contract if there is evidence that as a part of the local custom these terms will be there in a contract.**

## Hutton v Warren [1836] 1 M & W 466

**Facts**: There was a custom which gave a tenant an annual allowance for seeds and labour. A tenant claimed these allowances on the cessation of his tenancy despite there being nothing written in the contract.

**Ratio: It was held that the custom was well founded and thus became part of the contract.**

### Officious bystander test

**General Principle: some terms which are not laid down in the contract, but which are assumed by both the parties to have been intended to be included because they are so obvious that they need be spelt out. The courts have developed two tests to determine the intention of the parties: the officious bystander test and the business efficacy test.**

**Shell v Lostock Garage** [1977] 1 All ER 481

**Facts:** There was a contract between Shell and a garage owner under which the garage owner could only purchase petrol from Shell. There was a 'price' among local petrol stations. He discovered that Shell was supplying other garages with petrol more cheaply. He argued that there must be an implied term in the contract that that Shell would not discriminate against him in the terms on which he was supplied.

**Ratio: The Court disagreed. They found no ground for a term being implied by fact. It was suggested that there are two conditions to be complied with before a term could be implied by law. Firstly the term would have to be common for the type of contract. Second there must be a gap in the contract to be filled. The court felt that this was not a sufficiently common type of agreement.**

**General Principle: the officious bystander test is used by the courts to imply a term of contract.**

**Shirlaw v Southern Foundries** [1939] 2KB 206

**Facts:** The Plaintiff was appointed as managing director of Defendant's company for a period of ten years. But he was asked to leave before this term expired.

**Ratio: It was held by the court that a term may be implied where it is so obvious that it goes without saying. The court further added that there was an implied term that D would not remove P from his directorship during that period, since any such removal would automatically terminate his appointment as managing director. In the Court of Appeal, McKinnon LJ (with whom Goddard LJ agreed) said a clause to be implied in a contract should be such that had an officious bystander asked while the contract was being made "But what about so-and-so?", the parties would testily suppress him with "Oh, of course".**

**Business Efficacy Test**

**General Principle: the business efficacy test covers the terms which one party claims must be implied in the contract in order to make the contract work.**

**The Moorcock** (1889) 14 PD 64

**Facts**: The defendants made an agreement to allow the plaintiffs to use their wharf. Although not stated in the contract it was known that it was likely that any ship moored there would ground at low tide as there was a ridge of hard ground below the mud. The contract did not expressly mention that the boat would be moored safely. The ship was damaged when it grounded. The plaintiffs brought an action for damages on the basis that there had been a breach of the contract.

**Ratio: The Court of Appeal implied a term into the contract that the boat would be moored safely to give the contract business efficacy. For the contract to be workable, a term regarding the suitability of the river for mooring had to be implied into the contract. The court held that the defendants had warranted that the moorage was safe. Therefore, the action was successful.**

**Term implied by Law**

**General Principle: there are certain terms which are required by law to be present in contracts even though the parties do not want these terms.**

**Liverpool City Council v Irwin** [1977] AC 239

**Facts**: The council owned the tower block of which the defendants were tenants. The flats were in a poor state of repair due to vandalism, the lifts failed, the rubbish chutes were blocked and the lights often did not work. Nothing was said in the tenancy agreement as to who had responsibility for the maintenance of the common parts of the building. The tenants argued that there must be an implied term to make the council responsible for these things.

**Ratio: the HL decided that there was an implied term that the landlords should keep the property in reasonable repair but the tenants lost because their lordships decided that the council had achieved this and could not be constantly expected to carry out repairs when damage is done by vandals and by the tenants themselves.**

**Terms implied by statue**

**Sale of Goods Act 1979**

Section 12: Implied terms about title, etc.
(1)In a contract of sale, other than one to which subsection (3) below applies, there is an implied term on the part of the seller that in the case of a sale he has a right to sell the goods, and in the case of an agreement to sell he will have such a right at the time when the property is to pass.
(2)In a contract of sale, other than one to which subsection (3) below applies, there is also an implied term that—
(a) the goods are free, and will remain free until the time when the property is to pass, from any charge or encumbrance not disclosed or known to the buyer before the contract is made, and
(b) the buyer will enjoy quiet possession of the goods except so far as it may be disturbed by the owner or other person entitled to the benefit of any charge or encumbrance so disclosed or known.
...
(5A) As regards England and Wales and Northern Ireland, the term implied by subsection (1) above is a condition and the terms implied by subsections (2), (4) and (5) above are warranties.]

**Section 13: Sale by description**

(1) Where there is a contract for the sale of goods by description, there is an implied term that the goods will correspond with the description.
(1A) As regards England and Wales and Northern Ireland, the term implied by subsection (1) above is a condition.

**Section 14: Implied terms about quality or fitness**

(1)Except as provided by this section and section 15 below and subject to any other enactment, there is no implied term about the quality or fitness for any particular purpose of goods supplied under a contract of sale.
(2)Where the seller sells goods in the course of a business, there is an implied term that the goods supplied under the contract are of satisfactory quality.
(2A)For the purposes of this Act, goods are of satisfactory quality

if they meet the standard that a reasonable person would regard as satisfactory, taking account of any description of the goods, the price (if relevant) and all the other relevant circumstances.

(2B)For the purposes of this Act, the quality of goods includes their state and condition and the following (among others) are in appropriate cases aspects of the quality of goods—

(a) fitness for all the purposes for which goods of the kind in question are commonly supplied,

(b) appearance and finish,

(c) freedom from minor defects,

(d) safety, and

(e) durability.

(2C)The term implied by subsection (2) above does not extend to any matter making the quality of goods unsatisfactory—

(a)which is specifically drawn to the buyer's attention before the contract is made,

(b)where the buyer examines the goods before the contract is made, which that examination ought to reveal, or

(c)in the case of a contract for sale by sample, which would have been apparent on a reasonable examination of the sample.]

(2D)If the buyer deals as consumer or, in Scotland, if a contract of sale is a consumer contract, the relevant circumstances mentioned in subsection (2A) above include any public statements on the specific characteristics of the goods made about them by the seller, the producer or his representative, particularly in advertising or on labelling.

(2E)A public statement is not by virtue of subsection (2D) above a relevant circumstance for the purposes of subsection (2A) above in the case of a contract of sale, if the seller shows that—

(a)at the time the contract was made, he was not, and could not reasonably have been, aware of the statement,

(b)before the contract was made, the statement had been withdrawn in public or, to the extent that it contained anything which was incorrect or misleading, it had been corrected in public, or

(c)the decision to buy the goods could not have been influenced by the statement.

(2F)Subsections (2D) and (2E) above do not prevent any public statement from being a relevant circumstance for the purposes of subsection (2A) above (whether or not the buyer deals as consumer or, in Scotland, whether or not the contract of sale is a consumer

contract) if the statement would have been such a circumstance apart from those subsections.]
(3)Where the seller sells goods in the course of a business and the buyer, expressly or by implication, makes known—
(a)to the seller, or
(b)where the purchase price or part of it is payable by instalments and the goods were previously sold by a credit-broker to the seller, to that credit-broker, any particular purpose for which the goods are being bought, there is an implied term that the goods supplied under the contract are reasonably fit for that purpose, whether or not that is a purpose for which such goods are commonly supplied, except where the circumstances show that the buyer does not rely, or that it is unreasonable for him to rely, on the skill or judgment of the seller or credit-broker.

...

(6)As regards England and Wales and Northern Ireland, the terms implied by subsections (2) and (3) above are conditions.

**Section 15: Sale by sample**

(1)A contract of sale is a contract for sale by sample where there is an express or implied term to that effect in the contract.
(2)In the case of a contract for sale by sample there is an implied term—
(a) that the bulk will correspond with the sample in quality;
(c)that the goods will be free from any defect, making their quality unsatisfactory, which would not be apparent on reasonable examination of the sample.
(3)As regards England and Wales and Northern Ireland, the term implied by subsection (2) above is a condition.

**The Supply of Goods and Services Act 1994 amended the Sales of Goods Act:**

Section 15 A: Modification of remedies for breach of condition in non-consumer cases.

(1)Where in the case of a contract of sale—

(a)the buyer would, apart from this subsection, have the right to reject goods by reason of a breach on the part of the seller of a term implied by section 13, 14 or 15 above, but

(b)the breach is so slight that it would be unreasonable for him to reject them, then, if the buyer does not deal as consumer, the breach is not to be treated as a breach of condition but may be treated as a breach of warranty.

(2)This section applies unless a contrary intention appears in, or is to be implied from, the contract.

(3)It is for the seller to show that a breach fell within subsection (1)(b) above.

# Classification of Contractual terms of the Contract

- **Condition**
- **Warranty**
- **Innonomiate terms**

The law classifies the terms of the contract according to their importance and for this there are three kinds of contractual terms: conditions, warranties and innominate terms.

## Condition

**General Principle: when a condition of a contract is breached, the innocent party is allowed to regard the contract as repudiated and can also sue for damages.**

**Schuler v Wickman Machine Tools** [1974] AC 235
**Facts**: The defendants were bound to make weekly visits to six firms over the duration of the contract. This was the only term described as a condition of the contract. The term was one which could have serious consequences if it was breached, for example, when no visits were undertaken or could have a minor consequence, for example if only one visit was not carried out.
**Ratio: The House of Lords explained that the use of the word 'condition' gave the right to the other party to consider the contract as repudiated if the condition of the contract was breached, but this was only an indication. But even then the contract as a whole should be considered to discover the true intention of the parties. The Court refused to interpret the term as a condition as any breach of it would bring the contract to an end and this seemed unreasonable.**
**Application:** this seems logical as every breach of the condition, ranging from minor to serious would terminate the contract and it would be unreasonable to allow the contract to be terminated for a minor breach.

## Warranty

**General Principle: a warranty is a less important term than**

the condition and does not go to the root of the contract; the innocent party can only sue for damages but cannot terminate the contract.

**Poussard v Spiers and Pond** (1875-76) LR 1 QBD 410: an actress was under a contractual obligation to play in an operetta as from the beginning of its London run. The producers were forced to use a substitute for her, as she was ill until a week after the show opened.
**Ratio: the obligation to perform as from the first night was a condition and the breach of it entitled the other party to terminate the contract.**

**Bettini v Gye** (1876) 1 QBD 183
**Facts**: A singer was supposed to attend rehearsals six days before the start of performances. He was absent due to illness but arrived three days later.
**Ratio: This was a breach of warranty as the failure to attend rehearsals did not lead to a repudiatory breach of contract.**

**Innonomiate terms**

**General Principle: innominate terms are those which can be broken with either serious or minor consequences, depending on the nature of the breach that took place. If the effects of the breach are serious, it is considered as a condition and if it is trivial then it is considered as a warranty.**

**Hong Kong Fir Shipping v Kawasaki Kisen Kaisha** [1962] 2 QB 26
**Facts**: a ship was chartered for 2 years. There was an obligation to supply a ship that was 'seaworthy'. The crew were inept and the ship was old. The ship was frequently out of service for repairs. This led to a waste of 20 weeks. The agreement contained a clause that the 'ship was fitted for ordinary cargo service', the defendants could have brought an action for damages but they decided to terminate the contract. The plaintiffs then brought an action of wrongful repudiation stating that the defendants can claim damages but they cannot repudiate the contract.
**Ratio: The CA decided that there was a further category of terms known as innominate and the approach to be taken was**

to look at the effect of the breach and then decide whether it was sufficiently serious to be a breach of condition or not. As the breach was not serious in this case, the breach was not considered justified.

**Application:** the courts may find a condition to be a warranty even if the parties have called it a condition.

# Question and Answers

- Terms of Contract Essay Question
- Terms of Contract Problem Question

## Question

Evaluate the importance of terms within a contract according to their importance to the contract and the method of origin and consequence of breach.

## Answer

### Introduction

This essay will discuss the traditional view which is that each term of a contract, express or implied, is either a **condition** or a **warranty**, depending upon its importance with regard to the purpose of the contract. The question whether a term is a **condition** or a warranty becomes significant in cases of breach of contract.

The distinction between a condition and a warranty is that a condition is an important term 'going to the root of the contract'. On the other hand, a **warranty** is described under s. 61 of the Sale of Goods Act 1979 as:

> "an agreement with reference to goods which are the subject of a contract of sale, but collateral to the main purpose of such contract, the breach of which gives rise to a claim for damages, but not a right to reject the goods and treat the contract as repudiated".

As a general principle, if a promisor breaks a condition in any respect, however slight, the other party has a right to elect to treat himself as discharged from future obligations under the contract and to sue for damages immediately. If he does not exercise the right to elect to treat the contract as at an end (instead choosing to affirm the contract) he will remain bound by the contract, but can sue for damages with respect to the other party's breach. If, on the other hand, a promisor breaks a warranty in any respect, the only remedy available to the other party is to sue for damages; i.e. there is no right to treat the contract as at an end.

**Deciding whether it is a condition or warranty**

Since there is a stronger remedy available for breach of condition than for breach of warranty, it is not unusual for the parties to be in dispute as to whether a term is a condition or a warranty. The difference is conveniently illustrated by the following cases.

In **Poussard v Spiers and Pond** (1876) 1 QBD 410: an actress was under a contractual obligation to play the leading role in an opera as from the beginning of its London run. Owing to illness the actress could not attend the last rehearsal or the first four performances, and when she offered to take her part in the fifth performance the producers refused. The actress sued for wrongful dismissal, but the court said her participation in the first four performances was a **condition** fundamental to the contract, and its breach entitled the producers to treat the contract as terminated.

In **Bettini v Gye** (1876) 1 QBD 183: a singer was under contractual obligation to sing in a series of concerts and to take part in six days of rehearsals before the first performance. He arrived three days late, thus leaving only three days for rehearsals. The judge said this was not a fundamental condition. The undertaking to take part in the rehearsals for six days was a warranty and not a condition. The breach entitled the other party to damages but not to repudiate the contract.

**Calling it a "Term or Condition"**

The parties to the contract are free to classify the relative importance of the terms of their contract. However, even where the parties describe a term as a condition it is open to the court to hold that the parties could not have intended the term to have this effect.

One example of this is seen in **Schuler v Wickman Machine Tool Sales** [1974] AC 235: Wickman was given sole distribution rights in the UK of Schuler's panel presses for a period of four and a half years. Clause 7(b) of the agreement provided that:

> 'It shall be **condition** of this agreement that (i) (Wickman) shall send its representatives to visit (the six large UK motor manufacturers) at least once in every week for the purpose of soliciting orders for panel presses...'

Wickman's representatives failed to make a number of these visits and Schuler claimed that this failure was a breach of condition under clause 7(b) and, as such, was a material breach, as defined under clause 11(a) of the agreement, which entitled Schuler to determine the agreement. It was held by the House of Lords that clause 7(b) was not a condition as the parties could not have intended that a single breach, however trivial, would entitle the innocent party to terminate the contract.

The House of Lords in this case ignored the clear wording of the contract, ostensibly on the grounds that to interpret the particular clause as a condition was so unreasonable that it could not have been intended by the parties. However, Lord Wilberforce, in a dissenting judgment, was of the opinion that the express use of the word 'condition' should have been conclusive of the matter. Undoubtedly, if the use of the word 'condition' is not conclusive of the matter then this will create problems of uncertainty, not least that the innocent party will be unsure as to whether he has the right to terminate the contract for breach of that term.

**The modern approach**

The traditional distinction between conditions and warranties is no longer regarded as exhaustive. In **Hong Kong Fir Shipping Co v Kawasaki Kisen Kaishi Ltd.** [1961] 2 Lloyd's Rep 478 the Court of Appeal held that there are many terms which at the outset are neither conditions nor warranties but are of **an innominate or intermediate nature**. A minor breach of such a term will only amount to a breach of warranty but a serious breach thereof will allow the innocent party to terminate the contract and claim damages. This represents a more flexible approach and allows the court a good deal of leeway when dealing with cases where the purported innocent party is attempting to use a trivial breach in order to extract themselves from a contractual agreement which is no longer commercially advantageous.

In the **Hong Kong Fir** case the Court of Appeal took the view that the legal consequences of a breach of contract depend on the consequences of the breach or, to use the words of Diplock LJ 'the nature of the event to which the breach gives rise.' This is quite different from the traditional approach based on the distinction between minor terms (warranties) and important terms (conditions); the distinction resting on the intention of the parties at the time they made their contract. Admittedly, this analysis may promote justice as between the parties but such justice is achieved at the cost of certainty, in particular certainty as to whether the innocent party has the right to terminate the contract as a result of the breach.

## Question

Fred advertises in an antiques journal that he has an aeroplane for sale. The advertisement appears on 1 October and reads:

"A rare opportunity to acquire a collector's item: A bi-plane which belonged to the early flying ace, Sir George Ditcher, has come on the market for the first time. Sir George was an early member of the Royal Flying Corps and was the person upon whom Wiggles, the fictional flying hero, was based. £85,000 or nearest offer."

Boris, the owner of a museum dedicated to items connected with the First World War, contacts Fred on 15 October to discuss the sale. Fred shows Boris a large collection of letters written by Sir George Ditcher which describe an aeroplane of the same type as the one offered for sale as 'my little buzz bomb'. He also points out numerous letters written to Sir George by the author of the Wiggles books. On 31 October, Boris agrees to buy the aeroplane for £85,000 and a brief written contract is entered into which makes no mention of Sir George Ditcher or Wiggles.

Boris displays the bi-plane at his museum describing it as 'previously owned by Sir George Ditcher, the real life Wiggles'. It has now been established that, although he did fly it, the aeroplane never belonged to Sir George Ditcher and that there ten other people who had as strong a claim as Sir George Ditcher to be the basis of the Wiggles character.

Advise Boris.

## Answer

### Introduction

This paper aims to advise Boris of his position within the sale of a bi-plane, allegedly owned by Sir George Ditcher, for the sum of £85,000. After the sale, Boris discovered that the statements relating to Sir George Ditcher are unlikely to have been true. We will identify the potential issues and assess whether Boris is likely to have claim on the basis that the statements concerning Sir George Ditcher are terms of the contract.

1. Importance of the statement of sale regarding Sir George Ditcher.
2. Skill & knowledge of the defendant.
3. The written contract.
4. Conditions and warranties of their contract.
5. A modern approach to conditions and warranties.
6. Identify potential claim / conclusion

For Boris to have claim against Fred upon the discovery of the statement identifying Sir George Ditcher as the previous owner of the plane for sale and the relevance of the Wiggles books being based upon it would need to be identified that the above is, for all legal intents and purposes, not only a term of their contract of sale but whether this term is deemed to be a condition under the contract or a warranty.

## 1. Importance of the statement of sale regarding Sir George Ditcher.

Fred advertised the bi-plane for sale and in the advertisement states that "[the bi-plane] belonged to the flying ace, Sir George Ditcher, has come on the market for the first time". For this to be interpreted as a valid term of the contract, Boris would have to have made it clear that without this statement he would not have been interested in the purchase of Fred's bi-plane. The authority for this is in Bannerman v White where it was held that the plaintiff could claim for breach of contract on the basis that if the statement regarding the products quality were not made, they would not have bothered to inquire about the price. From the information provided we cannot determine whether Boris made any statement regarding the importance of the planes history (in regards to Sir George Ditcher).

Contrary to the above, Fred's lawyers may suggest that due to the subject matter (that of a plane nearing 100 years old), it would be implied that further verification would be required. The authority for this is in **Ecay v Godfrey** where the court held that in certain situations, it would be 'normally expected' that further investigation would be required. From this we can suggest that if there were no other mitigating terms, it would have been Boris's responsibility to independently verify the statements made by Fred.

## 2. Skill & knowledge of the defendant.

Fred produced a large collection of letters written by Sir George Ditcher which was claimed to be evidence describing the plane he was selling and a number of letters from the author of the Wiggles books to Sir George Ditcher (who at the time was claimed to be the inspiration for the books). Due to Boris's professional standing, that is the owner of a museum dedicated to items connected with the First World War, these can be identified as mere representations. The authority for this is in **Oscar Chess Ltd v Williams** where it was held that the seller of a vintage car, being sold to a dealer, was not responsible for an inaccuracy of the age as it was true to the best of his knowledge and based on information perceived to be true. While we do not know of Fred's qualification, we can assume that Boris is considered to be an expert in the field in which he owns a museum to collect similar items.

## 3. The written contract.

Boris and Fred enter into a 'brief' written contract to conduct the sale of the plane however this makes no mention of Sir George Ditcher or Wiggles. For the aforesaid statements to be considered terms of the contract it would require that they be shown to have been of the utmost importance. We can see this in **Evans & Sons Ltd v Andrea Merzario Ltd** where the court of appeal decided that because the plaintiff had specified the importance of the cargo not being carried 'on deck' and that the defendant had given oral assurance of this, that it was to be considered a term of the contract and overrule the standard contract. From the above we can see that if the importance of the statements relating to Sir George Ditcher where either made apparent or can be objectively seen as being apparent, they may be deemed a term of the contract. From the outset we can see the relevance in that the statement was used as a way of attracting potential buyers.

## 4. Conditions and warranties of their contract

For this term to be considered a condition of the contract it would need to be a term 'going to the root of the contract'. We can see this in **Poussard v Spiers and Pond** where it was held that due to the plaintiff being unable to attend the last rehearsal and first four performances, she had effectively breached a condition of her contract and the producers where able to terminate the contract.

Contrary to the above, a warranty is described by S.61 of the Sale of Goods Act 1979 as:

*"an agreement with reference to goods which are the subject of a contract of sale, but collateral to the main purpose of such contract, the breach of which gives rise to a claim for damages, but not a right to reject the goods and treat the contract as repudiated"*.

This can been seen in **Bettini v Gye** where it was held that a singer who had missed 3 days of a contracted 6 days of rehearsal was a trivial breach that would attract a claim for damages and not repudiate the contract.

## 5. The modern approach to conditions and warranties

The above is considered to be the traditional approach to what a condition and warranty are, due to the nature of the subject matter it is a possibility that it would be unconscionable for the contract to be repudiated on the basis of a breach of terms. This can be seen in **Hong Kong Fir Shipping Co v Kawasaki Kisen Kaishi Ltd** where the Court of appeal held that some terms are of "an innominate or intermediate nature" and that a minor breach of terms would amount to a breach of warranty but a serious breach would allow the innocent party to terminate the contract and that it would be best to assess the consequences of the breach, as quoted by Diplock LJ "the nature of the event to which the breach gives rise". Using the above we can suggest that while the breach of the term relating to Sir George Ditcher may be detrimental to Boris, the fundamental contract remains as in its standard form, that is, to purchase a bi-plane from the First World War.

## 6. Identify potential claim / conclusion

Using this paper to first confirm that there is an implied term within the contract of sale, we can see that identifying the term as either a condition or a warranty, in its traditional sense, may be difficult. However the underlying fact is that Boris has purchased an asset of value, albeit above the market value of a First World War bi-plane, and that to maintain a contract between the parties it would be logical that the term be considered a warranty and that Boris be able to claim damages.

# Chapter 10 Exclusion Clauses

## Exemption Clauses

A clause which seeks to exclude all liability for certain breaches, that would otherwise have been implied is called an exclusion clause and a limitation clause similarly seeks to limit liability for any breach of such a term. Moreover, the term, 'exemption clause' is used to cover both limitation and exclusion clauses. As a rule of thumb the exclusion clause completely excludes liability whereas the limitation clause only seeks to limit liability to a specific sum. The general rule is that the parties are free to determine the terms of their own contract, but the courts and Parliament do not look favourably on exclusion clauses and have found various ways of limiting their effect.

## Incorporation

Clearly no exclusion clause is valid if it is not part of the contract, and it is not part of the contract unless both parties agreed to it at the time. The clause can be incorporated in three ways: by **signature**, by **reasonable notice** and by a **previous course of dealing**.

## Signature

**General Principle: If a document is signed at the time of making the contract, its contents become terms of the contract, regardless of whether all the terms have been read and understood or not.**

**L'Estrange v Graucob [1934]** 2 KB 394, CA
**Facts:** The plaintiff ordered a slot machine from the defendant and signed a standard printed order form including (in very small print) a clause excluding any kind of warranty. The machine did not work, and P claimed not to be bound by the exclusion clause which she had not read.
**Ratio: The court held that signing the contract meant that the woman was bound by the exclusion clause.**
**Application:** In the absence of misrepresentation, a party who

signs a document is normally bound by its contents whether or not he has read them.

## Non-Est Factum

*Non est factum* (Latin for "it is not my deed") is a doctrine in contract law that allows a signing party to escape performance of the agreement. A claim of *non est factum* means that the signature on the contract was signed by mistake, without knowledge of its meaning, but was not done so negligently.

## Reasonable Notice

**While deciding whether a reasonable notice has been given, the courts generally look at when the notice was given, what was the form that it took, and how serious the effect of the exemption clause is. Hence, the timing, form and the effect becomes crucial.**

## Timing

**General Principle: if separate written terms are presented at the time of the contract being made, they only become a part of the contract if the recipient had reasonable notice of them.**

**Parker v South Eastern Railway (1877)** LR 2 CPD 416, CA
**Facts:** The Plaintiff left his bag in a railway cloakroom, paid 2d (two pence), and was given a ticket on which were the words "See back"; on the back of the ticket was a notice excluding liability for any package worth over £10. There was also a notice to the same effect visible in the cloakroom. The bag was lost, The Plaintiff sued, and defendant relied on the exclusion clause. The bag was worth £24 and the plaintiff claimed the amount from the railway company; the company claimed that their liability was limited to £10.
**Ratio: The Court opined that a party could be deemed to have had reasonable notice if they knew of the clause or if reasonable steps were taken to bring it their notice. The court further said it was a matter of fact whether or not the defendant had done all that was reasonably necessary to give notice of the clause, and in this case they had and therefore the**

train company was asked to pay only £10.

**Application:** the most important issue here is whether the recipient of the terms was aware of their existence.

**Olley v Marlborough Court Hotel** (1949) 1 KB 532

**Facts:** A married couple booked into a hotel for a week, and then went to their allocated room. On entering the room, they found a notice on the wall stating that the hotel does not accept any liability for the loss of the guests' property. While the couple was out, Mrs Olley's fur coats were stolen. The hotel relied on the words of the notice and disclaimed any liability.

**Ratio: The Court of Appeal rejected this argument and held that the notice had not been incorporated into the contract as it came to the couple's notice too late. The contract was made at the reception desk, and a new term could not be imposed on them in the room.**

**Application:** While deciding such cases the court analyses the transaction in terms of offer and acceptance to decide when the contract was complete. Hence, the terms should be delivered before the contract is complete.

**Thornton v Shoe Lane Parking [1971]** 1 All ER 686, CA

**Facts:** The Plaintiff parked his car in the defendant's car park, paying his money and taking a ticket from the automatic machine at the entrance. On the ticket, in small print, was a notice referring to conditions displayed in the car park; these were not visible from outside, and were quite lengthy, including one excluding liability for any injury to a customer. When the Plaintiff returned later to collect his car, there was an accident in which he was seriously injured, and he sued.

**Ratio: The Court of Appeal struck out this exclusion clause, holding (i) that so wide-ranging and unusual an exclusion called for exceptionally clear and explicit notice, and (ii) that in any case, the contract was complete when the money was put into the machine at the entrance, before there could be any possibility of reading the conditions.**

**Application:** The more onerous the term the more the more required greater degree of notice.

Form

General Principle: an exemption clause is only included into the contract if considerable notice was given before or at the time of contacting.

Thompson v LMS [1930] 1 KB 41, CA
Facts: The Plaintiff went on a railway excursion, and was given a ticket with the words "Excursion: for conditions see back". On the back was a notice referring customers to the conditions printed in the company's timetables (which cost 6d each); these conditions excluded liability for any injury. The Plaintiff was injured on the journey, and claimed damages.
**Ratio: The Court of Appeal said the ticket was a contractual document, and the fact that the Plaintiff could not read did not alter the legal position, as the clause had been brought to her attention and reasonable notice had been given. She should have realised that the special excursion price might imply special conditions.**

**General Principle: The document must be of a type which a reasonable person would expect to contain contractual terms.**

Chapelton v Barry UDC [1940] 1 All ER 356, CA
The Plaintiff hired a deckchair belonging to the defendant, paid the hire fee, and took a ticket without reading it. The chair collapsed and The Plaintiff was injured. The defendant relied on a clause printed on the ticket excluding liability for any injury in the event of 'any accident or damage arising from the hire of the chair'.
**Ratio: The Court of Appeal said that the ticket acted like a receipt- it merely acknowledged payment for the hire and in most cases was not received until after the hire sat in the chair. Hence, it was not a contractual document - no reasonable person in the circumstances would have thought it anything more than a receipt - so the clause had not been incorporated in the contract.**
Application: a document will be considered contractual if the party to whom it is given knows that it is intended to have that effect, or it in given in such circumstances that it provides reasonable notice of the fact that it contains terms.

## Effect

**General Principle:** the more unusual the term is, greater degree of notice is required to incorporate it.

**Interfoto v Stiletto [1988]** 1 All ER 348, CA
**Facts:** The defendant were an advertising agency who hired nearly fifty photographs from plaintiff; the photographs were supplied with a delivery note stating that they were to be returned within 14 days and setting out a number of conditions, including a "holding fee" of £5 per photograph per day for lateness. The defendant kept the photographs for nearly a month, and the plainntiff claimed the holding fee.
**Ratio: The Court of Appeal applied the principle in the Thornton case and said that where a contract includes any unusually onerous condition the party seeking to rely on it must show that it was fairly and reasonably brought to the notice of the other. The term should have been printed in bold type, for example, or a separate covering note sent drawing attention to it. The plaintiff was allowed to recover £3.50 per week for each transparency returned late.**

**Pervious Course of Dealing**

**General Principle: if two parties have previously made a series of contracts between them which contained an exemption clause, this clause may also apply to the subsequent transaction, even though the usual steps to incorporate the clause have not been taken.**

**Spurling v Bradshaw [1956]** 2 All ER 121, CA
**Facts:** The plaintiffs were warehousemen, and the defendant had dealt with them on many occasions. He delivered to them eight barrels of orange juice, and was sent a receipt which he did not read. When he came to collect the barrels he found them empty, but plaintiff pointed to an exemption clause on the receipt. The defendant argued that this clause could not be part of the contract because it was only sent to him after the conclusion of the contract. However, he admitted to have received similar documents during previous transactions.
**Ratio: The Court of Appeal said there had been a consistent**

course of dealing, and terms from the previous contracts could be implied in the present case as long as they were not inconsistent with express provisions.

**Application:** the clause is incorporated into the contract by the course of previous dealings between the parties.

## Contra Proferentem rule

**General Principle:** Any ambiguity or uncertainty in the interpretation of an exclusion clause, however contrived the ambiguity might be, is normally construed contra proferentem - against the party seeking to rely on it.

**White v Warwick** [1953] 2 All ER 1021, CA
**Facts:** The plaintiff hired a bicycle from the defendant under a written agreement which included a provision that "nothing in this agreement shall render the owners liable for any personal injuries. The Plaintiff was injured when the saddle tilted forward, and the Court of Appeal found the Defendant liable in negligence.
**Ratio: The exclusion clause was construed so as to exclude only the concurrent liability that would otherwise have arisen under the contract. Thus the Plaintiff was free to sue in negligence.**
**Application:** Where the words of the exemption clause are ambiguous they will be interpreted in the way which is least favourable to the party relying on the clause.

**Houghton v Trafalgar Insurance** [1953] 2 All ER 1409, CA
**Facts:** The plaintiff's five-seater car was damaged in a collision and he claimed on his insurance policy. The policy excluded liability for anything that might occur while the car was "conveying any load in excess of that for which it was constructed"; at the relevant time, the car was carrying six people, with one sitting on another's knee in the back.
**Ratio: The Court of Appeal said this clause was to be construed narrowly and the word 'load' refers to goods and not people; consequently the clause did not exclude the insurer's liability where the car was carrying too many people.**

## Contra Proferentem rule and exclusion clause

**General Principle:** Technically, the rule applies to all exemption clauses, but courts tend to apply it less rigorously on limitation clauses.

**Ailsa Craig v Malvern [1983]** 1 All ER 101, HL
**Facts:** Securicor agreed to provide a security service for certain ships moored in Aberdeen harbour. Because of their negligence one of the ships sank and took with it another ship. The main issue at the trial was the third party liability of Securicor, whose contract with AA included a clause limiting their liability "for any loss or damage of whatever nature arising out of ... failure in the provision of the services contracted for" to £1000.
**Ratio: The House of Lords unanimously upheld the validity of this limitation; Lord Fraser said the strict principles applied when construing exclusion clauses are not applicable in their full rigour when considering clauses merely limiting liability. The contra proferentem rule still applies, but so long as the clause is clear and unambiguous there is no reason to doubt that the other party assented to it.**
**Application:** Limitation clauses are more likely to express genuine intention of the parties as opposed to exclusion clauses.

## Statutory restrictions

Various statutory provisions invalidate or limit purported exclusion clauses. The Unfair Contract Terms Act 1977 (which in spite of its name applies to tort as well as contract), applies only to business liability. This includes government departments and other public authorities however international contracts, marine contracts, contracts for insurance, land, patents and copyrights, or for the formation of companies, are largely excluded. It deals with both exclusion and limitation clauses, including those which impose restrictive conditions such as clauses which deny liability unless notice of any complaint is given within a specified time.

## Dealing as a Consumer

**General Principle:** many of the provisions of the Act only apply where one of the contracting parties is dealing as a 'consumer'.

**R & B Customs Brokers v UDT [1988]** 1 All ER 847, CA
**Facts:** Plaintiff bought a car from a finance company, the defendant, and the contract excluded any implied conditions as to the car's fitness in relation to any business transaction. The car proved to be faulty, and Plaintiffs sued. The main issue was that the UCTA provision relied on would only apply if they were dealing as consumers.
**Ratio: The Court of Appeal said that where a transaction is only incidental to a business activity, a degree of regularity is needed before the transaction can be said to be "in the course of business". Since, the plaintiffs were buying a car for only the second or third time; they were entitled to be regarded as consumers.**
**Application:** The integral question to ask is whether the transaction concerned was actually an integral part of the business or merely incidental to it.

| Source of liability | Definition of liability (where relevant) | Effect on consumer | Effect on non-consumer |
|---|---|---|---|
| Negligence leading to death or injury | | void s.2(1) UCTA | void s.2(1) UCTA |
| Negligence leading to loss or damage | | acceptable if reasonable s.2(2) UCTA | acceptable if reasonable s.2(2) UCTA |
| Sale of goods with defective title | s.12 Sale of Goods Act 1979 | void (UCTA s.6(1)) | void (UCTA s.6(1)) |
| Sale of goods that do not match their description | s.13 Sale of Goods Act 1979 | void (UCTA s.6(2)a) | acceptable if reasonable (UCTA s.6(3)) |
| Sale of goods that do not match their sample | s.15 Sale of Goods Act 1979 | void (UCTA s.6(2)a) | acceptable if reasonable (UCTA s.6(3)) |
| Sale of goods that are of unsatisfactory quality | s.14 Sale of Goods Act 1979 | void (UCTA s.6(2)a) | acceptable if reasonable (UCTA s.6(3)) |
| Any other passage of goods where the goods are of unsatisfactory quality or do not match their sample or description | | void (UCTA s.7(2)) | acceptable if reasonable (UCTA s.7(2)) |
| Breach of standard-form contract | | acceptable if reasonable (UCTA s.3) | not affected |
| Misrepresentation | s.3 Misrepresentation Act 1967 | acceptable if reasonable (UCTA s.8(1)) | acceptable if reasonable (UCTA s.8(1)) |

**Table:** summary of the effect of UCTA on exclusion of liability

**Exclusion and Personal Injury**

**General Principle: Liability for death or personal injury resulting from negligence cannot be excluded or limited-clauses trying to do so will be considered void (s.2(1)).**

This included liability for negligence in contract and in tort.

**Thompson v Lohan [1987]** 2 All ER 631, CA
Facts: The plaintiff's husband was killed in an accident caused by the negligence of the driver in operating the excavator at the quarry. The Plaintiff sued both the owners and the hirers of the excavator, and succeeded against the hirer.
**Ratio: The Court of Appeal said that section 2 of UCTA was intended to prevent the exclusion of liability in negligence to the victim of the negligence( the plaintiff) and was not concerned with arrangements made to share liability with a third party.**
Application: negligence resulting in death or personal injury cannot be excluded in any case.

**Reasonableness Test**

**General Principle: Clauses which are subject to reasonableness under UCTA are only applied when the courts deem fit to do so.**

**Woodman v Photo Trade Processing (1981)** 131 NLJ 933
**Facts:** the plaintiff took photographs at a friend's wedding, and took the film to the defendant for processing. A sign on the counter limited the defendant's liability for lost or damaged films to the cost of replacement. The films were lost through the defendant's negligence. The plaintiff sued for the distress caused by the loss, these being the only photographs taken at the wedding in question.
**Ratio: The judge said the limitation was unreasonable after considering the facts of the case; the clause could have been reasonable if the processor also offered a premium service, which cost more but offered better protection.**
Application: the clause has to be reasonable to be considered as an exemption clause.

**Smith v Eric Bush [1989]** 2 All ER 514, HL
**Facts:** In an action brought by first-time house buyers against a surveyor who had negligently overvalued the property. The surveyor was trying to limit his liability for an inaccurate report on the plaintiff's house.
**Ratio: It was not fair and reasonable in the circumstances to allow the surveyor to disclaim liability to the purchaser for negligence where he was dealing with property at the lower end of the market and knew that the purchaser was unlikely to instruct another independent surveyor. Lord Griffiths drew attention to the evident inequality in bargaining power, the cost and trouble to first-time buyers of obtaining independent advice, the comparative simplicity (by professional standards) of the job to be done, and the ease with which the surveyor (but not the buyers) could have insured against the consequences of negligence.**
**Application:** the limitation could have been reasonable where the task was unusually difficult or complex.

**EU Directives**

The Directive on Unfair Terms in Consumer Contracts (Directive 93/13) came into effect on 1 January 1995, and the relevant UK regulations took effect six months later. However, it subsequently appeared that the original regulations had not properly implemented the Directive, and revised regulations (the Unfair Terms in Consumer Contracts Regulations 1999, SI 1999/2083) were made to replace them.

The Directive and the domestic Regulations are limited to consumer contracts (including oral contracts) for the supply of goods and services, including financial services (subject to some limitations), insurance and real property. They are wider than UCTA in that they apply to all types of clause, not only exclusion and limitation clauses. They are narrower as they apply only to consumer contracts - a consumer is defined as a natural person acting for purposes outside his trade, business or profession - and only to terms that have not been individually negotiated.

**Effect of 1999 Regulations**

Under the Regulations, unfair terms are not binding on the consumer. The rest of the contract remains perfectly valid provided that it is capable of existing without the 'unfair term'.

Schedule 2 of the Regulations sets out an indicative and non-exhaustive list of terms which may be regarded as unfair. These include terms which have the object or effect of -
(a) excluding or limiting legal liability for the death of or personal injury to the consumer;
(b) inappropriately excluding the consumer's rights in the event of total or partial non-performance by the other (the supplier);
(c) making the agreement binding on the consumer while leaving the provision of services by the supplier dependent on his own decision;
(d) allowing the supplier to retain a deposit paid by the consumer in the event of cancellation, without providing similar compensation for the consumer if the supplier cancels the contract;
(e) imposing any disproportiately high penalty on the consumer;
(f) allowing the supplier to cancel the contract at will, if no such right is given to the consumer;
(g) allowing the supplier to terminate a long-term contract without giving reasonable notice;
(h) automatically extending a fixed-term contract unless the consumer gives very early notice;
(i) binding the consumer by terms that he could not readily have known when the contract was made;
(j/k) allowing the supplier to alter the terms of the contract, except for some good (pre-specified) reason;
(l) allowing the price to be determined at some future date, unless the consumer has the right to cancel if the price is too high;
(m) giving the supplier the exclusive right to interpret any term or terms;
(n) limiting the extent to which the supplier is bound by his agents' actions, or imposing particular formalities;
(o) requiring the consumer to fulfil all his obligations even if the supplier does not fulfil his;
(p) allowing the supplier unilaterally to transfer his rights and obligations to a third party, to the consumer's detriment; or
(q) excluding or restricting the consumer's right to take legal action to enforce the contract (e.g. by requiring him to accept non-legal

arbitration or by imposing on him a non-standard burden of proof).

# Question and Answers

- Unfair Contract Terms Act 1979 Essay
- Exclusion Clause Problem Question

## Question

What, if any, are the differences in scope between the Unfair Contract Terms Act 1977 and the Unfair Terms in Consumer Contracts Regulations 1999?

## Answer

To fully answer this question we need first to look at the nature of exclusion clauses and the history behind this legislation. It is commonplace for a party drawing up a contract to seek to minimise the amount of liability that may be incurred in the performance of that contract. Contractual clauses that have this effect are usually called "exclusion clauses" or "limitation clauses". Exclusion clauses often attempt to exclude or limit liability for losses arising out of breach of contract, or for extra-contractual liabilities. Extra-contractual liabilities will often include losses for misrepresentation, or negligence in performing the contract.

On the one hand from a business point of view this limit on liability does make sound business sense. It could even be argued that it is logical for the consumer as well, say for example the provider of a service that is ineffective has to pay compensation for all the losses that arise from running a poor service, that cost will simply be passed on to the consumer. Nonetheless whatever the advantages of this argument, there are clearly exclusions that perpetuate an injustice so great that they can't be tolerated in a decent society. The archetypal case of this sort is Thompson v London Midland and Scottish Railway (1930)1. In this case, an elderly, illiterate woman bought a railway ticket which contained a reference to the railway company's standard terms and conditions. These included a statement that the railway would not accept liability for negligence. During the alighting of the train Mrs

Thompson fell and broke her leg. When she sued the railway in negligence, the exclusion clause was upheld, to the amazement of almost everybody. Mrs Thompson was an adult of full capacity, despite being unable to read, and had the notional freedom to either enter the contact or refrain. The courts had begun to develop common-law rules that helped exclusion clauses to be brought under control, however, cases like this made it clear that some sort of control was required.

When the Unfair Contract Terms Act (1977) ('UCTA') was drafted, it tried to balance freedom of contract (the long established principle that adults of full capacity who make contracts with each other should abide by them) against the need to prevent injustice. The UCTA deals with a limited set of precise types of exclusion, only exemption clauses. For example, it strikes out any attempt disclaim liability for death or injury, and this would probably have allowed Mrs Thompson to win her case. Efforts to disclaim liability for losses caused by negligence will be struck out if they don't pass the test of "reasonableness". Another main point is that the UTCA restricts those who wish to exclude liability for selling poor-quality, defective goods, or goods that the seller doesn't have a right to sell, say if they are stolen. Finally, it makes attempts to exclude liability for misrepresentation subject to a test of reasonableness. Whereas so far we have only looked at the English Law, at the same time the EC was also looking at legislation to control these types of clauses. This is how the Unfair Terms in Consumer Contracts Regulations 19992, however these two pieces of legislation have a number of important differences.

First, UTCCR only benefits with consumers whereas anyone can benefit under the 1977 act but there is most protection for consumers. For the UTCCR purposes, a consumer is any "natural person" acting outside the course of his business. In fact, s.3 of the Regulation defines "consumer" as meaning (only) "any natural person who [...] is acting for purposes which are outside his trade, business or profession". The very narrow phrase "natural person" implies that only individuals will benefit from UTCCR, whereas under UCTA businesses can trade as consumers if outside of their course of business. However although the UCTA 1977 introduced for the very first time the distinction between "consumer and "non consumer" the very definition of "consumer" in the UCTA leaves a lot to the interpretation the judges, so here we see the difference between the 1977 Act and the 1999 Regulations. In most instances it is not necessarily obvious what a consumer is and isn't, in a number of borderline situations. For example the case of **R and B Customs Brokers v UDT** the Court of Appeal held that a family firm that bought a car, partly for work and partly for social use, was a consumer for the purposes of UCTA. It isn't necessarily obvious what a consumer may be, in a number of borderline situations. Thus in **R and B Customs Brokers** would be excluded, unless they claimed as private individuals. There is, therefore, a difference between a `consumer' for UCTA purposes and for UTCCR purposes. There would, no doubt, be a large number of cases in which whether a person was a `consumer' or not would be decided the same way for both UCTA and UTCCR; but there are cases where it wouldn't. For example, in UCTA a person who buys at auction is, by definition, not a consumer. However, there is nothing in UTCCR that prevents a private individual buying at auction being a consumer.

So a second important difference is that the UTCCR deals not only with exclusion clauses, but any "unfair" term. The UCTA has a delicate balancing act to perform, that it only deals with exclusion clauses, and these are only one type of onerous contractual clause that causes problems. Consider the infamous case of **Interfoto v Stiletto** (1989). Here an advertising agency asked a photographic service to produce photographs for a presentation. The photographic service sent 47 transparencies to the agency for inspection, along with a contractual letter which had in its small print the statement that transparencies were to be returned within 14 days. If they were not, the service would levy a charge of £5 per negative per day. The agency forgot about the transparencies for a couple of weeks, and was rather surprised to receive a bill for £3,783. The Court of Appeal held that a term as onerous as this would have to be made very clear if it was to be enforced and the claimants had not done anything to bring it to the defendant's attention. As a result, the claim failed. This process of striking out a clause on the grounds of incomplete "incorporation" was one of the ways that the courts had sought to control exclusion clauses in the pre-UCTA days. While the Interfoto case showed that the courts were prepared to go through the whole process again for other types of onerous clause, this was hardly satisfactory.

In the UTCCR the possibilities of "unfair terms" come to light. An unfair term is any that imbalances rights and obligations significantly to the detriment of the consumer. Like UCTA's notion of "reasonableness", "unfair" is not defined, but there is guidance. For example, a clause might be unfair if it allows the business to terminate the contract at its discretion, without extending the same freedom to the consumer. Another example is a term allowing the business to vary the contract without the consent of the consumer. This idea of "unfairness" goes much further than UCTA's "unreasonableness". The UCTA does not prevent a contract containing terms that allow one party to vary its obligations, for example. However, UTCCR does nothing to control onerous terms in non-consumer contracts. This means that the defendants in the Interfoto case would not be able to rely on UTCCR to escape their bill. It still falls to the courts to handle situations like this on a case-by-case basis.

Third, UTCCR applies only to terms that have not been individually negotiated between the parties. A term that has been influenced by the consumer is, by definition, fair. UCTA does not define what it means to be reasonable, but it does give some guidance. Under the UCTA, the test of reasonableness does allow for consideration of whether the term was negotiated, but this is only advisory. A negotiated term can still be deemed unreasonable. The courts are to have regard for, among other things, the relative bargaining positions of the parties, whether the contract is negotiated or in standard form, and whether the party affected by the exclusion clause was offered an incentive to contract on particular terms. This approach allows the courts a lot of flexibility, and some surprisingly draconian exclusion clauses have been upheld. For example, in **SAM Business Systems v Hedley and Co** a software supplier was allowed to rely on an exclusion clause that allowed it to supply a thoroughly inadequate product. The court decided that the parties were of roughly equal bargaining power, and the purchasers could have attempted to negotiate better terms. The court also recognised that such clauses are ubiquitous in the computing industry. Had the purchaser been a consumer, the reasonableness test would not have applied; the exclusion clause would simply have been struck out, because it attempted to disclaim liability for supplying goods that are not suitable for their purpose.

Fourth the explanation of "unfairness" in UTCCR includes the phrase "contrary to the requirements of good faith". This seems be tricky as it implies that the drafter of a consumer contract has an obligation to contract in good faith. In English law we do not officially recognise the doctrine of good faith as other countries do. However, UTCCR comes from the EC, and the idea of contractual good faith is less unusual in other parts of Europe. There are very few cases which consider what "good faith" actually is in terms of consumer contracts, so it may be that this phrase adds little to our understanding of unfairness.

So there are clearly two major pieces of legislation that overlap, but not totally. Certain contractual arrangements are caught by both UCTA and UTCCR and handled the same. For example, both UCTA (certainly) and UTCCR (advisedly) would strike out a clause that attempted to disclaim liability for death or injury of a party. Situations like this should not cause any problems. Then there are contractual arrangements that are handled by one of the pieces of legislation and not the other. For example, UTCCR deals with onerous terms in consumer contracts, while these are beyond the remit of UCTA. Some contractual arrangements are within the scope of both UCTA and UTCCR, but are subject to different tests. For example, consider a term in a contract for supply of goods and services that tried to disclaim liability for faulty goods where the manufacturers were to blame for the faults. Such a term would be void under UCTA if the purchaser were a consumer, void unless reasonable under UCTA if the purchaser were a business, void if `unfair' under UTCCR if the purchaser is a consumer, and unaffected by UTCCR if the purchaser is a business. Since `unfair' is not the same as `unreasonable', these complications are even more opaque. Finally, some contractual injustices that cry out for redress are handled neither by UCTA nor UTCCR. For example, a large, powerful business can still impose onerous terms on a small business, and there is no statutory protection against these terms.

Aside from the problems of understanding which types of term in which strain of contract are caught by which piece of legislation, there is the additional problem that UTCCR goes beyond striking out unfair terms: it also establishes certain obligations on the contract those who draught contracts, to write in clear language. This may be no bad thing, but there is no similar rule for business contracts. To conclude, the law on statutory control of exclusion clauses is in a deplorable phase. Perhaps there needs to be a reassessment of this legislation to unify the UCTA and the UTCCR. More specifically, to amalgamate the rules corresponding to businesses and consumers and to supersede the "fairness" and "reasonable" tests with a common test to apply to all types of contract.

## Question

Kate parks her new sports car in Wood Lane private car park. When she entered the car park, she paid for her parking. Consequently, she has affixes a ticket to her window. When she returns to her car, she discovers that her car has been seriously dented.

She complains to the management of Wood Lane private car park about the damage to the car. The management, while sympathetic, point out the terms and conditions on the back of the ticket which state that "management is not responsible for any damage" and that "cars are parked at owners' risk".

Discuss the validity of the exclusion/exemption clause in the terms and conditions of the ticket at Wood Lane private car park.

## Answer

### Introduction

This paper will first discuss the liability that has arisen. Second it will discuss the incorporation of the exclusion clause. It will then discuss construction of the exclusion clause. It will then discuss statutory controls such as the Unfair Contract Terms Act 1977.

### Liability

Kate parks her new sports car in Wood Lane private car park. When she entered the car park, she paid for her parking. Consequently, she affixed a ticket to her window. When she returns to her car, she discovers that her car has been seriously dented. It is not clear from the question, by whom the dent has been caused by. If it has been caused by an employee or agent of the garage the garage will be liable for negligence that has caused damage.

Bailment is a temporary transfer of property to another for a limited time and for a specific purpose. The transfer of property in a bailment is only in regards to possession, not ownership. For cars, you turn over possession and care over to the lot, for example by giving a valet your car key. If you store your car in a lot for a prolonged period, but you maintain possession by keeping the keys or you pay a fee to park and retrieve your car on your own, you are likely not in a bailment situation.

If you are in a bailment situation, the lot owner has a duty to exercise reasonable care in safeguarding your vehicle. The owner would be liable if your windshield gets broken, someone crashes your car, some steals your car, or someone breaks into your car and the lot owner was not exercising reasonable care. For example, the lot owner cannot leave the keys in car and then not guard the car at all or leave windows open.

**Incorporation of Exclusion Clause**

Clearly no exclusion clause is valid if it is not part of the contract, and it is not part of the contract unless both parties agreed to it at the time. There are three ways in which an exclusion clause can become incorporated into the contract: signature, reasonable notice and pervious course of dealings.

*Signature*

The first way this can happen is through signature. This is demonstrated in the case of **L'Estrange v Graucob**[195] in which the court stated that in the absence of misrepresentation, where a party signs a document they will normally be bound by its contents whether or not he has read them. In the absence of misrepresentation, a party who signs a document is normally bound by its contents whether or not they have read them.

*Reasonable Notice*

The other way in which a term can become incorporated id through reasonable notice. Whether the term has become incorporated through this method will depend on the timing of any notice, the form it took and its effect. In respect of timing Kate has seen signs on Cheryl's premises which state. Kate has never requested sight of the terms and conditions. This would suggest it

---

[195] [1934] 2 KB 394

was brought to her attention before the contact was signed. This is essentially what the court is looking for and it has been demonstrated by many cases.[196] Secondly the form of the document that contains the clause must be a contractual document and not a receipt or note.[197] This appears to be satisfied. Lastly the effect of the clause is a determining factor. Lord Denning MR has famously said that the more onerous the clause, the better notice of it needed to be given. He went on to say: "In order to give sufficient notice, it would need to be printed in red ink with a red hand pointing to it - or something equally startling."[198]It appears that in the circumstances the court will agree incorporation has taken place through reasonable notice, although more information is needed to say for certain.

*Previous Course of Dealings*

The terms and condition will have most certainly been incorporated into this contract through the doctrine of previous course of dealings. The authority for this is the case of **Spurling Ltd v Bradshaw**[199] in which Denning, Morris and Parker LJ held that although the warehouse employees were negligent; their exclusion clause effectively exempted them as it had become incorporated as the two parties had traded on the same terms previously.

## Contra proferentem

Any ambiguity or uncertainty in the interpretation of an exclusion clause, however contrived the ambiguity might be, is normally construed *contra proferentem* - against the party seeking to rely on it. In **White v Warwick** [1953] 2 All ER 1021, the plaintiff hired a bicycle from the defendant under a written agreement which included a provision that "nothing in this agreement shall render the owners liable for any personal injuries". the plaintiff was injured when the saddle tilted forward, and the Court of Appeal found the defendant liable in negligence. The exclusion clause was

---

[196]*Thornton v Shoe Lane*Parking Ltd [1971] 2 QB 163; and *Olley v Marlborough Court Hotel*[1949] 1 KB 532
[197]**Chapelton v Barry Urban District Council** [1940] 1 KB 532
[198]**Thornton v Shoe Lane Parking Ltd** [1971] 2 QB 163 at 170
[199] [1956] EWCA Civ 3

construed so as to exclude only the concurrent liability that would otherwise have arisen under the contract. The plaintiff was able then to sue in tort.

**Statutory Control**

Various statutory provisions invalidate or limit purported exclusion clauses. The most important parts of the *Unfair Contract Terms Act 1977* (which in spite of its name applies to tort as well as contract), apply only to business liability. It deals with both exclusion and limitation clauses, including those which impose restrictive conditions such as clauses which deny liability unless notice of any complaint is given within a specified time.

Much of the Act is concerned with the protection of consumers, and a consumer is defined in s.12 as amended as a legal person who does not make the contract in the course of business, nor purport to do so, while the other party does. In the case of an individual that is enough; where the buyer is a corporate body the goods must be of a type normally supplied for private consumption. The definition excludes a person (even an individual) buying second-hand goods at public auction, as well as a person who obtains goods (even for private use) by using a cash-and-carry card at a wholesale warehouse.

In **R & B Customs Brokers v UDT** [1988] 1 All ER 847, the plaintiff bought a car from a finance company the defendant, and the contract excluded any implied conditions as to the car's fitness in relation to any business transaction. The car proved to be faulty, and the plaintiff sued. The Court of Appeal said that where a transaction is only incidental to a business activity, a degree of regularity is needed before the transaction can be said to be "in the course of business". The plaintiff who was buying a car for only the second or third time was entitled to be regarded as consumers. Kate will be deemed a consumer.

Under section 2(2) Unfair Contract Terms Act 1977. The garages exclusion of liability will only be valid if it satisfies the test of reasonableness as contained in section 11 of Unfair Contract Terms Act 1977.The reasonableness test is contained at s.11 of

UCTA and refers you to the matters specified in schedule 2, where there are 5 guidelines for the application of the reasonableness test:

The first guideline is equality and the strength of the bargaining positions of the parties. Are the parties relative to one another? The leading case on this point is **St Alban's City and District Council v ICL** where the crucial factor in deciding an exemption clause was not reasonable was that ICL was a massive computer company dealing with a small local council. The second is choice i.e. whether the customer received an inducement to agree to the term or had the opportunity to enter a similar contract with other persons but without a similar clause. Did the customer have any choice than to deal with this company? In **St Alban's** there was no choice as the software was not available anywhere else. This guideline also talks about inducements as in **Woodman v Photo Trade Processing**. The third is knowledge, i.e. whether the buyer knew the existence and extent of the term. The fourth guideline is time and the last is whether the goods were manufactured, processed or adapted to the special order of the customer.

# Chapter 11 Misrepresentation

## What is actionable misrepresentation?

Jill Poole states an actionable misrepresentation to be: an unambiguous, false, statement of fact (or law), addressed to the party misled, which is material and induces the contract, and causes loss.[200] Any pre-contractual statements made by the parties during negotiations can be referred to as **'representations'**. 'Representations' are statements of fact (or law) and any false statement of fact is a **'misrepresentation'**. If the untrue statement of fact made by one party has been relied on by another party before entering into the contract, it renders the contract voidable.

### Ambiguous statement

**General Principle: The representation must be an unambiguous false statement of fact.**

**McInerny v Lloyds Bank Ltd** [1974] 1 Lloyd's Rep 246(CA)
**Facts:** The plaintiff wanted to sell some companies to Mackay on a condition that the payment is guaranteed by the defendant bank. The bank directly replied to the plaintiff and stated that they were not allowed to give such a guarantee under the Banking regulations and the only available option was to set up an irrevocable credit. After the contract was concluded, Mackay only paid the first two instalments. The plaintiff claimed damages bringing an action for misrepresentation.
**Ratio: The bank could not be held responsible for the interpretation taken by the plaintiff, because on reasonable construction, the bank had not given any of the assurances which were requested. Hence there was no ambiguity.**

### Statement of Fact

**General Principle: To be actionable the representation must be a statement of fact and cannot be an opinion.**

**Esso Petroleum Co Ltd v Mardon** [1976] 2 All ER 5

---

[200]Poole, Jill. *Textbook on contractlaw*. Oxford UniversityPress, 2012.

**Facts:** Mardon took a lease of a petrol station with the aid of a loan from Esso after being assured by Esso's representative that the annual sales would be 200,000 gallons of petrol per year. The estimate was not revised when the council changed the entrance to the garage from the main road to a side road. Annual sales were about 1/3rd of the estimate given and the garage was uneconomic to run. Mardon could not repay the loan and Esso sought repossession of the garage. Mardon counter-claimed on the basis of negligent misrepresentation. Esso argued that as there had never been a garage on the site before, the estimate had merely been a statement of opinion.

**Ratio: The Court of Appeal said that in this case the estimate was a statement of fact. Since, Esso's representative had substantial experience and skill in estimating potential sales.**

**Application:** The statement must be one of fact; simply delivering an opinion will not lead to misrepresentation.

**Statement of Law**

**General Principle: A statement of law can also give rise to an actionable misrepresentation.**

**Pankhania v Hackney LBC** [2002] NPC 123
**Facts:** A buyer of a car park was informed by Hackney LBC that the car park could be let out on a contractual license. However, after the car park had been purchases once, it was covered under a protected tenancy under the Landlord and Tenant Act 1954.

**Ratio: The Court held that the legal status of the tenancy had been misrepresented which constituted a misrepresentation of law as the other party had relied on this statement before entering into this contract.**

**Silence**

Generally, mere silence does not amount to an untrue statement of fact and will not give rise to an actionable misrepresentation. However, there are a few exceptions to the general rule: Half-truths, ongoing silence and contract of utmost good faith.

**Half Truths**

Half-truths, are continuing representations and contracts requiring utmost good faith.

**General Principle: It is misleading to make statements which are true in themselves but they misleading because they do not reveal the whole truth.**

### Dimmock v Hallett[1866] LR 2 Ch App 21

**Facts:** A seller told a prospective buyer that the farms on the land were 'fully let' without disclosing that although the property is fully let the tenants were about to leave.

**Ratio: The Court held that not revealing this fact distorted the picture of the real situation and therefore there had been misrepresentation.**

**Application:** Even if the statement is true it can be considered to be a misrepresentation if it is a half –truth.

**Ongoing Silence**

**General Principle: If a statement was true when it was first made but subsequently becomes false before the contract is entered into, the representor is under an obligation to correct the statement. If he fails to do so, it will amount to misrepresentation.**

### With v O'Flanagan [1936] Ch 575

**Facts:** A doctor selling a medical practice told a prospective purchaser that the practice was worth £2,000 p.a. The statement was true at the time. However, he fell ill and the income was almost nothing at the time of the contract. The purchaser was not told.

**Ratio: The failure to disclose the change in circumstances was held to be a misrepresentation as he has continued to make a representation which has subsequently become false.**

**Contracts of Utmost Good Faith**

**General Principle: Sometimes the relationship between the parties gives rise to a duty of disclosure (i.e. car insurance contacts). These contracts are known as *uberrimaefidei* (utmost**

**good faith).**

**Tate v Williamson** (1866) LR 2 Ch App 55
**Facts:** The plaintiff who was a young man sought the advice of the defendant as he was heavily in debt. He advised the plaintiff to sell some land in order to raise money to pay his debts. The defendant then offered to buy the land for half its real value. Certain material facts that were known to the defendant were not disclosed to the plaintiff.
**Ratio: The Court held that there had been a misrepresentation as the defendant was under a duty to disclose all the material facts to the defendant.**

**Reliance**

**General Principle: For a misrepresentation to be applicable it must have been relied upon by the other party.**

**Horsefall v Thomas** [1862] 1 H & C 90
**Facts:** The vendor sold a gun to the purchaser which blew apart after 6 shots had been fired. The vendor had actively concealed a defect in the gun and this was a fraudulent misrepresentation.
**Ratio: The purchaser had not inspected the gun prior to purchase so although there had been a misrepresentation, the purchaser had not been aware of it and thus it had not induced the purchaser to buy.**

**Opportunity to discover the truth**

**Redgrave v Hurd** (1881) 20 Ch D 1
**Facts:** A solicitor was induced to buy a practice on the basis of an innocent misrepresentation as to the value of the practice and the property attached to it. The solicitor had the accounts made available to him, though he did not examine them.
**Ratio: He was able to rescind the contract despite the fact that the accounts would have revealed the untruth of the statements made to him.**

## Types of Misrepresentation

### Fraudulent Misrepresentation

**General Principle:** A fraudulent misrepresentation is actionable if the party relied on it before entering into the contract.

**Derry v Peek** [1889] 14 App Cas 337
**Facts:** Under a special Act of Parliament, a tramway company was empowered to operate certain tramways by means of animal power. It was also empowered to use mechanical power with the consent of the Board of Trade. It wanted to raise capital and issued a prospectus for the sale of shares stating that it had the right to use mechanical power. The plaintiff, relying on this, purchased shares. The company was later wound up because the Board of Trade refused to allow the use of mechanical power over the whole tramway.
**Ratio: The false statement in the prospectus was not fraudulent. The directors had honestly believed that obtaining consent was a pure formality.**

### Negligent Misrepresentation

**General Principle: In certain cases, damages may be recovered for a negligent misstatement which causes financial loss.**

**Hedley Byrne v Heller & Partners** (1964) AC 465
**Facts:** The plaintiffs were asked for credit by Easipower. It was decided to ask Easipower's bankers for advice as to the financial standing of the company. The defendants, who were aware of the purpose behind the request, stated carelessly that the company was financially sound.
**Ratio: The defendants owed the plaintiffs a duty to take care to make sure that statement was accurate, but there was no liability in this case because of a disclaimer enclosed with the credit reference.**

## Innocent Misrepresentation

**General Principle:** Even innocent misrepresentation is actionable in certain cases if the other party relied on it.

**Redgrave v Hurd** (1881) 20 Ch D 1
**Facts:** A solicitor was induced to buy a practice on the basis of an innocent misrepresentation as to the value of the practice and the property attached to it. The solicitor had the accounts made available to him, though he did not examine them.
**Ratio: He was able to rescind the contract despite the fact that the accounts would have revealed the untruth of the statements made to him.**

## Remedies for Misrepresentation

### Rescission

**General Principle: Rescission is an equitable remedy which sets the contract aside and puts the parties in a position where they were when the contract had not taken place.**

**Long v Lloyd** [1958] 1 WLR 753
**Facts:** The plaintiff purchased a lorry. After the first journey some defects were found but when they were pointed out to the defendant he offered to meet half the costs of repair. This offer was accepted by the plaintiff. The following day on the second journey the lorry broke down and serious defects were discovered.
**Ratio: It was held that since the plaintiff had affirmed the contract by accepting the assistance with the repairs after the first journey and lost the right to rescind.**

### Indemnity Payment

Sometimes the courts order payment of money known as indemnity which is not the available for obligations which arise from the contract.

## Damages

Damages awarded by the courts will vary according to whether they were fraudulently negligently or innocently made.

### Fraudulent Misrepresentation & Negligent Misrepresentation

**If the misrepresentation is fraudulent then damages will reflect that and damages will be recoverable under the tort of deceit.**

**If the misrepresentation is negligent (and the claim is in tort) then damages are recoverable under Hedley Byrne v Heller & Partners (1964) AC 465 principle. If the claim is in contract, then you have to look at the Act i.e. the claim for damages will be under s. 2(1) Misrepresentation Act 1967.**

Section 2(1) Misrepresentation Act 1967

Where a person has entered into a contract after a misrepresentation has been made to him by another party thereto and as a result thereof he has suffered loss, then, if the person making the misrepresentation would be liable to damages in respect thereof had the misrepresentation been made fraudulently, that person shall be so liable notwithstanding that the misrepresentation was not made fraudulently, unless he proves that he had reasonable ground to believe and did believe up to the time the contract was made the facts represented were true.

### Innocent Misrepresentation

**General Principle: If the misrepresentor can prove the he had reasonable ground to believe the representation was true, it will be regarded as innocent and damages awarded will reflect this.**

Under s.2(1) Misrepresentation Act 1967

Where a person has entered into a contract after a misrepresentation has been made to him by another party thereto and as a result thereof he has suffered loss, then, if the person making the misrepresentation would be liable to damages in respect thereof had the misrepresentation been made fraudulently, that person shall be so liable notwithstanding that the misrepresentation was not made fraudulently, unless he proves that he had reasonable ground to believe and did believe up to the time the contract was made the facts represented were true.

**General Principle: If the damage cannot be undone by rescission then damages are used as a remedy under s.2 (2) Misrepresentation Act 1967.**

Under s.2(2) Misrepresentation Act 1967 the remedies for an innocent misrepresentation are rescission or damages in lieu of rescission. The claimant cannot claim both. Damages are assessed on normal contractual principles.

**East v Maurer [1991]** 2 All ER 733
**Facts:** The plaintiff purchased one of 2 hairdressing salons owned by the defendant following a misrepresentation by the defendant that he would not be working in the second salon very often and he would be working abroad. He continued to work in the second salon with the result that the clients from the first migrated to the second.
**Ratio: Damages were awarded for the profit the plaintiff might have made had he bought a different salon in same area. It was lower than if the defendant had warranted he would not work in the second salon and damages had been for breach of contract.**

**Remoteness of Damages**

**General Principle: The Courts use 'remoteness of damages' test to calculate damages to award to the aggrieved party.**

**Smith New Court Securities Ltd v Scrimgeour Vickers (Asset Management)** 1996] 4 All ER 769
**Facts:** The plaintiffs bought over £23 million of shares in the Italian company Ferranti on a fraudulent misrepresentation that there were other active purchasers in the market, which was not the case. Unknown to either party, the shares in the company were lesser than the market price because Ferranti was also defrauded by a man who sold a company to Ferranti for a large amount of

money. Once this was exposed to the market, the share prices collapsed and the plaintiffs incurred a loss of over £11 million. The question before the Court was whether the damages must be restricted to what they had paid over the market price or whether they could recover the whole of the loss that they had suffered.

**Ratio: The House of Lords held that the plaintiffs could recover the whole loss as the damages had to be assessed to include all the losses flowing naturally from the original fraud.**

**Application:** The Court will check whether the loss was flowing directly from the fraud.

# Question and Answer

- Misrepresentation Problem Question

## Question

Jack is considering buying his aunt Jess's house as an investment. During the negotiations, Jess states, "This house is worth £200,000 and I've had two separate valuations from estate agents verifying that, but since I love you so much I'll sell it to you for £180,000." Jess has not received any valuations from estate agents and the house is worth only £120,000. Jack buys the house for £180,000. Two weeks after Jack has completed the sale and moved into the house, he discovers that Jess did not receive any valuations from estate agents. The same week, Jack discovers that the value of the house has been reduced to £80,000 due to serious damage caused by the collapse of a supporting wall. At this point, a buyer offers £80,000 for the house. Jack does not sell the house until three months later, when Jack only receives £75,000 for the house because of a general fall of the property market.

Advise Jack.

## Answer

### Introduction

This is an advice for Jack regarding the purchase of his Aunt Jess's house. It will discuss whether the contract can be set aside on grounds of misrepresentation, rather than on grounds of breach of contract. This advice will thus discusses the following: whether misrepresentation is established, the type of misrepresentation, the remedies available to Jack and the summary of advice.

### Term or representation

Jack's aunt Jess during the pre-contract negotiations made several statements, the main one being: *"I've had two separate valuations from estate agents"*. The second was the value of the house was *"worth £200,000"*. The third being silent about the defective wall.

The latter two statements stem from the first that a valuation had been carried out. If in fact a valuation had been carried out it would have given Jack a clear indication of i) the value of the house; ii) and the condition of the house, thus exposing any defects. Would these statements have become terms? Quite possibly. But the expected market value did not appear on the contact; neither did any defects or the soundness of the house. Therefore this advice advises on the assumption that the aunt's statements are representations, the following advice thus discusses whether these representation are actionable misrepresentations.

## The misrepresentation

The following statement of Jess gives rise to a potential claim for misrepresentation: *"This house is worth £200,000 and I've had two separate valuations from estate agents verifying that"*. Poole defines an actionable misrepresentation as: *"an unambiguous, false, statement of fact made to the claimant, which induces the claimant to enter into the contract with the statement maker."*[201]If the above elements are established Jack may have an arguable case for misrepresentation which can make the contract voidable.

## Unambiguous statement

The statements made by Jess about both the existence of valuations and the market value of the house was unambiguous and did not lend itself to misinterpretation on the part of Jack. In order to form the basis of a claim the representation must indeed be clear, keeping in mind that the representor may not be liable on the grounds that the representee unreasonably interpreted it. In **McInerny v Lloyd'sBank Ltd**[202]the Court of Appeal held that the representor may not be liable when the representee misconstrues the representation[203]. Here Jack has believed Jess in what she is saying and not unreasonably constructed neither the value of the house or the fact that a valuation has been carried out. He has been categorically been told this.

---

[201]Poole, Jill. *Textbook on contract law*. Oxford University Press, 2012, at 515
[202](1974) 1 Lloyd's Rep 246
[203] McInerny v Lloyd's Bank Ltd [1974] 1 Lloyd's Rep 246

## False Statement

Jack discovers that Jess did not receive any valuations from estate agents. To be actionable misrepresentation the representation must be substantially false, as opposed to substantially correct. In **Avon Insurance Plc v Swire Fraser Ltd**[204], Rix J stated: *"[A] representation may be true without being entirely correct, provided it is substantially correct and the difference between what is represented and what is actually correct would not have been likely to induce a reasonable person in the position of the claimants to enter into the contracts"*. Therefore Jess saying the valuations existed to justify the market value of£200,000 was a false statement which ultimately induced Jack

## Statement of existing fact

Poole explains that to be actionable, a representation must be a statement of fact. Factual statements have to be distinguished from statements which are not actionable such as: statements of opinion, future intention as well as instances of silence.[205]

## A statement of opinion

Although a statement of opinion is not a statement of fact, it may be considered a statement of fact if it is proved that the representor did not believe in it or if a reasonable man with the knowledge of the representor would not have held. In **Smith v Land and House Property Corporation**,[206] Bowen LJ held:

> *"Where the facts are equally well known to both parties, what one of them says to the other is frequently nothing but an expression of opinion...But if the facts are not equally known to both sides, then a statement of opinion by the one who knows the facts best involves very often a statement of material fact, for he impliedly states that he knows the facts that justifies his opinion."*

---

[204](2000) 1 All ER (Comm) 573
[205] Poole, Jill. Textbook on contract law. Oxford University Press, 2012. 523
[206](1884) 28 ChD 7 (CA)

As Jess said the house was worth £200,000 she could argue that this was merely her opinion. But using the above authority, Jack can argue that since her opinion was backed by the fact there was a valuation to verify this. She is saying she has the expert opinion of a valuation; this makes the statement one of fact rather than opinion.

**Statement of valuation and silence about the wall**

Jess's false statement about the existence of a valuation leads to the non-disclosure of the defect in the wall. These are linked. Indeed, if a valuation was carried out, it would have informed Jack about the state of the wall and certainly factored it into the evaluation of the market price of the house. As a result, the value of the house has been reduced to £80,000 due to serious damage caused by the collapse of a supporting wall, Jack may argue that Jess's lack of disclosure about the state of the wall at the time of the negotiations amounts to silence, which may be considered a misrepresentation under the circumstances at hand.

Silence does not generally amount to misrepresentation, according to the principle of *caveat emptor*. Thus a claim on the ground of misrepresentation may not be based on it. The case **Keates v The Earl of Cadogan**[207] defines this area of law. The Court established the principle that there is no general duty of disclosure and that it is justified that such a general duty would lack precision as it would not be possible to define which facts would have to be disclosed in advance. Thus Jess has no general duty to disclose facts that may impact Jack's willingness to enter into the contract. The case **Sykes v Taylor-Rose**[208]further establishes that the courts will assess what duty of disclosure exists on a case by case basis.

However, one line of argument that Jess and her lawyer may attempt to use is that a valuation was being sought, however did not happen in time. As we will see later, this is the only way she can show she had reasonable belief in the statement (an argument she will have to make when arguing remedy). If the court accepts a

---

[207](1851) 10 CB 591
[208][2004] EWCA Civ 299

valuation was sought then at the beginning of negotiations, where a statement is made which is true but which, prior to entering into the contract becomes false, the representor is under an obligation to correct the representation. If Jess then fails to inform Jack that no valuation has been done and allows Jack to enter into the contract still believing that a valuation has been carried out then she will be liable for misrepresentation.

In **With v O'Flanagan**[209] a man selling his medical practice stated at the beginning of the negotiation that it was worth a certain price. During the course of the negotiations the price fell dramatically and the man did not inform the buyer of that fact. The court ruled that by his silence about the change of price he had made an ongoing representation[210].

Using the above authority the fact that Jess has not told Jack that there is no valuation and this is inconstant with the obligation where a continuing representation is made which becomes false. The same applies to the valuation where one did not materialise at the time of sale. Indeed, had the valuations happened, the defect in the wall would have been exposed. It may be Jess already knowns about the defect in the wall, but remaining silent about it does not constitute actionable misrepresentation because the duty of disclosure does not extend to physical defects in the property itself. It may be that the loss of value to the house because of the wall could still be recoverable as it stems from the misrepresentation about the valuation.

**Statement addressed to the party misled**

Jess and Jack negotiated the contract face to face and Jack is thus aware of the representation. For the misrepresentation to be actionable, the representation must be addressed to the party misled. The authority for the law is the case **Peek v Gurney**[211]. It is thus established that Jess addressed her statements to Jack.

---

[209][1936] Ch 575
[210]Bigwood, R. (2005). PRE-CONTRACTUAL MISREPRESENTATION AND THE LIMITS OF THE PRINCIPLE IN WITH V. O'FLANAGAN. *The Cambridge Law Journal, 64*(01), 94-125.
[211](1873) LR 6 HL 377

## Statement inducing the contract

In order to be actionable misrepresentation, the representation must have been at least one of the reasons Jack entered into the contract. The authority on the law is the case is **Edgington v Fitzmaurice**[212]. Jack was induced into entering into the contract and paid the stated price for the house because Jess had stated that the valuations had taken place and that in turn the price of the house was validated by expert opinion. There was no other inducement.

If Jess wishes to prove that Jack bought the house independent of her representation, the burden of proof is on her to disprove Jack's claim. Indeed, the representor has to prove that the representee did not rely on the representation to enter the contract, according to **Peekay Intermark Ltd & Anor v Australia & New Zealand Banking Group Ltd**[213] (2006). Based on the facts of the case it is unlikely that Jess would successfully prove that her representation was immaterial in Jack's decision to enter into the contract. As we will now discuss, had Jack conducted his own valuation of the house Jess chances to dismiss Jack's claim would have been greater.

## Opportunity to discover the truth

Jack could have carried out his own independent valuation about the house, yet he did not, relying instead on Jess statement about valuations. The case of **Attwood v Small**[214] establishes the principle that when a representee conducts his own independent investigation about the representation, he will no longer be considered to have relied on it but instead on his own analysis. Since Jack did not conduct independent valuation of the house, Jess may not claim that Jack relied on his own judgement.

Moreover, the fact that Jack did not conduct his own investigation does not render his reliance on the representation immaterial. The case **Redgrave v Hurd**[215], establishes that are presentee has no

---

[212](1885) 29 Ch D 459
[213](2006) EWCA Civ 386
[214](1838) 6 CL & F 232
[215](1881) 20 Ch D1

obligation to verify the statement of the representor and that he may have relied on the misrepresentation to enter the contract. In addition, the case, **Smith v Eric S. Bush**[216], details the law, specifying that the more commercially aware are presentee is the more it is expected that he investigates the representation and conversely, the least commercially aware the representee is the less he is expected to investigate the representation. Thus we can conclude using the authorities above that as this not a commercial transaction and Jack was private buyer purchasing the house from his Aunt he had no duty to conduct own investigations. In addition, it would be reasonable for Jack to have trusted his aunty. Then again this is the sale of a house as an investment worth £200,000 and this size of investment warrants a valuation through survey in our current volatile housing market. Although any solicitor conducting Jack conveyance would insist on an independent valuation, this advice nevertheless considers there was no duty on Jack to carry out a valuation.

**The type of misrepresentation**

We must now consider the type of misrepresentation that has occurred, because this will have an effect of the outcome of the remedy available.

Fraudulent misrepresentation was articulated by Lord Herschell in the House of Lords when he decided the case **Derry v Peek**[217]and defined fraud as follows:

> "...it must be shown that a false representation was made (a) knowingly, or (b) without belief in its truth, or (c) recklessly, careless whether it be true or false."

The burden of proof is on the representee to establish that the elements above are present that is that the representor knew his statement was not true, or did not believe it was true or was reckless about its truth. As we do not know what Jess's state of mind was when she said *"this house is worth £200,000 and I've had two separate valuations from estate agents verifying that..."*it

---

[216](1990) 1 AC 831
[217](1889) LR14 App Cas 337

is unlikely that fraudulent misrepresentation may be established. The facts provided do not appear sufficient to base a claim on the tort of deceit.

Section 2(1) of the Misrepresentation Act 1967[218] provides:

> *"Where a person has entered into a contract after a misrepresentation has been made to him by another party thereto and as a result thereof he has suffered loss, then, if the person making the misrepresentation would be liable to damages in respect thereof had the misrepresentation been made fraudulently, that person shall be so liable notwithstanding that the misrepresentation was not made fraudulently, unless he proves that he had reasonable grounds to believe and did believe up to the time the contract was made that the facts represented were true."*

According to the definition of a negligent misrepresentation above, a negligent misrepresentation is a misrepresentation which Jess may believe but has no "reasonable grounds to believe." Also, the case **Howard Marine & Dredging Co. Ltd v A. Ogden & Sons (Excavations) Ltd**[219] further details that at the defendant must substantiate his beliefs. According to the authorities above the burden of proof moves to Jess to prove that her belief the house was worth £200,000 was grounded on serious evidence[220]. If she proves this the misrepresentation will be deemed innocent misrepresentation, according to **Thomas Witter Ltd v TBP Industries Ltd**[221]. To conclude it is likely on a balance of probabilities that the misrepresentation will be negligent because on the papers there is no reason offered for her false statement. Also, where Jess is found liable for a negligent misrepresentation under S(2), Jack will be able to claim the same level of damages as if it the misrepresentation had been fraudulent. Indeed, the case **Royscott Trust Ltd v Rogerson**[222] confirms that liability in damages cover all losses consequential to the misrepresentation.

---

[218]Section 2(1)Misrepresentation Act 1967
[219](1978) QB 574
[220]Sealy, L. S. (1978). Contract—Damages for Misrepresentation. *The Cambridge Law Journal, 37*(02), 229-232.
[221](1996) 2 All ER 573
[222](1991) 2 QB 297

Based on the above elements, this advice recommends that Jack bases his claim on s.(2) of the Misrepresentation Act 1967.

**The remedy**

According to Poole, the effect of misrepresentation is to render the contract voidable but not void and rescission is available for misrepresentation under the Section 2(2) and generally, rescission will be awarded only where the parties can be restored to their original position by returning all the property transferred between the parties under the contract.[223]As there has been negligent misrepresentation, Jack would have been entitled to rescind the contract with Jess.

However, this option is not available to Jack for he has sold the house for £75,000 and according to **Clarke v Dickson**[224]this prevents him and Jess to be restored to their original pre-contract positions.

Thus Jack can only claim damages, under Section 2(2) of the Misrepresentation Act 1967. Damages for fraudulent misrepresentation are potentially the greatest available for misrepresentation. However, it must be borne in mind that an action for negligent misrepresentation, under s2(1) MA 1967, will often match those that would be available for fraudulent misrepresentation, if Jess cannot prove she had reasonable belief in the statement.

The damages that are recoverable are everything that stems from the misrepresentation. According to **William Sindall plc v Cambridgeshire County Council**[225] liability for damages under section 2(2) are interpreted as meaning "*the difference in value between what the claimant was misled into believing he was acquiring and the value of what he in fact received.*" Jack starting cost was £180,000. He cannot recover what he was told the house was worth because he did not pay this amount (£200,000). He cannot recover loss of profit (£20,000) because it does not stem

---

[223]Poole, Jill. *Textbook on contract law*, Oxford University Press, 2012, at 536
[224](1858) EB & E 148
[225](1994) 1 WLR 1016

from the misrepresentation. He can arguably recover for the loss of £40,000 because the wall collapsed and this was the decrease in value, and as this was a direct result of the misstatement about the valuation which would have informed him of the wall and the state of the house. If he knew about the true value and the defect he would probably not have entered into this contract. The shortfall of £5,000 will not be recoverable as this is attributable to the market forces and not the misrepresentation. Therefore, the total he will recoup is £75,000 from the sale of the house plus £40,000 due to the collapse of the wall. This amounts to £115,000. Thus he has made a loss of £65,000.

**Summary of advice**

The advice proposes that Jack places a claim for damages for misrepresentation under Section 2(1) of the Misrepresentation Act 1967. If the courts find that the misrepresentation is material, Jack may be awarded the damages flowing from the misrepresentation that is £40,000.

# Chapter 12 Mistake

## Mistake

Various mistakes may occur in the negotiations leading to the formation of a contract, and they are not all treated the same. We distinguish three kinds of mistake, though different writers use different names and different classifications. A common mistake, we shall say, occurs when both parties make the same mistake (eg as to the existence, ownership or nature of the subject-matter of the contract). A mutual mistake occurs when each party is mistaken as to the intentions of the other in respect of the contract, and a unilateral mistake occurs when just one party is mistaken as to the identity or intention of the other, or as to the nature of a document being signed. A mistake renders a contract void.

## Common mistake

Two kinds of common mistake render the contract void: *res extinca* and *res sua*. If the contract concerns *res extinca* - that is, the subject matter of the contract no longer exists, or which never existed at all, then the contract is void.

**General Principle: a common mistake will only render a contract void if it amounts to a fundamental mistake.**

**Bell v Lever Brothers** [1932] AC 161, HL
**Facts:** Bell and Snelling had been appointed chairman and vice-chairman of a company controlled by Lever brothers. Their contracts were for five years but before this their posts were made redundant and compensation was agreed. Lever Brothers later discovered that both men had committed breaches of their contract and they could have been dismissed for misconduct .The Company sued to recover the compensation what was paid. Both the men had forgotten the mistakes and were under the opinion that the contracts were valid, and had not tried to defraud the Lever Brothers in anyway.
**Ratio: The House of Lords said the contract was valid in spite**

of the common mistake as to the security of the employment: there was no deliberate deception and the common mistake as to quality was not enough. Lord Atkin claimed that a contract would be void if both parties were mistaken "as to the existence of some quality which makes the thing without the quality essentially different from the thing as it was believed to be".

**Application:** Only a mistake as to quality of the subject matter is not enough to render a contract void (unless it is a fundamental mistake as to subject matter).

**General Principle: a contract will be void for a common mistake if the mistake is due to the fault of one of the parties.**

**Couturier v Hastie (1856)** 10 ER 1065, HL
**Facts:** A contract was made for the sale of a cargo of corn which (unknown to either party) had already been sold.
**Ratio: The House of Lords did not declare the contract void directly as the Court held that it is a common commercial practice to buy "a risk" rather than a cargo as such but it denied the seller's claim for payment.**
**Application:** the contract will be rendered void if there has been a common mistake.

**Scott v Coulson** [1903] 2 Ch 249, CA
**Facts:** A person took out an insurance policy on the life of a person who (unknown to either party) was already dead.
**Ratio: The Court of Appeal held the contract was void due to the presence of a common mistake.**

**General Principle: A contract involving a common mistake as to *res sua*, where the subject matter already belongs to the supposed buyer, is also void. The seller is giving no value for the consideration given by the buyer.**

**Cooper v Phibbs (1867)** LR 2 HL 149, HL
**Facts:** The Plaintiff leased a salmon farm from the Defendant which, it later emerged, was the Plaintiff's property all the time.
**Ratio: The House of Lords held the contract void for common mistake, but made an order in its equitable jurisdiction that Defendant should have a charge on the property based on the**

**value of the improvements he had made.**
**Application:** There can be no contract in such cases because the subject matter of the contract already belongs to the buyer.

## Mistake as to Quality

**General Principle: A mistake as to quality will not affect the validity of a contract.**

**Bell v Lever Brothers** [1932] AC 161, HL
**Facts:** Bell and Snelling had been appointed chairman and vice-chairman of a company controlled by Lever brothers. Their contracts were for five years but before this their posts were made redundant and compensation was agreed. Lever Brothers later discovered that both men had committed breaches of their contract and they could have been dismissed for misconduct .The Company sued to recover the compensation what was paid. Both the men had forgotten the mistakes and were under the opinion that the contracts were valid, and had not tried to defraud the Lever Brothers in anyway.
**Ratio: The House of Lords said the contract was valid in spite of the common mistake as to the security of the employment: there was no deliberate deception and the common mistake as to quality was not enough. Lord Atkin claimed that a contract would be void if both parties were mistaken "as to the existence of some quality which makes the thing without the quality essentially different from the thing as it was believed to be".**
**Application:** Only a mistake as to quality of the subject matter is not enough to render a contract void (unless it is a fundamental mistake as to subject matter).

## Cross- Purpose Mistake

This occurs when both the parties are mistaken but they are mistaken about different things. Two types of cross- purpose mistake: mutual mistakes and unilateral mistakes.

## Mutual Mistakes

**General Principle: Where each party is mistaken as to the**

intentions of the other, there is no consensus ad idem and hence no contract.

**Raffles v Wichelhaus** (1864) 159 ER 375, Exchequer
**Facts:** The plaintiff sought to enforce a contract for a cargo of cotton "ex Peerless out of Bombay". In fact there were two ships of that name, sailing from Bombay some months apart, and the parties had understood things differently.
**Ratio: The court held the contract was void for mutual mistake, and gave the judgment in the favour of the defendant.**

**Scriven Bros v Hindley** [1913] 3 KB 564, Lawrence J
**Facts:** The Plaintiff offered various amounts of hemp and tow at auction, and put up two lots with identical markings. The defendant inspected one, found it to be hemp, and bid for the other on the assumption that it was hemp too. Since the price of hemp is considerably higher than that of tow, the auctioneer realised the mistake but said nothing.
**Ratio: Although at first this appears to be a unilateral mistake, in that the second bale did objectively contain tow, the judge found a mutual mistake in that one could not state with certainty which commodity formed the basis of the contract. The catalogue description of the lots was not clear and a reasonable person could easily have believed that two bales of hemp were being offered; the contract was therefore void.**
**Application:** when a contract is concluded with one party thinking correctly but the other party thinking wrongly- neither was aware that they were at cross- purposes – then the contract will be rendered void.

**General Principle: From the available evidence if a reasonable man would infer the existence of a contract in a given sense, in spite of a mutual mistake, the contract can be binding on both the parties.**

**Smith v Hughes (1871)** LR 6 QB 597, QB
**Facts:** The Plaintiff offered some oats for sale, and the Defendant agreed to buy them. The Plaintiff knew they were new oats and thought that was what the Defendant wanted however the Defendant wanted old oats and thought that was what he was getting.

Ratio: The Court of Queen's Bench said the contract was valid, since the two minds were ad idem on the purchase and sale of oats, and at variance only as to their quality. The contract was quite clear - it was for a quantity of oats, a sample of which the Defendant had inspected - and there had been no misrepresentation, so the Plaintiff could not rely on a mistake induced by his own carelessness. Where a specific article is offered for sale without any express or implied warranty, said Cockburn CJ, and the buyer has every opportunity of inspecting the goods for himself, the principle caveat emptor applies.

Unilateral mistake

General Principle: A unilateral mistake occurs when just one party is mistaken as to some aspect of the contract, and the other is or is presumed to be aware of this mistake, then the contract will be rendered void.

Hartog v Colin & Shields [1939] 3 All ER 566, Singleton J
Facts: The defendant offered to sell 30000 hare skins to the Plaintiff and quoted a certain price "per pound", and the Plaintiff accepted. This was an error: the price should have been "per piece", and since all the preliminary negotiations had been on a "per piece" basis (as was the custom of the trade). On realising their mistake, the sellers refused to deliver the skins and were sued by the buyers for breach of contract.
Ratio: The judge dismissed the Plaintiff's claim for delivery at the quoted price as he could not reasonably have supposed that the offer expressed the defendant's real intention, and must have known it to be a mistake.
Application: there will be no contract if the buyers were aware of the seller's mistake.

General Principle: If the unilateral mistake is as to the identity of one of the contracting parties, where the identity of the other party is of fundamental importance, will render the contract void.

Shogun Finance v Hudson [2004] 1 All ER 215, HL
Facts: A rogue bought a car on hire purchase from a dealer,

producing a driving licence (probably stolen) that showed a false name. The finance company carried out the normal credit checks against the name on the licence, and subsequently approved the loan. The rogue sold the car to an innocent purchaser and subsequently defaulted on the loan. [Note: the Hire Purchase Act 1964 provides that a person who buys in good faith from a "hire purchaser", believing him to be an outright owner, acquires a good title.

**Ratio: The Court of Appeal and the House of Lords decided that Company was entitled to repossess the car: they clearly intended to hire the car only to the person whose credit they had checked, and the rogue had not acquired any title that could be transmitted to the purchaser. Moreover, the Hire Purchase Act did not apply because the contract between the fraudster and the purchaser was invalid.**

**Mistaken Identity**

**General Principle: A party seeking to avoid a contract on grounds of mistaken identity, even as a misrepresentation must therefore show that he intended to contract with some particular person other than the one with whom he contracted.**

**Cundy v Lindsay** (1878) LR 3 AC 459, HL
**Facts:** A rogue Blenkarn, writing from 37 Wood Street, purported to represent the highly respectable firm of Blenkiron & Co (123 Wood Street) and so obtained goods from the plaintiff without paying for them, selling them on to defendant who bought them in good faith. When the plaintiff sought to recover the goods (which had never been paid for) the issue before the court was whether there was a contract between the plaintiffs and Blenkarn. It there was, Blenkarn would have become the owner and would have been able to transfer ownership to the defendant.
**Ratio: The House of Lords held that there was no contract between Blenkarn and the plaintiffs, because they had intended all along to deal with Blenkiron & Co and not with a Mr. Blenkarnof whom they had never even heard. Hence, the contract was rendered void.**

## Face- to- face Principle

**General Principle:** where there has been a face- to-face contract between the contracting parties, there is a strong presumption that each party wants to contract with the other.

**Ingram v Little** [1961] 3 All ER 332, CA

**Facts:** A man called on two sisters, the Plaintiffs advertising a car for sale and agreed to buy it, persuading the Plaintiffs to accept a cheque by claiming to be a Mr Hutchinson of a certain address. Having checked the address in the telephone directory, the plaintiff reluctantly took the cheque and allowed the man to take the car. The man disappeared and the cheque bounced, and the plaintiff sought to recover the car from an innocent third party to whom the man had sold it.

**Ratio: The Court of Appeal said the offer to sell by cheque had been made only to Mr Hutchinson; the contract of sale was therefore void and the plaintiffs were entitled to the car.**

**Application:** even though the contract had been concluded face-to-face it was considered to be void.

## Mistake relating to documents

When there is a mistake relating to a written document there are two special remedies: *non est factum* and rectification.

## Non est factum

Where a person signs a document believing it to be something totally different from what it actually is, then the common law remedy of *non est factum* can render the contract void.

## Rectification

Where a part of the written document is alleged not to reflect accurately the intention of the parties, rectification may be used to alter the written document so that it coincides with the true intention of the parties.

**Bates v Wyndham's Lingerie** [1981] 1 All ER 1077, CA
**Facts:** The Defendant held a lease from the Plaintiff, whose terms included an option to renew the rent agreed between the parties or determined by arbitration. Through a clerical error on the Plaintiff's part, the second renewal omitted the reference to arbitration. The Defendant was aware of this omission but said nothing. When the time came for the next rent review, the Defendant refused either to agree to the Plaintiff's proposed rent or to submit to arbitration. The Plaintiff therefore sought rectification of the contract, and the Defendant counterclaimed for a declaration that they were entitled to occupy the premises rent free until the lease expired.
**Ratio: The Court of Appeal ordered rectification. Where one party knew the document did not give effect to the parties' intention, he was estopped from resisting rectification in order to take advantage of the other's error.**
**Application:** the remedy of rectification only applied if the contract has been put down in writing.

# Question and Answer

- Mistake Problem Question

## Question

Assume that Skywards Ltd are granted planning permission to build their office block. As the block promises to be the tallest building in Manchester, it receives much local press coverage.

Irmina, a supplier of building materials, is contacted by Michael, who introduces himself as the chairman of ReachSkywards Ltd. Michael tells Irmina that his company needs to place a large order for various building materials, but that, until financing arrangements are concluded, this will have to be on credit. Irmina mistakenly believes that ReachSkywards is the company she has read about in the local papers, who are building the tallest office block in Manchester. As such, she thinks that there is little risk in allowing Michael to have credit. Consequently, they enter into a contract, and Michael takes delivery of the materials. Payment is to be made a month later. However, Michael does not pay. When Irmina, by now quite worried, tries to contact Michael she discovers her mistake. She phones Michael, who tells her, "too bad – sue us if you like, but there is a long list of creditors ahead of you! Those materials are ours now."

Advise Irmina (ignoring any issue of criminal liability).

## Answer

### Introduction

This paper advises Irmina on her position in relation to her agreement with Reachskywards Limited. The most desirable option for Irmina would be to put forward a successful argument to the effect that her mistake as to Michael's identity negatives her consent to the contract, rendering the contract void *ab initio*. This would allow Irmina to obtain the return of her goods from Michael. This paper will therefore examine the case law in this area in order to determine whether it is advisable for Irmina to pursue such an argument. This paper will then put forward the remedies available to Irmina as a result of Michael breaching the contract.

## Mistaken Identity

Where there is a genuine mistake as to the identity of one of the contracting parties, and this mistake is of fundamental importance, the mistake will render the contract void *ab initio*.[226]Should Irmina be able to show that her mistake, in thinking that Michael from Reachskywards Limited was in fact from Skywards Ltd, was of fundamental importance to her entering into the contract then she may be able to succeed in such an argument.

The most recent case involving mistaken identity **Shogun Finance Ltd v Hudson**[227] draws a distinction between contracts made *inter presentes* (face to face) and contracts made *inter absentes* (non-face to face, i.e. in writing). As it is not strictly clear from the facts provided in relation to the agreement between Irmina and Michael from Reachskywards Limited, how their contract was concluded, it is necessary to look at both scenarios in turn. This paper will then conclude having determined whether Irmina would succeed in such an argument.

The cases that will be examined all involve the goods being passed on to a third party, as it is not suggested that a third party is involved in Irmina's situation this paper will not examine this aspect of these cases.

### *Inter presentes*

Where two parties enter into a contract *inter presents* the legal principle is that there is a *prima facie* presumption that the parties intend to contract with the person in front of them, notwithstanding the fact that there has been a mistake.[228]The burden of rebutting this presumption falls on the party claiming that there has been a

---

[226] Catherine Elliot and Frances Quinn, Contract Law (7th edn, Pearson Education Limited 2009) 218
[227] [2004] 1 A.C. 919
[228] Michael Furmston, Cheshire, Fifoot&Furmston's Law of Contract (15thedn, Oxford University Press 2007) 310

mistake.[229] As Irmina would therefore carry this burden it is necessary to consider her likelihood of success in rebutting the presumption.

In **Phillips v Brooks Limited**[230]and **Lewis v Averay**[231] the innocent parties were unsuccessful in rebutting the *prima facie* presumption that they had intended to deal with the person in front of them. The courts concluded that although they may have been mistaken as to the identity of the other party, this was not of fundamental importance. The mistake that both innocent parties had made was a mistake as to the attributes of the other parties, namely their creditworthiness, which was not enough to render a contract void *ab initio*.

In **Ingram v Little**[232] however, although the facts were very similar to **Phillips v Brooks Limited** and **Lewis v Averay**, the innocent party was successful in rebutting the *prima facie* presumption. The courts found that the identity of the other party was of fundamental importance to the Ingram sisters, as they only agreed to the contract after checking the identity of the other party. The contract was as a result rendered void *ab initio*.

The irreconcilable decisions reached in these *inter presentaes* cases that relate to very similar facts, made this area of law uncertain,[233] until they were considered in *Shogun Finance Ltd v Hudson*. Lord Nicholls and Lord Phillips of Worth Matravers both preferred the dissenting judgement of Devlin LJ in **Ingram v Little** which was in line with the decisions in **Phillips v Brooks Limited** and **Lewis v Averay,** and Lord Millet and Lord Walker went even further, being of the opinion that *Ingram v Little* had been wrongly decided.[234] As a result of the *obiter* in **Shogun Finance Ltd v Hudson** it is clear that *Ingram v Little* will not be followed. There is now certainty that the presumption that parties in *inter presentaes* cases intend to deal with the person in front of them is a strong presumption that will be very difficult to rebut,

---

[229] ibid
[230][1919] 2 K.B. 243
[231][1973] 1 W.L.R. 510
[232][1961] 1 Q.B. 31
[233] Ewan Mckendrick, Contract Law (8[th]edn, Palgrave Macmillan Law Masters 2009) 58
[234] ibid

just as in **Phillips v Brooks Limited** and **Lewis v Averay**.

Therefore if the agreement between Irmina and Michael from Reachskywards Limited was made *inter praesentes* then it is likely that the court would find that Irmina had intended to contract with him, despite her mistake in thinking that he was from Skywards Limited. They would be unable to conclude that her mistake had been one as to identity, thus rendering the contract void *ab inito*. They would instead conclude that the mistake made by her was one as to his attributes, his creditworthiness, thus leaving the contract intact.

*Inter absentes*

Where two parties enter into a contract *inter absentes* the courts look to the construction of the written document(s) to determine whom the parties intended to contract with, the legal principle is that there is a presumption that the parties intended to contract with the persons named in writing.[235]Therefore if Irmina and Michael made their agreement in writing then her success in a mistaken identity argument would fall on whether the written communication contained the name of Reachskywards Limited or Skywards Limited. This can be seen from the cases of **Cunday v Lindsay**[236], **King's Norton Metal Co Ltd v Edridge, Merrett & Co Ltd**[237] and **Shogun Finance Ltd v Hudson**.

In **Cunday v Lindsay** a rogue by the name of Blenkarn wrote to Lindsay, purporting to be from a firm by the name of Blenkiron & Co who was known to Lindsay by reputation. The written communication contained the name Blenkiron & Co, as a result the court found that Lindsay had intended to contract with Blenkiron & Co. The court stated that Lindsay could not have intended to contract with the rogue Belnkarn as he was unknown to Lindsay and was not named in the written communication. As Blenkarn had induced Lindsay into entering into the contract by misrepresenting his identity, at the time of making the contract Blenkarn was aware of Lindsay's mistake. As a result the contract

---

[235] Janet O'Sullivan and Jonathan Hilliard, The Law of Contract (4[th]edn, Oxford University Press 2010) 57
[236](1877-78) L.R. 3 App. Cas. 459
[237](1897) 14 TLR 98

was found to be void *ab initio* for mistake, as Blenkiron & Co was not aware of the agreement.

An additional requirement for a mistaken identity argument to succeed is that there is an identifiable third party with whom there was an intention to contract with. In **King's Norton Metal Co Ltd v Edridge, Merrett & Co Ltd** a rogue named Wallis, had placed an order in writing to King's Norton, purporting to be from a company named Hallam & Co. This company was unknown to King's Norton prior to them receiving the order. In determining whom King's Norton had intended to contract with the court again looked to the construction of the written communication. The documents contained the name of Hallam & Co, as there was no separate entity known to King's Norton by that name the court found that they could not have intended to contract with anyone other than the person writing the letters to them. Therefore there was found to be a valid contract between King's Norton and the rogue Wallis, who had deceived them by use of a trading name rather than by pretending to be from another existing company known to them. The only mistake that had been made was a mistake as to the attributes of the other party, which was not enough to render the contract void *ab initio*.

In **Shogun Finance Ltd v Hudson** a rogue went into a car showroom purporting to be an individual by the name of Mr Patel, an individual worthy of credit, with him he had a driving licence to prove 'his' identity. The finance company ran a credit check on Mr Patel, satisfied he was worthy of credit they entered into the finance agreement with Mr Patel and allowed the rogue, whom they believed was Mr Patel, to take the vehicle. The court again looked to the construction of the written document and determined that the finance company had intended to contract with Mr Patel, who was named in the written document, and not the rogue. As a result the contract was found to be void *ab initio* for mistake, as Mr Patel was not aware of the agreement.

When applying these principles to the facts provided which relate to Irmina and Michael's agreement, it appears as though the written communication would contain the company name of Reachskywards Limited, rather than Skywards Limited. Michael introduced himself to Irmina as the chairman of Reachskywards

Limited. Irmina mistakenly thought that this was the company that she read about in the local papers (Skywards Limited). However this was not as a result of a misrepresentation on the part of Michael and there is nothing to suggest that Michael would have been aware of Irmina's mistake. As a result Irmina would be unsuccessful in arguing that she had been mistaken as to the other party's identity. She would be found to have intended to contract with Reachskywards Limited, therefore a contract a valid contract would have been concluded between the parties. Her mistake would be deemed to be a mistake as to the attributes of Reachskywards Limited, their creditworthiness, which would leave the contract intact.

If however the facts were different and the written communication between Irmina and Michael contained the company name of Skywards Limited, as they are a separate entity known to Irmina, it would be very likely that the courts would concluded that Irmina had intended to contract with Skywards Limited and therefore the contract would be void *ab initio* for mistake, as Skywards Limited knew nothing of the agreement.

**Breach of Contract**

It can be deduced from the facts provided that a valid contract exists between Irmina and Michael. (Reachskywards Limited). On this basis, it is advisable for Irmina to make a claim for an action for an agreed sum as a result of the breach of contract.[238]It is unclear from the facts provided as to the exact terms agreed between the parties. Should Irmina have expressly incorporated a 'reservation of title' clause into the contract, which is common practice in the building trade, then she would instead be able to reclaim possession of the goods.[239]

---

[238] Elliot and Quinn, op.cit. 357
[239] P.S. Atiyah, John N. Adams and Hector Macqueen, The Sale of Goods (11[th]edn, Pearson Longman 2005) 470

# Chapter 13 Frustration

If, after a contract is made, something happens, through no fault of the parties, to make its performance impossible, the contract is said to be frustrated and all the obligations arising under the contract come to an end. Broadly, there are three ways in which a contract becomes frustrated: when the performance of the contract impossible, when the contract becomes illegal and if the performance of a contract becomes pointless.

**What will lead to frustration?**

**Impossible**

**General Principle: If a contract lays down a particular method for the performance of the contract, and if that becomes impossible to carry out then the contract may be frustrated.**

**Nickool and Knight v Ashton Edridge & Co** (1901) 2 KB 126
**Facts:** A contract for the sale of cottonseed explicitly specified that 'the cottonseed was to be shipped per steamship Orlando from Alexandria ...during January' However, the Orlando could not make the journey to Alexandria from the Baltic in January.
**Ratio: The majority of the Court of Appeal agreed that the contract required performance in a stipulated manner and hence claimed that the contract was frustrated since this could not be done. However, in certain cases even though a method of performance has been stated in the contract, the contract can be interpreted as accepting an alternative method if necessary, and then the contract will not be considered frustrated if the stated method of performance is impossible.**
**Application:** A contract may become frustrated if the method of performance stated in the contract becomes impossible to perform.

**Illegal**

**General Principle: If after a contract has been formed, a change in law renders its performance illegal then the contract becomes frustrated.**

**Fibrosa Spolka Akcyjna v Fairbairn Lawson Combe Barbour Ltd** (1942) 2 All ER 122

**Facts:** In this case Fairbairn was contracted to manufacture machinery for Fibrosa, a Polish company in July 1939. By September 1940, parts of Poland were under German occupation, including the area to which the machinery was to be delivered.

**Ratio: The contract was considered to become frustrated on the grounds of the ban on trading with the enemy.**

**Pointless**

**General Principle: A contract may become frustrated when a supervening event makes performance of a contract completely pointless.**

**Krell v Henry** (1903) 2 KB 740

**Facts:** The defendant had contracted with the plaintiff to rent a suite of rooms in Pall Mall on the day of the coronation. The coronation procession was visible from the room, and the defendant had intended to sell tickets to people wanting to watch the procession. The contract did not mention the coronation but the high price reflected the importance of the day. When the coronation did not take place, the defendant did not want the room, but the plaintiff sued for rent.

**Ratio: The Court of Appeal held that even the contract was still capable of being performed it was frustrated when the coronation did not take place as 'it was the foundation of the contract'. The court held that a contract will be frustrated in cases where, 'the event which renders the contract incapable of performance is the non-existence of an express condition and is essential to the contract's performance'.**

**Application:** a contract will be frustrated when an express condition of a contract ceases to exist.

**What will not lead to frustration?**

**Contractual Provision**

A contract will not be frustrated if the contract makes provision for such a type of event which might otherwise frustrate the contract. For example, the inclusion of a *force majeure* clause enables the parties to the contract to allocate risks in relation to these events and allows the contract to continue in circumstances which would have otherwise amounted to frustration of the contract.

**Contract more onerous**

**General Principle: A contract is not frustrated due to the fact that performance has become more onerous or expensive.**

**Amalgamated Investment and Property Co Ltd v John Walker & Sons Ltd** [1976] 3 All ER 509 **Facts:** The defendants advertised a property as being suitable for redevelopment. Before the purchase the plaintiffs inquired whether the property was designated as being of special architectural or historic interest to which the defendants replied in the negative. However, unknown to the parties, the officials at the Department of the Environment listed the building as being of architectural and historic interest. The plaintiffs brought an action for rescission on the grounds of frustration.
**Ratio: The Court held that the doctrine of frustration did not apply because being listed is an inherent risk of which every buyer of a property should be aware. The performance of the contract has just become radically different from which has been undertaken by the contract and therefore is not frustrated.**

**Foreseen and foreseeable events**

**General Principle: when the event is something that the parties could have foreseen, it is generally assumed that the contract was made with the knowledge of the possibility of that event and therefore, it does not frustrate the contract.**

**Walton Harvey Ltd v Walker & Homfrays Ltd** [1931] 1 Ch 274
**Facts:** The defendants contracted to allow an advertising sign to be displayed on their hotel for a period of seven years. Before the seven years expired, the local authority demolished the hotel. The defendants maintained that this frustrated the contract.
**Ratio: The Court held that the defendants were liable to pay damages as they could have foreseen the risk of the local authority demolishing the hotel and should have made a**

**provision for that in the contract.**
**Application:** a foreseeable event does not frustrate the contract.

## Self- Induced Frustration

**General Principle: A contract will not be frustrated by any supervening event which is the fault of one of the parties to the contract.**

**The Super Servant Two** [1990] 1 Lloyds Rep 1
**Facts:** The defendants contracted with the plaintiffs to carry a drilling rig in of their two vessels, the Super Servant One and Two. Even before the contract could be carried out Super Servant Two sank; the defendants claimed that they wanted to use Super Servant Two for another contract and therefore the contract was frustrated.
**Ratio: The courts did not agree with this argument: the defendants had chosen to use the Super Servant One on the other contract. The decision also seemed to be based on the fact that the other contract was finalized after the contract with the plaintiffs was signed, and the defendants continued to negotiate the payments before deciding which contract to allocate to Super Servant One- hence, they were trying to use frustration to avoid an agreement.**

## Legal Consequences of Frustration

Once a contract is considered to be frustrated, it is automatically from the point at which the event occurred and the contract is understood to be discharged.

### Under the common law
If a frustrating event occurs under common law, the contract is terminated at the date of the frustrating event, irrespective of the wishes of the parties and the rights before the event are enforceable but no liability arises for obligations which would otherwise have accrued after the frustrating event took place.

This position was changed somewhat after the **Fibrosa** case.

**Fibrosa Spolka Akcyjna v Fairbairn Lawson Combe Barbour Ltd** (1942) 2 All ER 122

**Facts:** In this case Fairbairn was contracted to manufacture machinery for Fibrosa, a Polish company in July 1939. By September 1940, parts of Poland were under German occupation, including the area to which the machinery was to be delivered.
**Ratio: The House of Lords considered the injustice of the common law rule and stated that where there has been a total failure of consideration then the money paid could be recovered but the money due and payable need not be paid.**

### Frustration under statute

The Law Reform (Frustrated Contracts) Act of 1943 deals with obligations arising prior to the frustrating event.

### Obligations to pay money

Section 1(2) *All sums paid or payable to any party in pursuance of the contract before the time when the parties were so discharged (in this Act referred to as "the time of discharge") shall, in the case of sums so paid, be recoverable from him as money received by him for the use of the party by whom the sums were paid, and, in the case of sums so payable, cease to be so payable:*

*Provided that, if the party to whom the sums were so paid or payable incurred expenses before the time of discharge in, or for the purpose of, the performance of the contract, the court may, if it considers it just to do so having regard to all the circumstances of the case, allow him to retain or, as the case may be, recover the whole or any part of the sums so paid or payable, not being an amount in excess of the expenses so incurred.*

The aforementioned section builds on the **Fibrosa case** by providing that the money paid before the frustrating event can be recovered, even though the failure of consideration may be partial. It further explains that money payable (which was due before the day of the frustrating event but was not paid) ceases to be payable.

### Obligations other than to pay money

Section 1(3) *Where any party to the contract has, by reason of anything done by any other party thereto in, or for the purpose of, the performance of the contract, obtained a valuable benefit (other than a payment of money to which the last foregoing subsection applies) before the time of discharge, there shall be recoverable from him by the said other party such sum (if any), not exceeding the value of the said benefit to the party obtaining it, as the court considers just, having regard to all the circumstances of the case and, in particular,—*

*(a)the amount of any expenses incurred before the time of discharge by the benefited party in, or for the purpose of, the performance of the contract, including any sums paid or payable by him to any other party in pursuance of the contract and retained or recoverable by that party under the last foregoing subsection, and*

*(b)the effect, in relation to the said benefit, of the circumstances giving rise to the frustration of the contract.*

Therefore, if a party has received a valuable benefit under the contract before the frustrating event took place may be required to pay a sum for it. The court has to identity and value the benefit conferred and then to decide the 'just sum' to be awarded.

# Chapter 14 Remedies

This chapter deals with remedies that are available to the aggrieved party when there is a breach of contract. Without a remedy, a right would be of no value. Many remedial responses when a breach of contract occurs have evolved over the years.

## Equitable Remedies

These remedies are not available as a right but are provided at the court's discretion, which takes into account the parties' behaviour and the overall facts of the case.

## Specific Performance

A decree of specific performance is issued to the defendant compelling him to carry out his obligations under the contract. Generally, specific performance is available where the payment of a sum of money would not be an adequate remedy. Specific performance is, therefore, an appropriate remedy in cases of breach of contract for the sale or lease of land. The granting of this decree is however exercised on some well- established principles.

**General Principle:** **Where the damages are only nominal, specific performance may be ordered to prevent the other party from being 'unjustly enriched'.**

**Beswick v Beswick** (1968) AC 58
**Facts:** The plaintiff's husband sold his business to his nephew on a condition that an annual return allowance would be paid to him and after his death to his widow. After the husband's death the nephew went back on his promise and refused to pay the allowance to the window.
**Ratio: Even though the husband had clearly intended that his window would benefit from the contract, the court held that since she was not a party to the contract she could not sue the nephew on her behalf. However, the window was allowed to sue as the executor of her husband's estate. Moreover, since the husband had not suffered any loses the damages would be nominal. It was unjust for the defendant to get all the benefits**

under the contract without performing his part. Consequently, specific performance was ordered.

**Application:** Specific performance is used by the Courts to prevent one of the parties to the contract from being unjustly enriched.

**General Principle: Courts will not resort to specific performance if it can cause great hardship or unfairness to the defendant.**

**Patel v Ali** (1984) Ch 283

**Facts:** The plaintiff requested specific performance on a contract of sale of a house. The claim was delayed for a period for four years and in this time the seller's husband had gone bankrupt and she had become disabled. As a result of this, moving house would be very difficult for her as she needed to be close to family and friends.

**Ratio: Under these circumstances, the court ordered damages instead of specific performance.**

**General Principle: Courts will not order specific performance for contacts which by their very nature are unlikely to be a subject for an order of specific performance.**

**Co-operative Insurance Society Ltd v Argyll Stores (Holdings) Ltd** (1997) 3 All ER 297

**Facts:** The plaintiffs were developers of a shopping centre. They granted a 35 year old lease to the defendants to operate a Safeway supermarket in the largest shopping unit. This was central to the success of the shopping centre as the customers coming to the supermarket would generate business for the other neighbouring smaller shops. The lease therefore contained a clause to keep the supermarket always open and only allowed for closure for a maximum of four months during the lease. In 1995, the supermarket was losing money and decided to close it down even though 20 years remained on the lease. The plaintiffs sought an order for specific performance.

**Ratio: The House of Lords held that the impact on the smaller shops was not sufficient to justify ordering someone to run an uneconomic business. Lord Hoffmann distinguished between contracts requiring someone to carry on an activity over a**

period of time and contracts for results. In the latter case, the court only had to look at the end result. This distinction was used to explain the fact that specific performance could not be ordered in this case as it would require constant supervision by the court.

**Application:** Specific performance will not be ordered in relation to contracts which involve breach of an obligation to perform a series of acts which would need the constant supervision of the court.

## Injunction

An injunction normally orders the defendant to refrain from carrying out a particular act.

**General Principle: When considering an application for a mandatory injunction the court applies the balance of convenience test and may refuse the remedy if the defendant would lose a lot more by restoring the original position that the claimant would gain.**

**Page One Records Ltd v Britton** (1968) 1 WLR 157

**Facts:** The defendants were a very well-known pop group called The Troggs who employed the plaintiff as their manager and promised not to employ anybody else. Later, they wanted to terminate the agreement and the plaintiff responded by seeking an injunction to stop the group from taking another manager.

**Ratio: The court refused to grant the injunction on the grounds that its practical effect would force the group to employ the plaintiff as their manager as they would not be able to work without a manager.**

## Damages

An award for damages is the usual remedy for a breach of contract. The aim is to compensate the claimant for the damage, loss or injury he has suffered as a result of the defendant's breach.

### Non-Pecuniary Damages

Under the law of contract, damages usually aim to compensate for pecuniary loss. This has been a major point of distinction between the law of contract and the law of tort; however, in reality there are many cases where damages for mental distress have been awarded.

### General Principle: Damages for mental distress are not awarded in commercial contracts

**Addis v Gramophone Co Ltd** (1909) AC 488
**Facts:** The plaintiff had been employed as a manager of a company in India. He was wrongly sacked for dishonesty. He brought an action claiming that his dismissal had been harsh and humiliating and he had been ostracized by the British community in Calcutta. As a result he had suffered mental distress and pain.
**Ratio: The House of Lords held that he could recover the usual damages for loss of salary and commission but not for injury to his feelings caused by the way in which he was sacked from his job.**
**Application:** This principle has been amended by recent cases where mental distress has been compensated.

### General Principle: The court will award damages for mental distress where the whole purpose of the contract was pleasure, relaxation and peace of mind.

**Jarvis v Swan Tours** [1973] 1 All ER 71
**Facts:** The plaintiff was a solicitor who had booked a two week winter sports holiday that was described in the brochure as 'house party'. The brochure claimed that there would be a welcoming party, afternoon cakes and a yodelling evening. However, nothing turned out as it was described in the brochure.
**Ratio: Lord Denning explained, "It is true that he was conveyed to Switzerland and back and had meals and bed in the hotel. But that is not what he went for. He went to enjoy himself with all those facilities that the defendants said he would have. He is entitled to compensation for the loss of those facilities and for the loss of is enjoyment".**
**Application:** Lord Denning changed English law to allow damages for mental suffering.

### General Principle: Damages will be given even for contracts

where a major object of the contract is pleasure, relaxation and peace of mind.

**Farley v Skinner** [2001] UKHL 49
**Facts:** Mr. Farley wanted to buy a house in the Sussex countryside to spend his retirement. He paid a chartered surveyor, Mr. Skinner, to survey the property and specifically asked if the nearby Gatwick Airport will cause noise. The surveyor was negligent in carrying out his work and advised Mr. Farley that 'it was unlikely that the property will suffer greatly from the noise'. After spending considerable amount of money on property repairs, Mr. Farley moved into the property, he discovered that the house was badly affected by the aircraft noise, especially during weekends. He sued the surveyor and claimed non-pecuniary damages for the loss of amenity caused due to the aircraft noise.
**Ratio: The House of Lords held that it did not matter that the object of the contract with the surveyor was not entirely to give peace and relaxation, but it was a major and important part of the contract.**
**Application:** The court said that the absolute upper limit would be £10,000 in damages for this type of loss of enjoyment.

### Limitation on Awards for Damages

The award for damages aims to put the aggrieved parties in the position they would have been had the contract been performed, however there are three limitations: causation, remoteness and mitigation.

### Causation

The claimant must establish a causal link between the defendant's breach of contract and his loss in order to recover damages.

**General Principle: A person will only be liable for losses caused by their breach of contract.**

**County Ltd v Gironzentrale Securities** (1996) 3 All ER 834
**Facts:** The plaintiff's bank agreed to underwrite the issue of 26 million shares in a publicly quoted company. The defendants were stockbrokers who had been employed by the plaintiffs to approach

the potential investors. The brokers breached the contract, in due course the plaintiffs lost nearly 7 million as some 4.5 million shares ( as the price of the shares had fallen). They sued the stockbrokers and the main issue was whether their loss could be attributed to the defendant's breach of contract.

**Ratio: The Court of Appeal held that the broker's breach of contract remained the most important cause of the plaintiff's loss and the breach does not need to be the only cause. The defendants were liable to pay damages.**

**Remoteness of Damages**

There are a few losses that even though result from the breach of contract but are considered too remote from the breach for it to be fair to expect the defendant to compensate the claimant for them.

**General Principle: The remoteness of damage test was laid down in the famous case of Haxley v Baxendale.**

**Hadley v Baxendale** (1854) 9 Ex 341
**Facts:** The case concerned the delivery of an important piece of equipment used by a mill, which had been sent away for repairs. The equipment was an iron shaft which was delivered a few days after its due date. This meant that the mill had stood idle for a few days as it could not work without it. The mill owners tried to claim the loss of profits they could have made in the time between the agreed delivery date and the actual delivery date.

**Ratio: The court laid down two situations where the defendant is liable for loss cause by the breach of contract a) Loss which would arise naturally, 'in the usual course of things' from the breach of contract b) Moreover, loss 'as may be reasonably be supposed to have been in contemplation by the parties at the time when they made the contract, as the probable result of the breach'. The fact that the mill could not work without the shaft is not a loss that can cause in the normal course of things because they could have had a spare; nor could any such loss be said to be within the contemplation of the defendants, because the mill owners had failed to make it clear that the mill could not work without the shaft.**

**Application:** It is important to inform the other contracting party of any circumstances that would affect performance, to prevent the subsequent loss being found too remote.

**Transfield Shipping Inc of Panama v Mercator Shipping Inc of Monrovia, The Achilleas** [2008] 4 All ER 159 **Facts:** Transfield chartered The Achilleas from Mercator. However, Tranfield was late in the re-delivery of the ship. Mercator had entered into another charter-party which was to follow immediately after the ship's return. Due to the volatility in the shipping charter market, Mercator had to accept a much lower price for the charter- party after the late delivery of the ship. Mercator argued that they should be compensated for the reduced rate of hire for the duration of the subsequent charter. Transfield argued that their liability was only limited to the reduced rate of hire for the period of late delivery.
**Ratio:** **The Court agreed with Transfield and stated that Transfield cannot be held responsible for the drop in the market rate.**
**Application:** The test for remoteness in contract appears to be that the loss must have been in the reasonable contemplation of the parties as *'not unlikely'* to occur.

**Mitigation**

Claimants cannot just sit back and allow losses to pile up and expect the defendant to pay compensation for the whole amount if there is something they could have reasonably done to prevent further losses.

**General Principle: The claimants are under a duty to mitigate their loss, and cannot recover damages for losses which could have been avoided if reasonable steps had been taken.**

**British Westinghouse Electric and Manufacturing Co v Underground Electric Rail Co** [1912] AC 673 **Facts:** The appellants had contracted with the respondents to supply electricity turbines. The turbines that were delivered did not match the specifications of the respondents; the respondents replaced these with highly efficient ones made by a different manufacturer. They were so efficient that the replacement machines paid for themselves in a short time. They claimed damages for the cost of replacing the turbines.
**Ratio: The House of Lords rejected this claim. It was held that**

the respondents had greatly mitigated their loss and had been so successful that almost all the losses had been recovered. Hence, they were only entitled to damages for the period of time when the turbines were running inefficiently.

**Application:** You must be able to show you have taken steps to minimise your losses and not let them escalate and spiral out of control.

## Contributory Negligence

**General Principle: Where the claimant's fault has contributed to the losses he has suffered, then the amount of damages he can recover for the breach of contract may be reduced due to his contributory negligence.**

**Forsikringsaktieselskapet Vesta v Butcher** [1986] 2 All ER 488

**Facts:** The plaintiffs, a Norwegian insurance company, entered into a contract of reinsurance with the defendant to insure them against claims to the value of 90 per cent, of the risks under a contract to insure a fish farm in Norway. The contract contained a safety clause requiring the insured to keep a 24-hour watch on the site but that clause was not complied with. A severe storm led to the loss of a large number of fish. The plaintiffs brought an action against the defendant claiming to be indemnified to 90 per cent, of the settlement.

**Ratio: Hobhouse J identified the following categories of obligation: a) where the defendant's liability arises from a breach of strict contractual duty, b) where the defendant's liability arises from a contractual obligation which is expressed in terms of taking care , but it does not correspond to a common law duty to take care which would exist in the given case independent of contract and c) where the defendant's liability in contract is the same as his liability under the tort of negligence which arises independently of the contract. The court held that contributory negligence can be used as a defence in the third category but not in the first or second.**

**Application:** The Law Commission recommended in 1993 to use contributory negligence as a defence even in the second category (but not in the first one).

## Other Remedies in Contract

## Quantum Meruit

Where work has been done or goods supplied but no payment has been received and cannot be obtained under a contract, an action is called a *quantum meruit*. It is based on restitutionary principles and is different from damages, since it pays for performance but does not compensate for loss.

**General Principle: Where there is a precise provision for remuneration, a quantum merit cannot be used to change the price even if extra work is done.**

**Gilbert and Partners v Knight** (1968) 2 All ER 248
**Facts:** Knight employed a firm of surveyors for supervising work on a building for £30. The surveyors did more supervision than asked and submitted another bill of £105 for the additional work. Knight refused to pay the extra £105.
**Ratio: The Court agreed with him as the original contract had fixed the payment and it was still in existence.**

# Question and Answers

- Remedies Problem Question

## Question

Helen decided to set up a business as a potter. She entered into a contract with a local builder, Eric, to convert her shed into a potting studio, complete with wheel and kiln. The contract was for £15,000 and provided that the work would be finished by 30 June. However, Eric had problems with labour and did not complete the work until 30 September. Helen had to cancel a number of pottery jobs over the summer, including a lucrative contract for a dining set of her pottery in the restaurant at Lowclere, a local stately home and the sale of the pottery at Lowclere's gift shop. The cancellation of these jobs in the summer season has caused Helen significant mental distress.

Advise Helen.

## Answer

### Introduction

This essay will discuss the opportunity for Helen to obtain damages in the context of a local builder's delay in the delivery of her potting studio. The goal of her claim is for her to be in the position she would have been in had the contract been performed properly. We will discuss the following losses:

1. Cancelation of Pottery jobs at Lowclere gift shop
2. A lucrative contract for a dining set
3. Mental distress

### Cancelation of Pottery jobs

We will discuss Helen's pecuniary loss in connection with the cancellation of pottery jobs at the gift shop. These are expectation loss. Using **Barries and Davis** as an authority, Helen may place a claim on the expected profits had the contract been properly performed. We now discuss the remoteness, mitigation and causation requirements. **Hadley v Baxendale** provides a test to assess the remoteness element of the claim. The claimant needs to establish that the loss naturally flew from the breach and that it was foreseeable that the loss would occur. As the builder is a local builder and was probably aware that Helen was running a pottery business and had ongoing contracts to provide local shops with her products we argue that is was foreseeable that she would incur some loss as a result of the delay. We argue that the loss naturally flew from the delay. **Quinn v Burch Brothers** establishes that the breach must be the cause of the loss. According to the facts the loss is caused by the delay. Finally, Brace v Calder establishes that the claimant has a duty to mitigate the loss. Thus Helen has to establish that she took steps to mitigate her loss. On the facts of the case we argue that there is not much she could do to mitigate the loss resulting from the delay. Thus Helen may place a claim for damages based on the loss of profits she would have realised had the pottery studio be ready on time.

**Anglia TV** provides that a claim for damages may be based on the investments incurred by the claimant in the context of the contract when losses are not materially measurable. Since Helen losses are measurable and the damage appears to be appropriate remedies to compensate Helen for her losses we do not advice Helen to place a claim for damages based on reliance.


**Cancellation of a lucrative contract**

We will discuss Helen's pecuniary loss in connection with the cancellation of a one-time pottery job for the restaurant. Using **Hadley v Baxendale** test, we argue that although the loss of this job resulted from the delay, it is debatable whether it was foreseeable that it would occur. Based on the facts, the builder may not have been aware of this specific contract. In **Victoria laundry** the courts held that only the loss of contemplated profits could be recoverable, but not the loss resulting from a cancelled contract which the defendant was not aware of. **Chaplin v Hicks** establishes that damages may be claim for loss of opportunity. We argue that Helen may claim that the contract for the restaurant constituted a chance for her to develop a new market segment of made-by-order pottery jobs and that the delay resulted in her missing that opportunity, even though the losses are speculative. Based on these authorities on the balance of probabilities we argue that Helen may not be able to claim damages for the loss of this specific contract.

**Mental distress**

We will discuss Helen's mental distress in connection with the builder's delay in setting up the pottery studio. This is non pecuniary loss occasioning distressed as defined in **Addis Gramophone** where the courts held that damages may not be claimed for mental distress. However, **Farley v Skinner** established that some compensation may be claimed if significant disturbance results from the loss. Jarvis v Swan tours established that damages may be claimed for distress if the object of the contract involves leisure and relaxation. On the fact Helen may not rely on this authority to place a claim since the contract does not pertain to a leisure activity.

We argue that besides the financial loss incurred Helen's distress is not material as she may not point to a specific disturbance, such as noise or the impossibility to use an item properly. Thus we argue that Helen may not claim damages for mental distress.

The End

Printed in Great Britain
by Amazon